Political Leadership in New Zealand

Political Leadership in New Zealand

Edited by

Raymond Miller

and Michael Mintrom

Auckland University Press

Auckland University Press
University of Auckland
Private Bag 92019
Auckland
New Zealand
www.auckland.ac.nz/aup

© the contributors, 2006

ISBN 1 86940 358 4

National Library of New Zealand Cataloguing-in-Publication Data

Political leadership in New Zealand / edited by Raymond
Miller and Michael Mintrom.
Includes bibliographical references and index.
ISBN: 1-86940-358-4
1. Political leadership—New Zealand. 2. New Zealand—
Politics and government. I. Miller, Raymond, 1953-
II. Mintrom, Michael, 1963- III. Title.
320.0993—dc 22

Printed by Printlink Ltd, Wellington

Contents

Foreword

Our world of global interconnectedness characterised by uncertainty, unpredictability and increasing mistrust has brought about a new and intensified period of change. This unrelenting change has created a prevalent concern about a lack of leadership to overcome these compelling challenges. Many of the significant current and emerging challenges are of a political nature and will require more and better political leadership.

There is an unfortunate tendency to think of leadership as a romantic simplicity. However, it is important to appreciate that leadership is complex, and if we are to develop more effective political leadership, then we need to take the time to reflect on and understand it.

Political Leadership in New Zealand takes seriously the responsibility of reflecting on and understanding political leadership. Its publication is a timely reminder that political leadership is not automatically conferred through a position or a title; rather, it manifests itself through transformative thinking and learning.

The New Zealand Leadership Institute is committed to enhancing the understanding of leadership in New Zealand and is proud to have played a role in the initiation of this book through its support of the planning workshop in June 2004.

The Institute is profoundly interested in creating a nexus between academic theory, research and practice to transform the understanding and practice of leadership in New Zealand.

This excellent book achieves this goal and creates a platform for the type of conversations that can lead to more and better political leadership. I congratulate Raymond Miller and Michael Mintrom and their fellow authors on this important initiative which has the capacity to create both more understanding and action.

Lester Levy
New Zealand Leadership Institute

Introduction

ONE

Political Leadership
in New Zealand

**Raymond Miller
and Michael Mintrom**

We all know that leadership is vital to collective action, but the causes and extent of that influence are more difficult to assess. When great human achievements are being recorded, the dominant actors almost always capture our attention. Leadership is essential for the attainment of success in business, farming, medicine, scientific research, the performing arts and sports. In every case, through their efforts, effective leaders work with others to identify and achieve certain goals. Just as leadership is fundamental to other human activities, so it is an essential ingredient of politics and government. Yet, in contrast to the wealth of knowledge that has been accumulated over time in other fields, the only certainty about political leadership is how little we actually know. This book is designed to help close that gap, focusing on political leadership in New Zealand.

While political leadership is often depicted in ways that invite ridicule, if not contempt, leaders are indeed capable of having a profound impact on the quality of our everyday life. In New Zealand, there are those who bemoan the lack of leadership talent in all sectors of society. This is partly a reaction to change: change in the economy and electoral and political systems; change in the ethnic composition and size of the population; and change in the international and global context. Not all of these changes are directly related to politics, but they do have political ramifications. For example, who would doubt the potential impact on the reputations of political leaders of rising oil prices, international terrorism, the war in

Iraq or a public backlash against immigrants and refugees? Inevitably, each of these developments has consequences not only for leaders, but also for their followers and the entire process of government.

Interest in leadership has never been greater than it is today. The reasons are complex and include heightened feelings of anxiety and powerlessness, as well as an awareness of the need for security, both personally and as local and national communities. But powerlessness is also a product of the complexities of our technological age. There are those who believe that power should be the responsibility, not of the non-expert masses, but of professionally trained leaders. According to this view, while mass participation could be justified before the advent of modern technology, the electronic age created a need for specialised leadership by the political, bureaucratic and technocratic elites. Even if we regard this view to be inherently undemocratic, the overall trend is unmistakable. As a result of the growing influence of the mass media, especially television, the focus of attention has been shifting away from political institutions and policies and towards 'personal' leadership (Foley 1993), a trend that comes into particularly sharp relief during elections, when, through such methods as public opinion polls, studio interviews and leaders' debates, the perceived qualities of individual leaders and the strength of their appeal to a mass electorate become the central focus of the campaign.

The Study of Political Leadership

In contrast to the literature on other forms of leadership, especially business leadership, the literature on political leadership is surprisingly small and narrow in scope. Early research tended to be presented in the form of biographies of 'great' political leaders, however greatness might have been defined. Typically, such studies explored the life and times of individual leaders, focusing on the reasons for their success. Prominent subjects included prime ministers, presidents and other elite figures. However, in more recent times it has become clear that the study of political leadership requires us to do more than chronicle or analyse the careers and actions of particular individuals. As a result, attention has begun to be directed more towards theories of leadership, an approach that depicts leaders as rational actors and encourages us to think beyond their personal attributes and achievements. Inevitably, such an approach invites the drawing of comparisons and the making of normative judgements about the relative performances of leaders one with another. It also broadens our understanding of political leadership, reminding us that leadership efforts are always influenced by contextual factors.

The study of political leadership has much to learn from other forms of leadership, especially in the fields of business and commerce. Until recently, political leadership and business leadership were travelling on quite divergent paths. Whereas political leadership was primarily concerned with the relationship between leaders and the mass electorate, the focus of business leadership is said to have been on organisational structures and hierarchies of power (Kellerman 1999). As a result of three major developments, these longstanding differences have either become blurred or have completely disappeared. In New Zealand, the first development was the neo-liberal transformation of the economy and public service, a result of which was the forging of new and significant links between the public and private sectors. At the height of reform in the 1980s and 1990s, the public sector was both restructured and inculcated with private sector values, approaches and personnel. In the new environment of economic deregulation and fiscal restraint, it was made clear that the state's resources had to be managed with greater prudence and care.

A second development that strengthened the linkage between the study of political and business leadership has been the gradual emergence of a more business-oriented political elite. Globalisation, access to higher education, and the information revolution have contributed to an increase in the number of politicians with a background in the professions or in business. In New Zealand, most Members of Parliament now possess a range of management and technical skills barely conceived of a generation or more ago. Whereas prime ministers and parliamentarians once came disproportionately from the manual occupations, such as farming, manufacturing or a skilled trade, a vast majority of today's politicians boast a university degree, often in law or commerce, together with significant prior experience in senior management positions in the private sector. In New Zealand, the first university-educated prime minister of the modern era was John Marshall, a lawyer, who entered the role in 1972. Subsequent prime ministers have included an economist, accountant, lawyer, constitutional law professor and university lecturer.

Third, the adoption of a proportional electoral system in New Zealand in 1996 raised questions about the relevance of traditional conceptions of political leadership. Rather than perpetuating the highly partisan and combative leadership common under the Westminster system of government, the new Mixed Member Proportional (MMP) voting system required a more consultative and conciliatory style of leadership, especially in light of the consolidation of the multi-party system and advent of coalition government. The collapse of one coalition and the premature termination of another sheeted home the importance of a management style that is less adversarial and more open and inclusive than under single-party government arrangements. As a number of commentators have pointed out, leaders are more likely to be successful under proportional electoral systems if they are reconcilers rather than mobilisers, coordinators rather than charismatic crusaders, and consensus-builders rather than advocates of majority rule.

Despite the growing convergence between the skills required of a successful political leader and those found in other sorts of leader, there are some obvious differences. Political leadership involves a level of accountability rarely if ever seen in other categories of leadership. Not only are party leaders able to be replaced by the politicians of their party at any time, they are ultimately answerable to the collective judgement of the voting public. In New Zealand, this occurs every three years. On a more frequent basis, of course, political leaders are subject to robust scrutiny by the mass media and their political opponents. And while the literature on business leadership tends to distinguish between leadership and management, with leadership requiring vision and an ability to transform, and management being primarily concerned with process and efficiency (Storey 2004), management is generally regarded to be an integral feature of political leadership. Indeed, much of the success of political leaders hinges on their performance in both micro and macro management. In New Zealand now, effective prime ministers must balance the needs of a complex array of frequently competing groups, including consultants, advisers, cabinet colleagues, coalition partners, backbench MPs, public servants and the voting public.

While the architects of neo-liberal reform in New Zealand may not have achieved their ultimate goal of creating a minimalist state, as a result of their actions there was a diffusion of power in the direction of government corporations, crown agencies, district health and school boards, local and regional government, voluntary service bodies, and Maori tribal and sub-tribal authorities. With the advent of MMP, the opportunities to exercise political leadership increased still further. On recommending the new electoral system for New Zealand in 1986, the Royal Commission on the Electoral System had predicted that it would produce fairer representation among the various parties, fairer representation of women and special interests, and fairer representation of minority groups, including Maori. As well as achieving these objectives, the new electoral system resulted in a strengthening of the role of parliament and its select committees *vis-à-vis* the executive branch of government. Instead of just two parties and party leaders as in the past, parliament now has up to seven or eight. It also has leaders representing the previously under-represented or excluded groups, including women, Maori, Pacific peoples and Asians.

A Framework for Studying Political Leadership

Of the many possible approaches that could be taken to studying political leadership, the most common involves focusing on the holders of particular positions. Prime ministers, as the leaders of governments, and other leaders of political parties exhibit political leadership by definition. Focusing on these office holders therefore accords with common sense and appears quite defensible. The basic contention is that if you want to study political leadership, then you should study political leaders. Everybody knows that prime ministers are political leaders. Studying their backgrounds, tracing the steps in their political careers, analysing their leadership styles and discussing their achievements in office can generate many insights into political leadership. However, this method of identifying instances of political leadership carries the risk that political leadership will be defined narrowly as the activities of people in elected positions of political authority. We think good grounds exist for expanding our understanding of political leadership and where it might be found. The key is to recognise that political leadership involves a range of specific activities. There is no question that these activities are undertaken by people holding high-profile positions in government and in parliament. But many of these activities are also undertaken by people who, while well known in specific contexts, are not nationally recognised, and are not subject to the continuous glare of media attention.

When political leadership is viewed primarily as a set of activities, rather than as the actions of people in predefined leadership positions, the process of political leadership becomes the central object of study. As a result, many new opportunities are opened up for gaining insights into the nature of political leadership. The contexts in which political leadership occurs – including those well-understood leadership roles – remain critical to the analysis. But they are no longer taken as given and it is understood that people can serve as political leaders without holding formal positions of authority. Here we present a framework for this more inclusive approach to studying political leadership. The framework contains three basic questions relating to the actions of leaders, the importance of context and the role of followers. These are: What does political leadership involve? How does political context matter? And how significant are followers? The framework incorporates the expectation that each of the three elements influences – and is influenced by – the other two. Figure 1 portrays the basic relationships. Next, we discuss each element in turn.

FIGURE 1: **Elements of Political Leadership**

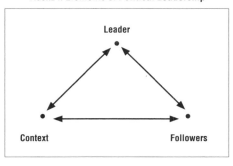

Question 1: What does political leadership involve?
One of the most fundamental components of leadership is the ability to offer something that people want. In addition to promising a range of material benefits, leaders gain the right to lead by helping those around them to make sense of their immediate world, especially when that world is subject to uncertainty and change. If we accept that leaders are in the

business of creating certainty in uncertain environments, this helps us to understand many aspects of contemporary politics. Demand for certainty should result in a tendency for political leaders to be selected according to collective judgements about the quality of the information that they provide about themselves and their ability to act in the collective interest. Put another way, we might say that political leaders are selected on the persuasiveness of the narratives or visions that they offer people in given contexts. Politicians running for elected positions understand this well. They know that they must present a set of convincing messages that connect with the voters. Often, messages are considered most convincing when the politicians concerned can claim to have relevant experience and can show themselves to have a range of things in common with key sections of the electorate. But here, style of presentation can be as important – if not more important – than the substance of the message. Actions need to be given meaning. A crucial role for the leader, then, is to offer people easily accessible and believable interpretations of who they are, what they stand for and how they will act to promote the interests of the whole. This explains why issues of credibility and trustworthiness surface so often during elections, and why commentators and members of the public search endlessly for insights into a potential leader's character.

The requirements that political leaders offer persuasive stories and pass basic credibility tests also hold for those serving in non-elected positions. Leaders who mobilise others to engage in civic actions of one kind or another often do so by offering leadership by example. The act of putting the interests of the group above your own narrow interests can send powerful messages about your commitment to a cause (Hermalin 1998). For example, leaders of industrial action often put their jobs at risk because they believe in a larger goal. At other times, people will put their own safety and security on the line, by marching at the head of demonstrations intended to publicise group struggles. No matter where they are positioned in the broader polity, political leaders need to signal their conviction and their commitment to those around them. The more they do this, the more believable their messages become.

While there is no magical formula for leadership success, it is fair to say that there are certain personal qualities that most effective leaders have in common. Because leadership occurs in a social context, leaders are likely to display highly developed social skills, including empathy, sound judgement, courage in the face of adversity, an aptitude for solving problems and an ability to instil confidence. But as well as intrinsic qualities, leaders are expected to have a highly developed understanding of the political context, especially the requirements of winning and holding power. Through a combination of natural ability and training, they learn that leadership involves an ability to persuade, partly through effective use of the mass media, but also through public speaking, debating and one-to-one communication. In the end, however, success has much to do with having a keen sense of timing, or, in the words of one study, being 'blessed with incredibly good fortune . . . coinciding with the misfortunes of their rivals' (Marbach 1979, 2).

Question 2: How does context matter?
Leadership occurs in many different contexts. Since we have argued that political leadership can be exercised by individuals regardless of whether or not they hold formal positions of authority, it is critical that we discuss the ways that leadership and context typically interact. At the most basic level, context serves to open up or limit opportunities for the exercise of leadership. Consider the tragic terrorist attacks of 11 September 2001. These created chaotic scenes in lower Manhattan and generated fear and anxiety among many Americans. The context called for political leadership. The mayor of New York City, Rudolph Giuliani, and the president of the United States, George W. Bush, immediately recognised the enormity of the crisis. As holders of key positions of political authority, they acted rapidly to manage the situation. Their displays of political leadership contained two key components. First, they encouraged others to calmly and decisively do the work needed to restore order. Second, they convinced the public that, even though a devastating set of events had just occurred, collectively, the citizens of New York and the citizens of the United States had the wherewithal to overcome adversity. Within a context characterised by tragedy, chaos and uncertainty, Giuliani and Bush acted to restore people's faith and hopes. They exhibited political leadership by offering certainty, by drawing strength from the past and projecting positive images of the future. This awful set of circumstances allowed each of these politicians the opportunity to present themselves as strong, decisive and calm. They thus offered leadership by example in quite extreme circumstances.

Well over a century before the events of 11 September 2001, the Englishman Lord Bryce (1889) posed the question of why, in the United States, great men are not chosen as presidents. Although today we might question Bryce's definition of greatness, he observed at the time that one reason why great men are not chosen as presidents is that, in quiet times, such leaders are not absolutely needed. The immediate context creates the conditions within which political leadership can be displayed. In peaceful and unremarkable times, it might well be that people who have the capacity to exhibit greatness are not required to do so. In extraordinary times, people in particular positions of authority might be placed under great pressure to exhibit political leadership. When this happens, people who previously might not have been credited with exceptional leadership ability might respond in ways that show their deeper capacity for effectively guiding collective action. Alternatively, such circumstances might prove the downfall of people who, in less challenging times, appeared quite competent as leaders, simply because they were not put to any significant test.

We contend that leaders in any circumstances work hard to reduce uncertainty, thereby creating conditions that allow others to be far more productive and creative than they would otherwise be. Viewed in this way, we see that political leadership often involves working with others to create new laws, institutions and organisations in society so that people can productively coexist. In studying political leadership, we need to pay close attention to how changes in ideas, technologies, structures, power relations and interests serve to constrain or open opportunities for leadership. The key challenge is to understand how certain base conditions shape the goals and actions of political leaders and how those leaders then work to shape the context in ways that accord with their broader goals.

Some recent contributions to the study of leadership have paid careful attention to context and offer insights that we might build upon when considering political leadership in New Zealand. Karl Weick (1995) has argued that complex problems cry out for leadership. In contrast to the rational-comprehensive view of decision-making that is often portrayed in public policy analysis and decision theory textbooks, Weick contends that decision-making is always heavily conditioned by context. In Weick's view, people are limited in their rationality and in their capacity to make perfectly informed decisions. Applying this model of decision-making in organisations to the consideration of leadership, Weick (2001) has proposed that leadership be thought of as 'the legitimation of doubt'. Confronted by difficult circumstances, leaders find ways to promote creative problem-solving within the collectivity. According to Weick, the leader who acknowledges that he or she does not come with all answers to all problems creates exciting possibilities for others to wrestle with and address public problems. In a similar vein, Ronald Heifitz has argued that leaders distinguish themselves in any given context by 'getting on the balcony' (1994, 252). By this, Heifitz means that leaders are able to act within a given context while at the same time standing above it, reflecting on the whole scene and determining how specific actions of specific individuals serve to help or hinder collective action. Linked to this perspective, Heifitz contends that a key task for the leader involves 'giving the work back to the people' (1994, 262). Like Weick, Heifitz sees enormous value in the leader empowering others to work on the solving of collective problems. In both instances, the leader must have the self-confidence to take charge, even when the situation is riddled with uncertainty. Further, they must stand ready to coordinate the actions of others towards a set of common goals even when the context may make it impossible to clearly articulate those goals at the outset.

Earlier, we discussed aspects of the political context in New Zealand and some of the fundamental changes that have occurred in that context over the past two decades. Changes in the global economy and changes in international politics have opened opportunities for political leadership in New Zealand that are quite distinct from the past. Here, we believe that complexity has created opportunities for political leaders to empower others. Meanwhile, changes in the electoral system have again created uncertainty and opened opportunities for political leaders to forge new kinds of political coalitions. The economic policy reforms of the 1980s and 1990s, along with continuing changes in economic conditions, have again created distinctive, interesting and challenging contexts within which local and national political leaders must operate. Finally, increased immigration and greater self-consciousness among Maori and Pacific peoples have created political dynamics that pose challenges and opportunities for political leadership in many locations within the broader polity.

Question 3: How significant are followers?

James MacGregor Burns (1977, 274) defined leadership as 'leaders inducing followers to act for certain goals that represent the values and the motivations . . . of both leaders and followers'. In this definition, leaders are inseparable from followers. But, while inseparable, leaders and followers are clearly distinguishable one from the other. Burns argued that four key distinctions can be drawn. First, it is the leader who creates the linkages that allow communication to occur between leader and followers. Second, the leader is more skilful in determining the needs and motives of followers, and anticipating their responses to actions. Third, the leader takes the dominant part in maintaining the relationship and pursuing shared goals. Finally, and most importantly, the leader addresses the wants and needs of followers. In so doing, the leader serves as an independent force in the lives of the followers. While leaders and followers are inseparable then, is seems clear that leaders engage in the more significant actions. But followers matter and the role they play in the leadership process requires investigation.

Much has been made of the role of political leaders in inspiring their followers with a sense of vision about the better times and conditions ahead. However, as the example of New Zealand demonstrates, leadership will only be successful if that vision is a two-way process that also involves those who follow. During the 1980s and 1990s, successive governments attempted to impose their economic and social welfare reforms on a profoundly cynical electorate. As a result, political leadership suffered from an absence of public confidence and trust. This gave rise to the emergence of several new parties, most of which were breakaway movements from Labour and National. As well as causing a steep decline in electoral support for the two major parties, with close to half of all voters either abstaining or supporting a minor party, the inattentiveness of political leaders to the wishes of followers resulted in a majority vote in two successive referendums to replace the existing electoral system with a proportional system of representation. Indeed, it is fair to say that today's multi-party parliament and government only exist because of a failure to recognise that political change is a product of a symbiotic relationship between leaders and followers – despite their uneasy relationship, each needs to be attentive to the needs and interests of the other. The example emphasises that, without followers, leadership has neither meaning nor purpose.

This tension between the impulses of the leader with an independent vision and the necessity to be responsive to the needs of one's followers is perhaps best reflected in the *trustee* and *delegate* models of political representation. The trustee model originates with the British political theorist, Edmund Burke. According to Burke, political decisions are best left to the independent judgement of the individual politician, who is equipped to decide what constitutes the national interest. In contrast, the role of ordinary citizens should be restricted to electing representatives capable of exercising sound judgement and protecting the interests of the nation. Whereas the trustee model recognises the right of individual leaders to exercise their own independent judgement, the delegate model is based on the assumption that political leaders will act at the behest of – rather than on behalf of – their constituents.

A variety of factors have served to ensure that the delegate model of leadership is now most prevalent in New Zealand, as elsewhere. Rising levels of education, the decentralised role of the state in society and the strong role that the mass media plays in political communication have empowered citizens. Increasingly, the followers have come to see that the fortunes of leaders will rise and fall with their ability to act in ways consistent with the followers' needs. Greater democratisation has resulted in the phenomenon of many self-appointed opinion-leaders seeing themselves as spokespeople for the masses and engaging in continual critique of traditional political leaders. Of course, in this climate the tenure of any given critic is also uncertain. A poor choice of subject for discussion on talkback radio, or use of a few inappropriate words, can greatly tarnish the reputation and influence of media commentators. Yet all of this speaks to the power of followers and the very real constraints that followers place on the range of actions leaders can take. Further, the power of followers can be observed directly and indirectly in the ways that popular discourse and shared norms of appropriateness serve to mark out those people who might be acceptable within particular leadership positions and those who would not be. Prejudice and popular notions of what it takes to be a leader have always made it difficult, if not impossible, for some people to seriously aspire to significant leadership positions. This has been changing, but the power of followers remains strong in this negative way and deserves close examination.

The framework for studying political leadership presented here portrays leadership as a process. Within this process, the actions of political leaders cannot be understood without giving careful consideration both to the context in which they occur and the characteristics and expectations of would-be followers. Explicit within the framework is the notion that political leadership can be exhibited in many contexts and that it is not simply the domain of people who happen to hold positions of political authority. This framework is designed to be flexible and open to application in a range of specific contexts. Next, we introduce a variety of ways of exploring political leadership in New Zealand. While not exhaustive, these different approaches to understanding political leadership give a sense of the opportunities that now exist for the exercise of political leadership in New Zealand. The case study chapters that comprise the remainder of the book show how combining elements of this framework with rich contextual evidence can generate many insights into political leadership as it is currently being practised in New Zealand.

Political Leadership in a High-Stakes World

Political leadership is understood to be important, yet surprisingly few systematic studies have been undertaken of just how political leadership is practised in a range of contexts. Beyond the important biographical studies of parliamentarians and prime ministers that have long been produced in this country, we know very little about the nature of political leadership in New Zealand. The study of politics in New Zealand has been missing a fundamental component. This book is intended to address that gap and to establish an agenda for the on-going analysis of political leadership in New Zealand. This is an excellent time to be studying political leadership because, more than ever, we live in a high-stakes world. As old ways of conducting international relations subside, as new threats appear, and as the global economy becomes more integrated, major challenges emerge for the leaders of every economy and democracy in the world, large or small. Love it or hate it, New Zealand is closely integrated into that high-stakes world. This world begs for high-quality, decisive leadership, leadership that reduces the uncertainty inherent in this context and opens possibilities for ordinary people to make the very most of their lives while contributing to collective projects. New Zealand's current political leaders and the political leaders of the future face many opportunities for shaping the destiny of this country and its people. Thinking hard about the lessons that leaders and followers alike might draw from the present times is essential work. As the following chapters attest, it is also interesting and engaging work.

Bryce, J. (1889) 'Why Great Men Are Not Elected President', in J. Bryce, *The American Commonwealth*, 2nd edn, London, Macmillan, chapt. 8.

Burns, J. M. (1977) 'Wellsprings of Political Leadership', *American Political Science Review*, 71, 266–75.

Heifetz, R. A. (1994) *Leadership Without Easy Answers*, Cambridge, MA, Belknap Press.

Hermalin, B. E. (1998) 'Toward an Economic Theory of Leadership: Leading by Example', *American Economic Review*, 88, 1188–206.

Foley, M. (1993) *The Rise of the British Presidency*, Manchester, Manchester University Press.

Kellerman, B. (1999) *Reinventing Leadership: Making the Connection Between Business and Politics*, New York, State University of New York Press.

Marbach, J. (1979) *The Anatomy of Power: An Enquiry into the Personality of Leadership*, London, W. H. Allen.

Storey, J. (ed.) (2004) *Leadership in Organisations: Current Issues and Key Trends*, London, Routledge.

Weick, K. E. (1995) *Sensemaking in Organizations*, Thousand Oaks, CA, Sage.

Weick, K. E. (2001) 'Leadership as the Legitimation of Doubt', in W. Bennis, G. M. Spreitzer and T. G. Cummings (eds), *The Future of Leadership*, San Francisco, Jossey-Bass.

Leadership and Identity

TWO

Constructing New Zealand in the World

David Capie

This chapter explores how political leaders play a role in constructing an identity for New Zealand in world affairs. Its analysis focuses on three comparatively recent prime ministers: Norman Kirk, Robert Muldoon and David Lange. It examines how each leader worked within a specific international and domestic context to influence and shape the way New Zealand is seen in international politics. It concludes with a brief examination of contemporary leadership in foreign affairs and the challenges and opportunities that confront leaders in an MMP environment.

A wide range of actors can have an impact on New Zealand's foreign relations. These can include the respective Ministers of Foreign Affairs, Defence and Trade Negotiations, senior diplomats, business people and even representatives of NGOs. Why then focus on prime ministers? This chapter argues that prime ministers are qualitatively different actors. They are important international players in their own right, even if they care little for foreign policy issues. They play a key role in shaping foreign policy and present a 'New Zealand face to the world' if only by virtue of their position as leaders of the government. Only prime ministers attend meetings such as the annual Asia–Pacific Economic Cooperation (APEC) Leaders' Meeting, the Commonwealth Heads of Government Meeting (CHOGM) or the Pacific Forum. Although the one-time practice of New Zealand prime ministers also holding the Foreign Affairs portfolio has declined in recent years and is unlikely to be revived, the prime minister remains a central figure when it comes to representing New Zealand's interests and policies in international affairs (Henderson 1997, 75).

Prime ministers do more than simply advocate for New Zealand policy abroad. As individuals, they represent a kind of symbolic bridge connecting the domestic and the international realms. How they are seen by the world in part colours perceptions of New Zealand as a state. As former Secretary of Foreign Affairs Frank Corner has written, 'we are the components with whom the leader we have chosen must interact; then on our behalf he [sic] must also interact with the world. The ideas, attitudes and style projected by this leader will be perceived by the world outside our islands as reflecting what we New Zealanders are really like'(Corner 2001).

But while prime ministers play this important 'bridging' role in world affairs, scholarship on leadership in New Zealand has largely focused on domestic politics. A notable exception is the work of John Henderson, who has modified James David Barber's political psychology typology and applied it to Muldoon's style of foreign policy (Barber 1972; Henderson 1980). Other writers have made reference to foreign policy in functional analyses of David Lange's leadership (Hayward 2001; Miller 2005) but most have not focused their attention on foreign relations. While recognising that psychological and functional explanations of leadership can offer important insights, this chapter takes a different approach. It proceeds by looking at how political leaders interpret and define New Zealand's place in the world in four ways: first, by looking at the comparative level of interest and importance prime ministers attach to international as well as domestic politics; second, in the way that they define key relationships with friends and allies; third, by how they weigh calculations of interest against considerations of principle or a so-called 'moral' foreign policy; and, finally, in the way that, as individuals, their personality, strengths, weaknesses and idiosyncrasies have lent New Zealand's foreign relations a certain style or tone. It concludes that while prime ministers face constraints imposed by the external environment, they retain a great deal of freedom to influence foreign relations and define how New Zealand is seen in world politics.

New Zealand Prime Ministers and Foreign Policy

The extent to which New Zealand's prime ministers have embraced foreign affairs has varied enormously over time. Of the postwar leaders, Peter Fraser and Walter Nash stand out as having had a deep interest in world affairs. Fraser's personal diplomacy in the creation of the United Nations and in the drafting of the Universal Declaration on Human Rights helped him earn a legacy as the only New Zealand leader 'with a plausible claim to be recognized as an international statesman' (Bassett and King 2000, 296). Nash was similarly fascinated by international politics, having served as minister in Washington before becoming prime minister. But not all leaders possessed such an innate sense of curiosity about the world beyond New Zealand's borders. Fraser's successor, Sidney Holland, was known for his almost total lack of interest in foreign affairs and his extreme parsimony when it came to funding diplomatic posts abroad (McKinnon 1993, 114). Keith Holyoake adopted a similar position. According to Malcolm McKinnon, 'Like Holland, Holyoake . . . had no particular interest in foreign affairs and in this respect he was a characteristic conservative New Zealand Prime Minister' (1993, 149).

The three more recent prime ministers under consideration here – Kirk, Lange and Muldoon – all took a keen interest in foreign relations. Kirk's writings while in opposition often reflected on New Zealand's place in the world. He came to power with a keen desire to lay out a new vision for New Zealand's external relations. Members of his caucus recall that Kirk's attention had to be 'unriveted' from foreign affairs (Bassett 1976, 70).[2] In contrast, Robert Muldoon embraced foreign policy only later in his career. According to Barry Gustafson, before becoming prime minister, Muldoon 'had shown little interest or expertise in foreign affairs' but that 'changed dramatically' after winning the 1975 election (Gustafson 2000, 214). Muldoon never formally held the foreign minister's job, but in practice he dominated the portfolio. David Lange also served as foreign minister for his first term in office, recalling later that he enjoyed it more than he did being education minister in his second term, although it did not give him the same sense of achievement (Lange 2005, 219). Lange's staff remember a prime minister who 'revelled' in foreign relations, digesting reports and cables with great enthusiasm – especially any marked 'top secret' (Henderson 2005, p.136). Like many prime ministers, he enjoyed the travel and the opportunities to mix with world figures.

While Kirk, Muldoon and Lange all shared an interest in the projection of New Zealand's interests and identity abroad, their leadership styles and the policies they pursued varied enormously. In the sketches below, this can be seen in their divergent views on the role of power in world politics, the importance they attached to New Zealand's relations with its traditional allies and their beliefs about the role and proper purpose of diplomacy.

Norman Kirk

When Norman Kirk took office on 8 December 1972, New Zealand was struggling to find its place in a changing world. For most of the country's history since European settlement, foreign affairs had been defined by the relationship with London. New Zealand premiers and prime ministers were for the most part happy to defer to Britain when it came to foreign policy issues. The focus of New Zealand's foreign relations was on connections with the Empire and then the Commonwealth, ties that McKinnon aptly describes as 'international' rather than 'foreign' in nature (1993a). But after World War II, New Zealand's relationship with the United Kingdom began to change. In particular, after London announced its intention to seek membership of the EEC in 1961, New Zealand began to realise the need to diversify its economic ties. Defence relations with the United States, which since the signing of the 1951 ANZUS Treaty had replaced Britain as New Zealand's great power 'protector', were also thrown into question by the bloody and unpopular war in Vietnam.

Against this backdrop, Kirk came to office with ambitious plans for a 'new era' in foreign affairs and the self-proclaimed intention of pursuing 'a more independent foreign policy' (McKinnon 1993, 185). Living up to his reputation as a 'man in a hurry', Kirk threw himself into foreign policy matters, quickly issuing a four-page paper entitled 'New Zealand in the World in the 1970s'. Within two weeks he had announced the withdrawal of the last New Zealand troops from Vietnam and recognised the People's Republic of China. These decisions, he said, 'mark a significant change after years of equivocation, but they are only the first steps in working out a new, more independent foreign policy. We have a mind and a voice of our own and we intend to use them.' (Bassett, 26–7)

As both Prime Minister and Minister of Foreign Affairs, Kirk provided clear leadership within his government on foreign policy issues. His tenure signalled a cautious but significant change in relations with London and with Washington. He had 'no sense of his country being an appendage of Britain nor did he wish it to become an appendage of any other country' (Corner, 144). In 1974, Kirk used his Waitangi Day speech to address the question of New Zealand's changing relationship with Britain. He noted that the country had been slow to create 'a fully New Zealand civilization' in part because it did not have to react against Britain in a revolution, a coup or a war. But while New Zealand continued to look to the UK with 'respect, with friendship and yes, with love', he said Britain's move into Europe meant that 'we must draw more upon the spiritual and cultural strength of the people who make our nation' (Jeffries 2001, 115). Small symbolic changes reflected this new attitude. Kirk introduced the Royal Titles Bill, which changed the Queen's formal title from Queen of the United Kingdom to Queen of New Zealand. Upon becoming prime minister, he did not make the obligatory visit to London to visit Her Majesty, as was the tradition of the day (McKinnon 1993, 185).

As leader, Kirk saw a clear relationship between foreign policy and the evolution of New Zealand's national identity. According to Brian Easton, he understood 'foreign policy – in the Pacific, South Africa, nuclear disarmament, racism, foreign aid, and speaking on small independent nations – as contributing to national confidence' (Easton 2001, 186). This sense of growing confidence and independence manifested itself in a number of initiatives. Kirk had been one of the earliest advocates of a nuclear-free zone in the South Pacific as a means of stopping the testing of nuclear weapons in the region. As prime minister, his best-known initiative was to send a navy ship to protest at the French test site at Mururoa and to take action against France in the International Court of Justice. The issue not only reflected Kirk's strong opposition to nuclear weapons, but also his view that the Pacific was New Zealand's home. Kirk's speeches are rich with references to a growing Pacific identity. He called the United Nations 'the world's marae' (Kirk 1973b, 12), and used language and metaphors that broke with the anglocentric foreign policy discourse of his predecessors.

A second defining issue concerned a proposed tour by the racially selected South African rugby team scheduled for 1973. Before the 1972 election both parties had said they would not stop the tour from going ahead, but once in office Kirk changed his mind. He wrote to the New Zealand Rugby Union (NZRFU), urging them to cancel the tour and warning them that it could have an 'effect on New Zealand's broader international relations by reducing our credibility as a humane country with a successful multi-racial society, and opening us up to criticism in forums such as the United Nations' (Bassett, 37). After the NZRFU declined to cancel the tour, Kirk directed them to halt it. His intervention prompted rumblings of discontent around the country but, internationally at least, the decision had a positive result. One contemporary recalls that New Zealand's 'standing as a country, both at the United Nations and at the Commonwealth Prime Ministers' conferences, [rose] immeasurably. After years of vacillating on matters of race at international forums, New Zealand had at last taken a stand' (Bassett, 70).

Kirk's foreign policy reflected a strongly idealistic component. He sought to base New Zealand foreign policy on 'moral principles', describing this as 'the most enlightened form of self interest' (Kirk 1973b). While aware of the role of power in world affairs, he argued that even small countries could play a leadership role in the international system that was emerging after the Vietnam War. 'Small powers are important', he asserted.

> The small countries for whom the rule of law is imperative will work together, will move consistently in international forums in the pursuit of justice and the rule of law. I believe that not only can they succeed, but they will succeed in encouraging the great powers to relinquish strength and to seek justice, better relationships, and peace through cooperation and through a common community dedicated to the advancement of the human family. There are those who say that this is idealistic. But if there are no ideals then there is no hope (Bassett, 70).

Kirk was fortunate in terms of the context in which he made foreign policy. Domestically he had a sizeable majority, making it easier to contemplate new policy positions (McGraw 2002). Internationally, the end of the Vietnam War, and the growing atmosphere of détente, 'meant that Labour could take its initiatives in an atmosphere relatively free from party political bitterness or conflict with the United States or other allies' (McKinnon 1993, 177). China's admission to the UN in October 1971 made recognition of Beijing and the adoption of a 'One China' policy less complicated than it had been for earlier Labour leaders. The fact that Kirk's predecessor as prime minister, Jack Marshall, had secured a trade agreement with the EEC, including France, also gave Kirk much greater freedom of action on nuclear testing. But while this context made opportunities possible, political leadership was still required to make the case for new, sometimes unpopular policies that represented a break with tradition.

Kirk's success in making the case for change seems in part to have come from his personal qualities, that elusive aspect of leadership sometimes called charisma. One study has argued that, 'Kirk alone among post-war New Zealand politicians has been an inspiration' (Easton, 179). Michael Bassett recalls that, 'Kirk made an impact when he went abroad. He was good and unusual copy from a small country, quiet and supine, such as New Zealand had been for much of the previous twenty years' (Bassett, 70). A New Zealand diplomat recalls that Kirk 'cut a swathe' through the United Nations during a visit (McGhie 2005). Lee Kuan Yew remembered Kirk's 'gravitas', describing him in 1999 as 'by far the most impressive New Zealand Prime Minister I have known' (Corner, 146). In addition, Kirk's leadership benefited from an unusually strong relationship with his foreign ministry officials. His Secretary of Foreign Affairs, Frank Corner, recalls an 'unforgettable collaboration' between the prime minister and his ministry (ibid.).

Norman Kirk's short time as prime minister saw a combination of personal vision and leadership coincide with a period in world affairs in which New Zealand was able to stake out new ground in its key relationships and foreign policy priorities. While the change was incremental and resisted by some, the result was the cautious emergence of a new, more independent national identity on the world stage.

Robert Muldoon

A clear difference between the leadership of Kirk and Robert Muldoon can be seen in their views on the purpose of diplomacy. While Kirk saw foreign relations, at least in part, as an identity-building exercise, Muldoon is best remembered for his claim that 'our foreign policy is trade'. According to Simon Murdoch, 'his foreign policy had deep linkages to his concerns and fears about the New Zealand economy and its future' (2001, 153). Others recall that 'his foreign policy was simply an extension of his political approach at home. . . . His aims were as traditional and conservative as his policies at home and equally focused on what he saw as New Zealand's economic interests' (Hensley 2001, 143). One reason he kept the foreign affairs and trade portfolios together was that he believed foreign affairs would give trade negotiators better access to senior officials while abroad (Gustafson 2000, 214–15).

If Kirk was an idealist, Muldoon was deeply pragmatic. He did not see New Zealand as a potentially influential player in world politics; rather he worried about its vulnerability and weakness. Muldoon preferred realism to idealism and was highly critical of what he called the 'sanctimonious humbug' of a 'moral' foreign policy, whether pursued by Kirk or by US president Jimmy Carter (Gustafson 2000, 215, 217–19). Gerald Hensley has described Muldoon's foreign policy as being 'as scrappy, instinctive and matter of fact as the man himself . . . . He had no systematic view of New Zealand's interests abroad, indeed [he] would have distrusted such an approach' (Hensley 2001, 143).

But despite this pragmatism, Muldoon's view of relations with Britain conformed more closely to the traditional idea of 'loyalty'. Like many of his generation he had a deep sentimental attachment to Britain. Shortly after his election in 1975 he declared that his first overseas visit would be to London to see the Queen (Barber 2001, 229). His foreign affairs advisers told him there was no need to visit Britain on the way to Europe and that 'the idea that a New Zealand Prime Minister should visit the Queen before going to another country was an old-fashioned one'. Muldoon replied: 'I *am* old-fashioned' (Gustafson, 225). Britain became the focus of his foreign policy and central to his own personal diplomacy (Hensley 2001, 145). When Argentina invaded the Falkland Islands in 1982, Muldoon expelled the Argentine ambassador and dispatched a frigate to the Indian Ocean to free up a British vessel for the South Atlantic (McKinnon, 207–8). He published an article in *The Times* unambiguously entitled 'Why We Stand with our Mother Country' (Belich, 28). But if his leadership had 'anachronistic elements', it was also influenced by hard-headed calculations of interest (McKinnon 1993, 208). He saw Britain as a crucial conduit within the EEC and he continually lobbied London for extensions of New Zealand's trade privileges.

Muldoon's view of the United States was more complicated, but it was fundamentally based on the realist notion that, as a small state, New Zealand needed a powerful protector. His government reversed Labour's ban on nuclear-armed vessels visiting New Zealand ports. He urged the US navy to send ships (even when no visits were planned), arguing that New Zealand was 'totally vulnerable if we do not retain the freedom of the sea lanes'. As Gustafson notes, 'Muldoon was less concerned with the morality of nuclear weapons than with protecting New Zealand's security and trade' (Gustafson, 230–1). The prime minister frequently played up fears of an expanding Soviet presence in the Pacific and Indian Oceans, even surprising American officials with the strength of his views (McKinnon 1993, 198). Critics have suggested there was a strong whiff of expediency and domestic politics influencing his calls for ship visits, which allowed him to portray Labour's anti-nuclear position as soft on communism and a threat to ANZUS. But James Belich goes further, suggesting that Muldoon saw traditional alliance ties as 'rocks to cling to in changing times' (Belich, 437).

In terms of leadership style, Muldoon brought his 'blunt, confrontational' manner to his foreign policy (Gustafson, 217). His preferred diplomatic method was an uncompromising statement of what he considered to be New Zealand's interests. Occasionally he crossed the line, leading to a number of embarrassing gaffes. Chief among them was a speech in Sydney in 1977 when he derided US president Jimmy Carter as a mere 'peanut farmer' who did not understand 'the realities of America's place in the world' (Gustafson, 218). A visit to the White House was cancelled as a result and only great efforts by New Zealand officials got it rescheduled. Muldoon's undiplomatic language also caused difficulties in relations with African nations and Japan.

This confrontational style carried over into his relationship with his officials. The prime minister frequently ignored official advice when it did not fit with his worldview (Gustafson, 220). He liked to rely on his small advisory group rather than take the advice of the foreign ministry (Gustafson, 215–16). At his first Cabinet meeting he ordered that a separate Prime Minister's department should be created and that the Ministry of Foreign Affairs should be relocated away from parliament. Muldoon's relations with his first Secretary of Foreign Affairs, Frank Corner, were also cool. Corner was a great admirer of Kirk's and a strong supporter of his opposition to apartheid and nuclear testing. Corner personally disliked Muldoon and detested his equation of foreign policy with trade.

After the idealism of the Kirk years, Muldoon's leadership marked a return to a conservative tradition of Holland and Holyoake (McKinnon 1993, 221). Keith Jackson attributes the abrupt policy shift to a 'sudden and dramatic change in New Zealand's balance of payments situation' from 1974 onwards (Jackson 1980, 21). But without dismissing the importance of context, it seems inconceivable that Muldoon's personal beliefs about power and the role of traditional allies did not play a crucial role. The emphasis on Britain, the return of nuclear ship visits, the willingness to 'put domestic political perspectives ahead of foreign policy considerations' in terms of sporting contacts with South Africa, were not positions dictated by international circumstances (Gustafson, 233). Rather, they reflected Muldoon's personal preferences as leader. But this conservatism had its consequences. As Jon Johansson has concluded, 'Muldoon became a prisoner to his own worldview, trapped inside a nostalgic view of a New Zealand that was no more' (Johansson 2001, 277–8).

David Lange

David Lange's Labour Party was swept into power in July 1984 with a popular mandate to initiate change in domestic and foreign policy. A senior official recalls that '[t]here was a widespread sense, almost a 1935 feeling, that the former things had been swept away, that this was the start of a new era' (Hensley 2005). In foreign relations and security, 'the government passed overnight from the RSA generation to the baby-boomers' (ibid.).

In foreign policy, the focus of this new era was the government's anti-nuclear stance. The policy had its origins among environmental and peace groups and had been taken up with enthusiasm by the grass roots of the Labour Party. Ironically, while Lange would come to be intimately associated with the policy, he initially took a cautious position. He strongly opposed nuclear weapons and the logic of nuclear deterrence, but 'found it hard to accept that the Labour Party's policy required the exclusion of nuclear-powered ships' (Lange 2005, 157). While Lange worried about the electoral consequences of a policy that might be seen to threaten ANZUS, he was persuaded that a nuanced position would not go down well with the Labour Party faithful (Lange 1990, 33–34, 62–3).

The nuclear ships dispute and the collapse of the defence relationship with the United States has been called 'New Zealand's War of Independence' and is widely agreed to mark a seminal moment in the country's diplomatic history (McKinnon 1993). Despite that, there is still heated debate about some of the events that led to the breakdown of relations with the United States. There can be no dispute, however, that Lange was the central player and that his personal beliefs and style of leadership played a critical role in determining the outcome.

Lange's view of New Zealand's relations with major powers was closer to Kirk's than Muldoon's. In his memoirs, he recalls that 'I knew when I took the job as foreign minister that the connection to the United Kingdom which had coloured my childhood, while still valuable, had become less and less relevant. I did not want to replace it with dependence on the Americans' (Lange 2005, 220). But although Lange had protested against the Vietnam War and had been critical of US foreign policy, he was not a radical leader in his view of New Zealand's relations with the United States, at least not at first. He worked to find a compromise on the nuclear ships impasse, ensured continued cooperation on intelligence matters and made sure his government did not vote against US military action in Panama.

Lange's personality played an important role in exacerbating the nuclear ships dispute. The relationship between the new government and the United States was on the back foot from the beginning, with the Americans apparently under the misapprehension that Lange had asked for six months after taking office to find a way to allow ship visits. American officials later accused the prime minister of deliberately misleading them, but recent accounts by disinterested officials suggest the problem was more likely a misunderstanding (Norrish 2005).[3] New Zealand diplomats also complained that their efforts to find a compromise (at Lange's direction) did not receive any support from the prime minister. Lange's dislike for personal confrontation and his inability (or lack of interest) in building coalitions within his caucus seem to have been important. These contributed to a communications breakdown with his Cabinet colleagues and the rejection of the USS *Buchanan* in early 1985, the event that precipitated the collapse of ANZUS.

Although Lange did not play a leading role in the development of the anti-nuclear policy, his remarkable rhetorical skills made him the ideal salesman for the position that emerged after the rejection of the *Buchanan*. Despite declaring that New Zealand's policy was 'not for export' the greatest moment in the prime minister's political career came during his performance at the Oxford Union debate in March 1985. Lange remembered later that he did not know how the general public would respond to the breach with the United States, but 'wanted to say something about the nuclear-free policy which would make people at home proud of it' (Lange 2005, 208). His goal was to 'move public opinion away from its attachment to the American military alliance and make nuclear-free New Zealand a reality'. His performance in the debate was a triumph and turned out to be a pivotal moment. One recent essay on New Zealand's national identity concludes that, 'it is not being fanciful to think that in that speech there emerged a kind of confidence that has since spread to our other endeavours in the world' (Brown 2005, 15).

The banning of nuclear-armed and nuclear-propelled vessels marked a fundamental change in New Zealand's place in the world. It destroyed 'the made-in-London-or-Washington mould in which foreign policy had been cast for 40 years' (James 1992, 112). The policy may have been conceived in 'a muddling, uncertain way', but to supporters at least, it was 'a hugely positive step in helping us create a point of definition of the New Zealand character for the outside world' (Laidlaw 1999, 16). Yet whatever the merits of the anti-nuclear stance, it was not a replacement foreign policy. Lange was a remarkable advocate for the anti-nuclear position, but he had less of a vision of an alternative role for New Zealand in the world. In Margaret Hayward's terms, Lange had charisma, but he was not a 'transformational' leader (Hayward 2001, 208).

Some fragments of a new foreign policy stance did emerge and some reflected the prime minister's personal interests. Lange wanted to widen New Zealand's ties to the world. He reopened the High Commission in India that Muldoon had closed. He put emphasis on building relations with African states and symbolically opened a new High Commission in Zimbabwe. Lange's aim 'was to reach out to places where New Zealand interests had not traditionally been advanced or even represented'. He toured Africa in 1985 in an attempt to 'identify with the states which were in the front line of the struggle against apartheid and put our association with white South Africa behind us' (Lange 2005, 210). But many of these initiatives lacked commitment and, despite an attempt by Geoffrey Palmer to give greater emphasis to environmental initiatives when he succeeded Lange as leader, the foreign policy void was only partly filled when Labour left office in 1990 (James, 112, 119–20).

Leadership and Foreign Policy Today

What do the experiences of these three leaders say about the role of prime ministers in constructing a New Zealand identity in world affairs? First, prime ministers are now inescapably international actors. It is impossible to imagine a return to the days when leaders could delegate foreign policy to a trusted colleague and devote all their energies to domestic politics. Indeed, in a world of mass media, prime ministers are more and more likely to be asked to comment on and respond to events on the other side of the world. The more important the foreign policy issue, the more likely it is that the prime minister will address it, rather than the foreign minister or officials. In the current government, for example, Helen Clark has put her personal stamp on a diverse range of key foreign policy decisions, including the deployment of SAS troops to Afghanistan as part of the US-led 'war on terror', the decision not to join the war in Iraq and agreeing to sign the Southeast Asian Treaty of Amity and Cooperation (Clark 2005a).

The result of coalition negotiations following the 2005 election seems to confirm the continuation of this trend. Clark's naming of New Zealand First leader Winston Peters as foreign minister attracted criticism in some quarters, particularly because Peters would be a minister outside Cabinet. But although Peters holds the foreign relations portfolio, Clark seems extremely unlikely to reduce her active role in foreign policymaking. Indeed, one media commentator likened her role to that of an overseeing 'Super Foreign Minister' (Robinson 2005).

Second, context has been important in shaping the leadership of New Zealand prime ministers on foreign policy issues. All have been somewhat pragmatic in their foreign policy positions. All have attached great importance to trade and economic diplomacy. But, despite being a small state with limited resources, New Zealand political leaders have still been able to put their own mark on the country's foreign relations. Kirk had a broad vision of New Zealand's place in the world and was able to work in a remarkable partnership with his officials to move it forward. There is a tendency to exaggerate the extent of the changes that took place under his leadership, partly because of his untimely death, but his time in office was important in the way it represented New Zealand as a more independent state, at last beginning to reconcile its national identity with its geography.

In contrast, Robert Muldoon responded to a similar international context with a very different approach. His conservatism emphasised traditional ties and while his tendency to see foreign policy issues through a domestic lens paid dividends for him politically, it came at a cost to the country's image in the world. He found it hard to move away from the symbols that had been so important to New Zealand for so long, even though he could see the changes in the world that were coming about. This made the changes, when they did come, seem even more momentous than they were.

As leader, David Lange sought to use his rhetorical and communicative skills to embed the idea of a nuclear-free New Zealand as part of the country's national identity. His success was confirmed when the policy was adopted by the National Opposition shortly before the 1990 election and maintained throughout its time in office. Ironically, while the breakdown of ANZUS perhaps happened more by acts of omission than commission (and Lange's leadership was more pragmatic than is often remembered), the anti-nuclear position has become central to New Zealand's national identity. Lange's rhetorical powers helped shatter the 'traditional' foreign policy consensus, inaugurating a wholly new nationalist sense of independence in foreign policy (McKinnon 1993).

This identity continues to have resonance and power today. Helen Clark's refusal to join the US-led invasion of Iraq in March 2003 put her at odds with both the United States and New Zealand's closest ally, Australia, but reflected the same suspicion of power politics that underpinned the ANZUS dispute. When National leader Don Brash – who supported sending troops to Iraq – raised the prospect of repeal of the ban on nuclear propulsion during the 2005 election campaign, Clark was quick to condemn National's policy, saying it was 'not the New Zealand way' (Clark 2005b). In debates and interviews, Brash became more equivocal on the subject, saying National had no plans for a change in policy, and any change would first require approval in a referendum.

Like Norman Kirk, Clark has moved ahead cautiously with symbolic changes signalling a more independent national identity. Her government abolished royal honours, replacing them with indigenous equivalents. It ended the right of appeal to the Privy Council in London, establishing a Supreme Court in its place. Unlike her predecessors, Clark has also realised the role of a prime minister in constructing a New Zealand identity in the world must go well beyond a narrow understanding of politics or diplomacy. She has been enthusiastic to be filmed hiking in the South Island and her government has proven astute at using cultural diplomacy to portray New Zealand as a clean, green and technologically savvy nation. Clark's leadership has sought to not only consolidate the national identity that she inherited from former Labour prime ministers Kirk and Lange, but also to leave her own distinctive mark on the country's place in world affairs.

---

1   I am very grateful to Margaret Clark for letting me consult several chapters from her new book on David Lange before its publication. I am also grateful to Michael Mintrom, Sally Hill and Gerald McGhie for comments on an earlier draft and to Nataliya Mikhenker for research assistance.
2   Bassett adds that foreign affairs were 'particularly important to [Kirk]' (26) and that it was 'an area that was to remain exclusively [Kirk's] despite the appointment of an Associate Minister, Joe Walding' (22).
3   Merwyn Norrish, who was at the meeting between Lange and US Secretary of State George Schultz, concludes that Schultz 'heard what he wanted to hear' (2005, 151). John Henderson, who was not at the meeting, suggests that Lange probably did agree to work for a solution, 'but that this is not the same as promising a successful outcome'. He says, 'Schultz can be forgiven for not understanding "Lange speak". Lange seldom made definitive statements' (2005, 138).

Barber, D. (2001) 'Muldoon and the Media', in Margaret Clark (ed.), *Muldoon Revisited*, Palmerston North, Dunmore.
Barber, J. D. (1977) *The Presidential Character: Predicting Performance in the White House*, Englewood Cliffs, NJ, Prentice Hall.
Bassett, M. (1976) *The Third Labour Government: A Personal History*, Palmerston North, Dunmore.
Bassett, M. and M. King (2000) *Tomorrow Comes the Song: A Life of Peter Fraser*, Auckland, Penguin.
Belich, J. (2001) *Paradise Reforged: A History of the New Zealanders*, Auckland, Allen Lane.
Brown, R. (ed.) (2005) *Great New Zealand Argument: Ideas about Ourselves*, Auckland, Activity Press.
Clark, H. (2005a) 'Election campaign launch', 21 August, available at: http://www.labour.org.nz/labour_team/mps/members_of_cabinet/helen_clark/speeches_and_releases/campaignlaunch21aug2005/index.html
Clark, H. (2005b) 'New Zealand to accede to Treaty of Amity and Cooperation', Office of the Prime Minister press release, 9 May, available at: http://www.beehive.govt.nz/ViewDocument.aspx?DocumentID=22963
Corner, F. (2001) 'Kirk Presents a New Zealand Face to the World', in M. Clark (ed.), *Three*

Labour Leaders, Palmerston North, Dunmore.

Easton, B. (2001) *The Nationbuilders*, Auckland, Auckland University Press.

Gustafson, B. (2000) *His Way: A Biography of Robert Muldoon*, Auckland, Auckland University Press.

Hayward, M. (2001) 'A Comparison of the Leadership and Change Management Styles of Four New Zealand Prime Ministers, 1984–97', in K. Foley (ed.), *Leadership in the Antipodes: Findings, Implications and a Leader Profile*, Wellington, Institute of Policy Studies.

Henderson, J. (1997) 'The Prime Minister', in R. Miller (ed.), *New Zealand Politics in Transition*, Auckland, Oxford University Press.

Henderson, J. (2005) 'The Warrior Peacenik: Setting the Record Straight on ANZUS and the Fiji Coup', in M. Clark (ed.), *For the Record: David Lange and the Fourth Labour Government*, Palmerston North, Dunmore.

Hensley, G. (2001) 'Muldoon and the World', in M. Clark (ed.), *Muldoon Revisited*, Palmerston North, Dunmore.

Hensley, G. (2005) 'The Bureaucracy and Advisors', in M. Clark (ed.), *For the Record: David Lange and the Fourth Labour Government*, Palmerston North, Dunmore.

James, C. (1992) *New Territory: The Transformation of New Zealand 1982–94*, Wellington, Bridget Williams Books.

Jeffries, B. (2001) 'Kirk's Prime Ministership, 1972–1974', in M. Clark (ed.), *Three Labour Leaders*, Palmerston North, Dunmore.

Johansson, J. (2001) 'Muldoon and Character', in M. Clark (ed.), *Muldoon Revisited*, Palmerston North, Dunmore.

Kirk, N. (1973a) 'New Era, New Initiatives', Address to the Annual Conference of the United Nations Association of New Zealand, Victoria University of Wellington, 31 March 1973, Wellington, Ministry of Foreign Affairs.

Kirk, N. (1973b) 'Introduction', in the *Annual Report of the Ministry of Foreign Affairs for the Year Ending 31 March 1973*, Wellington, Ministry of Foreign Affairs.

Laidlaw, C. (1999) *Rights of Passage: Beyond the New Zealand Identity Crisis*, Auckland, Hodder Moa.

Lange, D. (1990) *Nuclear Free – The New Zealand Way*, Auckland, Penguin.

Lange, D. (2005) *My Life*, Auckland, Penguin.

McGhie, G. (2005) Personal communication with author, 22 October.

McKinnon, M. (1993) *Independence and Foreign Policy: New Zealand in the World since 1935*, Auckland, Auckland University Press.

McKinnon, M. (1993a) 'New Zealand External Relations in the Twentieth Century: "Foreign" or "International"?', in A. Trotter (ed.), *Fifty Years of New Zealand Foreign Policy Making*, Dunedin, Otago University Press.

McLeay, E. (2001) 'Rules, roles and leadership', in M. Clark (ed.), *Three Labour Leaders*, Palmerston North, Dunmore.

Miller, R. (1997) *New Zealand Politics in Transition*, Auckland, Oxford University Press.

Miller, R. (2005) *Party Politics in New Zealand*, Melbourne, Oxford University Press.

Murdoch, S. (2001) 'Muldoon and the World', in M. Clark (ed.), *Muldoon Revisited*, Palmerston North, Dunmore.

Norrish, M. (2005) 'The Lange Government's Foreign Policy', in M. Clark (ed.), *For the Record: David Lange and the Fourth Labour Government*, Palmerston North, Dunmore.

Robinson, G. (2005) Comment on Radio New Zealand, *Morning Report*, 19 November.

THREE

Globalisation and the Knowledge Economy

Jacqui True

Globalisation poses new and significant challenges to national identity and calls for innovative forms of political leadership. The New Zealand Information Technology Advisory Group recommended to the government in 2000 that if New Zealand 'does not seize the opportunities of the knowledge economy it will survive only as an amusement park and holiday land for the citizens of more successful developed economies' (ITAG 1999). Economic development in a globally competitive environment is dependent less on accumulating physical capital than on creating and deploying intellectual capital (with the assistance of financial capital). While information and knowledge have always been important for economic growth, we have entered an era in which the ability of individuals, firms, regions and nations to produce, circulate and apply knowledge is fundamental to their competitiveness in a global economy (Bryson et al., 1). This recognition poses some major challenges for political leadership in New Zealand. New Zealand is a comparatively small, highly open country where agricultural commodities still constitute the productive base of the economy. As Chris Tremewan argued at the first Knowledge Wave conference (2001), New Zealand needs to address its 'overdependence on low-value agricultural commodities in a world of low cost competitors' in order to achieve the government's goal of returning New Zealand to the top half of the OECD. Countries reliant for their wealth on physical resources will be progressively disadvantaged as globalised production becomes less based on physical inputs and more on knowledge inputs (Burton-Jones 1999, 15).[1] Political leadership that can communicate and leverage the opportunities of the global knowledge economy in a national setting may be the critical factor distinguishing the most successful states around the world.[2]

These contemporary changes in the production of knowledge and the globalisation of the economy raise a number of questions about political leadership in New Zealand. How has New Zealand responded to the exigencies of the knowledge-based global economy? What new forms of leadership are emerging to take up the challenges of the global knowledge-based economy? Have New Zealand political leaders from across the spectrum been successful in reshaping national political and economic space in an environment where investment and production are globalised? Is there a new consensus about the role of the state? And have new social identities and norms developed in light of these leadership efforts to promote knowledge-based economic growth in New Zealand? This chapter aims to address such questions. It consists of two main parts. The first part discusses the key challenges for political leadership in a globalising, knowledge-driven economy as seen by scholars of international business and political economy. This scholarship implies that success in a global knowledge economy demands both non-traditional political leadership by state actors and new forms of political leadership by non-state actors. The second part of the chapter considers three examples of political leadership in New Zealand that can be seen as nationally specific responses to contemporary globalisation and knowledge-based economic competition. These examples are the New Zealand government's Growth and Innovation Framework established in 2002 and two non-governmental initiatives, the 'Knowledge Wave' conferences and the subsequent creation of the New Zealand Institute, and the bilateral Australia–New Zealand Leadership Forum. The chapter assesses how far and in what ways both government and non-government political leadership has been able to address the local challenges of the global knowledge economy.

The purpose of this chapter is to describe and analyse New Zealand political leadership in the context of globalisation and knowledge-based economic growth. While this analysis is not explicitly prescriptive, it considers managing the country's engagement with the global economy to be one of the key tasks for New Zealand political leaders. Thus, the chapter does not see the option of disengagement with the global economy as desirable or even possible.[3]

Political Challenges in a Global Knowledge Economy

Implicit in a knowledge-driven global economy is the notion that knowledge is most powerful when it is shared, exchanged, networked, diffused and, in the process, expanded. A knowledge-based economy has a zero marginal cost because knowledge is not diminished when given away. In fact, more knowledge can be gained through exchange (Burton-Jones 1999; Dunning 1999). As the New Zealand Knowledge Wave conferences held at the University of Auckland declared, 'knowledge routinely creates new knowledge'. Knowledge is rarely owned or invested in one individual, firm or country. Indeed for firms to increase or deploy their own knowledge effectively they may have to complement this knowledge with that of other firms, and more often than not by way of some kind of collaborative agreement (Dunning 1999, 10). Knowledge production is socialised through collective intellectual commons and a networking logic. In today's economy it is also increasingly globalised across territorial boundaries and multiple locations (Jessop 2000). But precisely because innovation and the levers of innovation such as ideas, people and technology are becoming globalised, knowledge formation and power over knowledge have moved beyond the control of the nation-state. Martin Carnoy and Manuel Castells (2001, 11) argue that the state is less able to determine the means and ends of knowledge production because the discourse on knowledge is outside the state's control in a competitive global market and because information is much more accessible than it has ever been due to advances in technology and communications.

The social democratic state in particular is engaged in managing the contradictions of the knowledge-driven economy (Jessop 1990; see also Cox 1996). It must secure the international capital and investment in order to support domestic economic growth and social redistribution. But, more specifically, it must maintain socialised conditions for the production of knowledge in universities and schools while also creating the conditions for the commercialisation of that knowledge to develop a competitive economic advantage in the global economy. As Carnoy and Castells contend:

> It is mainly through . . . knowledge production and transmission that the state both maintains its legitimacy and shapes the national economic/political space in terms of global investment and production. The better the state can reintegrate its disaggregated workers into a smoothly functioning knowledge based society, the higher the potential return to global capital in those national and regional sites, and the more rapid the economic development in those sites (Carnoy and Castells 2001, 12).

There are advantages for small nation-states such as New Zealand in the globalising knowledge economy. First, from an economic perspective, this so-called borderless economy provides more opportunities for small countries to expand their markets and increase economies of scale (Ohmae 1999; Jacobs 1985). They can access the same multimedia technology and global networks as larger countries. Small countries are also more readily able to reinvent themselves in the global economy and they have less to lose in the process than larger countries. Second, and equally important, the knowledge-based global economy rewards the often unique nature of small countries and their products. Knowledge-based industries typically produce specialised goods and services that are priced on their brand sophistication rather than their lower raw cost (based on mass production). Global branding explicitly recognises the market value of diversity, including cultural, ethnic, aesthetic and lifestyle differences, and distinctive national and regional identities.

While the advantages of openness for sustaining economic growth and prosperity in a globalising world economy are clear, they require political leadership to harness and leverage them for the greatest national benefit. Scholars of international business and political economy have explored concepts of leadership and key challenges for political leadership in a globalising, knowledge-driven economy. They suggest that there may be common leadership strategies among firms and countries.

In a knowledge-based economy the traditional divides between business and political leadership are eroding. Indeed, Kellerman and Webster (2001, 500) consider globalisation the most 'consequential public policy phenomenon facing public leaders'. This is because knowledge-based global competition and the increased globalisation of political and economic decision-making have a direct impact not only on macro-economic management, trade and defence issues but on the whole range of so-called 'domestic' policy issues public leaders are expected to take a lead on (for example, employment relations, education, immigration, taxation, the environment, health care and poverty). As both business and political leaders confront a competitive global context, the leadership skills they need to succeed are similar (Kellerman 1999; see also Olins 1999). Common challenges include increasingly restive and demanding constituencies; a far more intrusive and aggressive media that can affect country bond ratings or firm share prices; more demanding and more public performance reviews; diminished respect for authority; the growing power of money and the rapid pace of change (Kellerman 1999, 161).

Among the knowledge economy challenges for business and political leaders set out in the scholarly literature, the need to foster networks for sharing and synthesising information is crucial. Knowledge production is often expensive, highly uncertain and quickly outdated (Dunning 1999). Networks for sharing knowledge can ameliorate these features of knowledge production and build the mutual capabilities of individuals and firms (Kellerman and Webster 2001, 491). Utilising networks for information and advice also effectively reduces the distance between markets and lowers the barriers to world trade. Kenichi Ohmae's (1999, 199) clarion call to firms rings true for states as well: 'The challenge for leaders over the next decade will be to speed the transition from the static boxes of the twentieth century value chains to the anarchic network of the twenty-first century model'. As Bevir (2003, 474) discusses with respect to the British state, the aim is to effect a shift 'from a world of risk-averse static organizations staffed by bureaucrats to one of complex networks within which social entrepreneurs create synergies and virtuous cycles'. Without such a shift in practices – that would involve many more New Zealand firms defining their global competitive edge and exporting to world markets – New Zealand faces a future in which it will be left behind by larger, high-growth economies that are close to major markets with skilled populations, such as China, India and Brazil, as well as Europe and the United States.

Such a networked approach to leadership involves a change from the past when government officials directed the national economy and innovation through policy decisions and incentives from the centre. Government can no longer engineer the economy in a competitive, knowledge-intensive environment. Rather, government's success in managing the economy is dependent to a large extent on its ability to leverage the resources and expertise of business and civil society partners. Increasingly, government leaders seek to maintain an 'arm's length' from the economy, brokering partnerships with other levels of government, private-sector businesses and 'institutions of collaboration' such as industry organisations, professional associations, chambers of commerce, trade unions, think tanks, technology transfer organisations and university alumni organisations (Porter and Emmons 2003). Although not directly controlling these partnerships, government can define the criteria by which they operate and are evaluated. Institutions of collaboration, in particular, promote the exchange of knowledge and information, fostering coordination among firms, and sometimes carry out joint collective projects. In New Zealand, new institutions such as NZBio, ICT NZ and the Screen Council are intended to serve these crucial roles in economic governance in order to realise the high, knowledge-based growth potential of the information and technology, biotechnology, screen production and design sectors of the national economy.

Political leaders, like business leaders, need to be able to create a sense of national (or firm) identity to unite an often amorphous networked and globalised national economy that no longer falls within clear-cut territorial boundaries. That identity, however, needs to be relevant in an increasingly knowledge-based economy, and flexible enough to adjust to ongoing changes in the ethnic, cultural and demographic makeup and activities of the national population. If it is to help position New Zealand in the global economy such a national identity needs to be inclusive, uniting all New Zealanders by recognising their diverse contributions to social and economic change. But that inclusive vision of nationhood also needs to acknowledge and 'create opportunities for fast-moving mavericks, entrepreneurs and unconventional risk takers', those whom New Zealanders and Australians have traditionally termed 'tall poppies' (Ohmae 1999, 195).

Scholars argue that along with the challenge of building collective identity, political and business leaders need to preserve the core skills and values that underpin the strength of their country/firm in the global knowledge economy. For government leaders this means, among other things, ensuring that knowledge is accessible and that all citizens are well educated. Global competitiveness, Ohmae (1999, 194) argues, is 'ultimately a race for brains and know-how, not for cheap labour'. Conventionally, both explicit and tacit knowledge has been seen as a fixed quantity codified in disciplines and by experts and 'hoarded' by elites or large firms (Castells 2000). This is especially the case in a small society with a unicameral political system such as New Zealand, where tacit knowledge and/or strong ties have been crucial to individual advancement and have often been tightly guarded. However, to have a stake in the global economy where knowledge is less a product than a dynamic and collaborative process, national societies and economies need to support the free exchange and diffusion of knowledge and know-how. One of the major leadership tasks therefore is to transform the education system from a mass-production, one-size-fits-all model toward one better designed for the diverse needs of individual learners and groups of learners (Gilbert 2005, 60–61). In New Zealand this is a particularly important task given the ethnic diversity of the population and the highly unequal educational and employment outcomes among ethnic groups (see Mintrom and True 2004). This disparity has implications for the future of the workforce and New Zealand's ability to sustain its recent economic prosperity.

Preserving core skills and values in a global knowledge economy also requires leadership to encourage throughout society an entrepreneurial attitude that can support national innovation and foster a renewed sense of national identity. Current governments seek to change dispositions that are not compatible with a culture of entrepreneurship and innovation through information and persuasion rather than through coercion and control (Bevir 2003; see New Zealand Government 2002). Rod Oram (2005b) contends that:

> All we need to do [in New Zealand] is value properly what we have – our creativity, innovation, culture and environment – figure out how to turn these into unique and highly profitable products and services, and learn how to sell them to the world.

Ohmae (1999) notes that as organisations become increasingly diverse and amorphous, the notion of who you are and what binds you together becomes a matter of strategic importance. A country such as New Zealand therefore cannot effectively negotiate and implement a new bilateral trade agreement with China or the United States without being driven by a clear sense of priorities, of how the 'free trade' agreement will advance long-term national interests and values. If they are to be successfully pursued, the conception and legitimation for economically liberal policies must always occur in a national context (Helleiner and Pickel 2004).

In a global economic environment, leadership involves thinking across different terrains simultaneously, locally, nationally and regionally as well as globally. The business literature refers to 'leaders without borders', and to leaders who are both generalists and globalists (Kellerman 1999). For political leaders in small countries there are opportunities to do well in a global context. New Zealand leaders, for instance, do not have the luxury of parochially disregarding the broader world. Yet although the relative smallness of their country/firm requires them to be close followers of global politics and markets, New Zealand leaders also need to keep in touch with local developments, which is somewhat easier in a smaller society than a larger one.

Political leadership in a knowledge economy that is increasingly globalised is both seemingly more important and more difficult to pin down. Taken together the leadership challenges of reframing our attitudes to knowledge, stimulating domestic innovation and entrepreneurship, capitalising on our uniqueness to build our identity and market niche and preserving our core skills and values involve the global transformation of New Zealand society and economy. Such transformative leadership may come from traditional political leaders, including prime ministers or politicians and bureaucratic agencies in central government. But increasingly political leadership for national economic gain is also the prerogative of corporate executives and business organisations, non-governmental think tanks and community groups. In the next section, I discuss three examples of how government and non-government actors in New Zealand have responded to the challenges of the knowledge economy and the difficulties of adapting the national society and economy to that globalising world.

New Forms of Leadership for Growing and Globalising New Zealand

The Knowledge Wave Trust

If adapting New Zealand society for the global knowledge economy demands a new form of political leadership, and a departure from government leadership directing the economy from the centre, then the Knowledge Wave conferences held at the University of Auckland attempted to generate this new leadership to bring about economic and social change. The first conference, Catching the Knowledge Wave, held in August 2001, aimed to engender widespread appreciation of the pivotal role that research-based knowledge will play in securing New Zealand's future prosperity. Half of the conference costs were covered by commercial sponsors, a quarter by the government and the remainder by delegate fees. In her opening address to the conference, Prime Minister Helen Clark stated:

> There can be no doubt that over a number of decades New Zealand's economic performance has not kept pace with that of other first world nations. The reasons are obvious. While others have been transforming their economies and societies through the application of knowledge and innovation, we haven't kept up with them. Our export profile resembles that of developing economies, not that of a developed economy. Our economy has not been generating the wealth required to keep us high in the first league.

The success of the first Knowledge Wave conference led to the creation of the Knowledge Wave Trust in 2001. Vice-Chancellor of the University of Auckland at the time, John Hood served as the chair of the Knowledge Wave Trust's nine-member executive board of directors. As an exemplar of public–private partnership, the board was an amalgam of business, political, academic and media interests. Members included the editor-in-chief of the *New Zealand Herald*, Stephen Tindall of the Warehouse and Chris Liddell of Carter-Holt Harvey/International Paper (now at Microsoft). The Trust also had a 35-member advisory board, comprising high-profile politicians, academics, business leaders, government officials and community leaders (Mintrom 2006).

A second Knowledge Wave conference, Knowledge Wave 2003 – The Leadership Forum, was held in February 2003. Hosted by the University of Auckland, this three-day conference was attended by 450 invited guests, people chosen for their roles as opinion leaders in government, business, education, Maoridom and the wider community, although the proceedings were telecast live. Like the 2001 conference, all but one or two of the keynote addresses and papers were given by renowned international speakers, experts on aspects of the knowledge economy who commanded high fees. These speakers for the most part had no prior experience or knowledge of the New Zealand economy or society. The Knowledge Wave Trust (Grant 2003) saw the conference as an opportunity for 'people from all sectors, age groups, and geographies can meet on an equal footing . . . to create lasting national networks to lead change and move the national agenda forward'. However, it is hard to see how the selected nature of the event, led by foreign not local leaders, could generate that kind of political commitment for national change.

Following their attempt at agenda-setting through the large-scale conference events, the Knowledge Wave Trust established a national policy think tank to carry forward the economic and social change agenda of the Knowledge Wave conferences. The New Zealand Institute (NZI) was thus launched in July 2004. Auckland-based, and headed by former Treasury economist David Skilling, the institute currently has an operating budget of around $1 million with four staff. It aims to lead public debate and policy change by generating 'world-class' ideas and solutions through evidence-based research on issues that will have a major impact on New Zealand's economic and social future. The institute runs as a private, not-for-profit organisation funded primarily through an annual membership fee. It is governed by an executive board of 33 directors made up mostly of members of the Auckland business elite. The NZI believes that:

> New Zealand is a country with vast potential and opportunity ahead of it. But we have to overcome a number of challenges if New Zealand is to face up to its full potential. Those challenges won't be met by recycling the same old solutions. We need new solutions and new ideas. We need a new generation of thinking.[4]

Since its establishment the New Zealand Institute has engaged in two major areas of research and advocacy. One area of research, a report on 'Creating an Ownership Society', proposed policy solutions, including government incentives, to help New Zealanders to save more and acquire assets. This research addresses the global knowledge economy challenges in two ways. First, it seeks to build New Zealanders' asset-ownership stake in the economy and thus to preserve the core economic values that can support the growth of New Zealand's competitive advantage in the global economy. Second, proposals for increasing New Zealanders' savings intend to create the conditions typical in globally competitive economies – i.e., household wealth – for greater domestic investment, productivity and growth in the New Zealand economy.

The New Zealand Institute's current research focus is on the international performance of the New Zealand economy (see Skilling and Boven 2005a, 2005b). This research aims to identify actions and policies that can help make New Zealand a genuinely global economy, where much more of 'national income is generated offshore and where New Zealand firms win systematically abroad'. Compared with other countries, New Zealand is not an export-oriented economy, with export/import activities equivalent to approximately 50 per cent of GDP. Yet, given the small size of the New Zealand economy and the already high economic participation rate, the Institute argues that both export activity and outward investment need to increase if the New Zealand economy is to grow or even to maintain the same level of growth of the past 15 years. Currently export-oriented firms have higher productivity rates than other firms; thus increasing exports could also lead to productivity increases across the board. NZI research has identified attitudinal and infrastructural barriers to expanding the number and size of New Zealand's export firms. Businesses, especially small and medium enterprises, need government to help identify potential export opportunities. Market information may be a constraint on growth especially when opportunities for expansion lie primarily in overseas markets. The New Zealand Institute is working to suggest public and private policy solutions to help New Zealand business develop strategies for accessing global markets and increasing offshore investment. This research has clear implications for addressing the local challenges of the global knowledge economy. It aims to spark public debate about an international strategy for New Zealand and influence government policy that could both increase firms' access to knowledge about markets and stimulate knowledge-based exports, which tend to generate higher returns than other exports.

The Growth and Innovation Framework

The New Zealand government has articulated its own view of the challenges of a global knowledge-based economy and how they might be addressed through the cross-government Growth and Innovation Framework. Established in 2002, the Growth and Innovation Framework (GIF) aims to redefine government as *governance* in an open economy, where knowledge-based innovation is the key driver of economic growth.[5] It was founded on the assumption that 'countries which generate and create and adopt new technologies grow faster than those which do not'.[6] In the view of Prime Minister Helen Clark, there are critical and important roles for governments to play in the economy, even though they exercise less formal regulatory power than in the past (New Zealand Government 2002). In launching the GIF the Labour-led coalition government defined those roles as being 'leadership, partnership, facilitation, brokerage, and funding and direct provision where appropriate'. In her 2004 speech to the International Labour Organisation, Helen Clark further elaborated on her government's perspective behind the Growth and Innovation Framework:

> Governments have a unique ability to develop strategies and bring a range of actors together to work for common goals. Securing our country's niche in the global economy in a way which builds high living standards for all is not a task which can be left to market forces. It requires clear and deliberate strategies both to grow the cake, and then ensure that it is fairly distributed (Clark 2004).

Representing a move beyond the 'silo model' of government, the four main components of the GIF are intended to integrate government policies through inter-agency collaboration and 'shared outcomes' (Managing for Shared Outcomes Development Group 2004). These components are strengthening the innovation system, developing and retaining skills and talents, increasing international connections and engaging with enabling sectors.[7] Initiatives to strengthen the innovation system involve efforts to build capabilities in firms and to create more high-growth, high-value firms. These efforts include encouraging supportive inter-firm networks and institutions of collaboration, and aligning research and development expertise with finance capital. Developing skills and talents for an increasingly knowledge-based economy has entailed realignment mainly in the tertiary education sector, working with business to build workforce skill levels through the expansion of the modern apprenticeship scheme and attracting and retaining talented people through immigration policies including the recent 'New Zealand Now' campaign to attract skilled expatriates back to New Zealand.

Another key strand of the Growth and Innovation Framework is to increase New Zealand's international connections. According to Prime Minister Helen Clark, New Zealand's future prosperity depends on the quality of its international linkages. It needs to be involved in the international trade in goods and services, and in attracting investment, people, new ideas and technology (Clark 2002). The New Zealand national economy is increasingly spread beyond fixed geographic borders through global networks of goods, services and people and the government seeks to shape this global environment to New Zealand's advantage. The implementation of this goal involves four main tasks: attracting quality foreign investment; aggressive export promotion that isolates those companies that have the ability to both grow quickly and grow their exports quickly; deepening international relationships and networks between countries, firms and researchers; and improved national branding of New Zealand offshore, through Tourism New Zealand's '100% Pure' advertising in key overseas markets. In order to project a New Zealand brand, the Labour-led coalition government has poured considerable resources into non-traditional economic spheres such as sports, film and tourism that represent New Zealand as an upmarket, innovative and dynamic economy. This global branding is intended to help New Zealand to attract and retain international investment and talented people.

The fourth main component of the GIF requires government to engage with enabling sectors that could have productivity-enhancing effects across the whole economy. This has meant focusing on the knowledge-based economic sectors considered likely to be winners in export markets. The GIF designates biotechnology, ICT, design and screen production as the four sectors potentially able to give New Zealand an overall competitive edge in the global knowledge economy. Probably the most important initiative of this GIF component has been the establishment of 22 industry clusters, private taskforces to develop industry-driven strategies for the four sectors. These taskforces have subsequently facilitated the creation of 'institutions of collaboration' such as NZBio and the Screen Production Council to strengthen the strategic focus and networks within each sector.

The ongoing implementation of the Growth and Innovation Framework is a clear indication that the New Zealand government recognises the challenges of adapting the national economy and society to a fast-changing, increasingly knowledge-based global economy. However, questions could be raised about whether there is sufficient government funding and infrastructural capital behind the GIF to effectively carry out its ambitious goals and if the GIF involves more than just rearranging the existing activities of government. A range of indicators around wellbeing, productivity, skills and talents, investment, innovation, entrepreneurship and technological change, international connectedness and the performance of the enabling sectors have been developed to monitor and benchmark progress on the GIF goals. These indicators should provide a solid basis for evaluating the outcomes of the strategy for growth through innovation and how they position New Zealand in the global knowledge economy. They should enable analysts to examine any potential trade-offs between economic growth goals and quality of life values, such as environmental sustainability and work/life balance.

The Australia–New Zealand Leadership Forum
The Australia–New Zealand Leadership Forum is a private-sector-led initiative (supported by government) intended to develop independent thinking for strengthening the bilateral relationship between Australia and New Zealand. Modelled on the Australia–US dialogues conducted since 1993, it involves an annual meeting of Australian and New Zealand delegations of leading figures from business, government, trade unions, academia and the media selected by their respective CEO chairs without political interference. Business leaders especially see the need to strategically position both countries to maximise their mutual advantage in the face of growing competition in the Asia-Pacific region and global economy.

At the inaugural Leadership forum held in Wellington in 2004, the Australian delegation, led by Qantas chair Margaret Jackson, pushed a bold agenda for a single trans-Tasman market. In their view, the single market has an inherent logic: 20 million Australians plus four million New Zealanders equals a 24-million-strong Australasian market. This agenda was further pursued at the 2005 Leadership Forum in Melbourne. Co-chairs Margaret Jackson and Kerry McDonald (Bank of New Zealand) in their joint statement emphasised the broad, very substantial benefits that could be achieved through greater Australian and New Zealand economic cooperation and integration.[8] They argued:

> Closer economic integration, including through joint regulation and harmonised standard setting, will facilitate trade and economic development in both countries. In an increasingly globalised world, where both countries face many of the same economic challenges, we need fewer barriers to trans-Tasman trade and a more efficient and competitive business environment if we are to compete successfully in regional and international markets.

The co-chairs stressed the important leadership role of business in promoting the benefits of economic integration to both the Australian and New Zealand communities and in achieving the changes. As well as the major 'single market' proposal, the Forum has also provided an opportunity for discussion on key issues relevant to the knowledge economy such as a common border, business and financial regulation, demographics and labour markets, and education and research.

Despite the large differences in the structures and regulatory frameworks of the Australian and New Zealand economies (see Oram 2005a), each delegation acknowledged that the current framework for economic relations, CER (Closer Economic Relations), established in 1981, is increasingly outdated in the fast-globalising world (see Mein Smith and Hempenstall 2005). However, while making some progress, so far the Forums have focused less on the big, strategic issues and tended to get bogged down in concrete, bureaucratic issues such as double taxation, ease of passport entry into Australia and revenue/budget matters.[9] The respective delegations are not well matched for consensus either. The New Zealand delegations, although private sector led, have been dominated by bureaucratic interests when a common Australia–New Zealand vision needs to be shaped by political leaders, not officials. By contrast, the Australian delegations have been dominated by corporate interests, although including a more diverse range of union and academic representatives. Nonetheless, the Australia–New Zealand Leadership Forum is the basis for developing a common regional response to the competitive demands of the global knowledge economy out of an already strong set of economic, political and cultural bilateral relations. For New Zealand, political leadership to promote a single Australasian market represents a crucial initiative in the context of falling standards of living that rank the average New Zealander as one third poorer than the average Australian.

Conclusion

Historically, one of the key tasks for politicians in New Zealand has been to create a sense of nationhood. Whether or not past leaders have been successful in that task, globalisation has major implications for efforts to forge national identity and cohesion today because it diminishes the significance of economic and political borders. But rather than heralding a homogenised world, globalisation provides new opportunities for constructing a distinctive national identity and political unity. Indeed, a coherent national vision for social and economic development is the foundation for success in the knowledge-based global economy.

The purpose of this chapter has to been highlight the importance of political leadership in adapting a national society and economy for the competitive challenges of the global knowledge economy. These challenges are so fundamental to the future wellbeing and prosperity of New Zealand that business and other civil society actors have not wanted to leave the job of political leadership to government alone. At the same time, the government has recognised that many economic and social processes are now global and beyond their control, and that it cannot lead an innovative New Zealand from above or from the centre. Increasingly, government must share political leadership with the private sector and broader civil society. Only together can these actors, employing 'soft power' strategies of information, persuasion and leadership by demonstration, move New Zealand to the cutting edge of a globalising world.

1   To take just one example of the growing importance of knowledge inputs: 'it has been estimated that 80 per cent of the value added in US manufacturing industry represented primary or processed foodstuffs, materials and mineral products, and 20 per cent knowledge, by 1995 these proportions had changed to 30 and 70 per cent respectively' (Dunning 1999, 8). Moreover, research and development expenditures in OECD economies increased three times the rate of output in manufacturing industry (1999, 9).

2   See Weiss (1998) and compare the experiences of Ireland, Singapore, Finland and New Zealand and their economic indicators on foreign direct investment, exports as a proportion of GDP, research and development spending, and productivity.

3   This chapter seeks to go beyond criticisms of the ideological nature of the knowledge economy discourse (see, for example, Codd 2005; Hope and Stephenson 2005; Roberts 2005) and does not share the anti-globalisation position of the New Zealand Green Party on trade agreements, for example, the future bilateral agreement between New Zealand and China.

4   See the website of the New Zealand Institute, www.nzinstitute.org.

5   The term governance signifies 'the shift from "state/government" to "multilayered governance", not only of states and markets but also of interstate relations and security' in response to the demands of a global knowledge economy and democratic, political contestations around the state (Rai 2004, 579).

6   'Strengthening the Innovation System', accessed 7 November at http://www.gif.med.govt.nz/aboutgif/innovation.asp.

7   Working with regions, assisting business development and strengthening infrastructure for economic development are also included as key components of the Growth and Innovation Framework.

8   The Joint Statement by Co-Chairs of the Australia–New Zealand Leadership Forum, April 2005, accessed 10 September at: http://www.mfat.govt.nz/foreign/regions/australia/leadershipforum/chairstatementapr05.html

9   Interview with an anonymous participant at the Australia–New Zealand Leadership Forum, 11 September 2005.

Burton-Jones, A. (1999) *Knowledge Capitalism: Business, Work, and Learning in the New Economy*, Oxford, Oxford University Press.

Bevir, M. (2003) 'Narrating the British State: an interpretative critique of New Labour's institutionalism', *Review of International Political Economy*, 10, 3, 455–80.

Bryson, J. R., P. W. Daniels, N. Henry and J. Pollard (eds) (2000) *Knowledge, Space, Economy*, London, Routledge.

Carnoy, M. and M. Castells (2001) 'Globalization, the knowledge society, and the Network State: Poulantzas at the millennium', *Global Networks*, 1, 1, 1–18.

Castells, M. (2002) *The Rise of the Network Society*, Oxford, Blackwells.

Clark, H. (2002) 'Growing an Innovative New Zealand', Prime Minister's Statement to Parliament, 12 February.

Clark, H. (2004) 'Speech to International Labour Organisation on the Social Dimensions of Globalisation', Geneva, May.

Codd, J. (2005) 'Education policy and the challenges of globalization: Commericialization or citizenship?', in J. Codd and K. Sullivan (eds), *Education Policy Directions in Aotearoa New Zealand*, Southbank, VIC, Thomson Dunmore Press.

Cox, R. W. with T. Sinclair (1996) *Approaches to World Order*, Cambridge, Cambridge University Press.

Crosby, B. C. (1999) *Leadership for Global Citizenship: Building Transnational Community*, New York, Sage.

Dunning, J. H. (ed.) (1999) *Regions, Globalization, and the Knowledge-Based Economy*, Oxford, Oxford University Press.

Gilbert, J. (2005) 'Catching the knowledge wave? "Knowledge society" and the future of public education', in J. Codd and K. Sullivan (eds), *Education Policy Directions in Aotearoa New Zealand*, Southbank, VIC, Thomson Dunmore Press.

Grant, A. (2003) 'Leaders From All Sectors Pool Ideas', *New Zealand Herald*, 17 February.

Helleiner, E. and A. Pickel (eds) (2004) *Economic Nationalism in a Globalizing World*, Ithaca, Cornell University Press.

Hope, W. and I. Stephenson (2005) 'Global capitalism and the knowledge economy: The New Zealand experience', in J. Codd and K. Sullivan (eds), *Education Policy Directions in Aotearoa New Zealand*, Southbank, VIC, Thomson Dunmore Press.

ITAG (1999) *The Knowledge Economy*, Wellington, Minister for Information Technology's IT Advisory Group.

Jacobs, J. (1985) *Cities and the Wealth of Nations*, New York, Vintage.

Jessop, B. (2000) 'The State and the Contradictions of the Knowledge-Drive Economy', in J. R. Bryson, P. W. Daniels, N. Henry and J. Pollard (eds), *Knowledge, Space, Economy*, London, Routledge.

Kellerman, B. and S. W. Webster (2001) 'The Recent Literature on Public Leadership: Reviewed and Considered', *Leadership Quarterly*, 12, 485–514.

Kellerman, B. (1999) *Reinventing Leadership: Making the Connection between Politics and Business*, Albany, State University of New York Press.

Managing for Shared Outcomes Development Group (2004) *Getting Better at Managing for Shared Outcomes: A Resource for Agency Leaders*, Managing for Outcomes Programme Office, Department of Prime Minister and Cabinet, Te Puni Kokiri, State Services Commission and the Treasury, retrieved from: http://www.ssc.govt.nz/upload/downloadable_files/mfso-resource.pdf

Mein Smith, P. and P. Hempenstall (2005) 'Changing community attitudes to the New Zealand/Australia relationship', paper prepared for the Australia–New Zealand Leadership Forum, April, accessed 7 November at: http://www.mfat.govt.nz/foreign/regions/australia/leadershipforum/uccjj.html

Mintrom, M. (2006) 'Policy Entrepreneurs, Think Tanks and Trusts', in R. Miller (ed) *New Zealand Politics and Government*, 4th edn, Melbourne, Oxford University Press.

Mintrom, M. and J. True (2004) *Framework for the Future: Toward Equal Employment Opportunities in New Zealand*, New Zealand Human Rights Commission.

New Zealand Government (2002) *Growing an Innovative New Zealand*, Wellington.

Ohmae, K. (1999) 'Strategy in a World without Borders', in F. Hesselbein and P. M. Cohen (eds), *Leader to Leader: Enduring Insights on Leadership from the Drucker Foundation's Award-Winning Journal*, San Francisco, Jossey-Bass.

O'Sullivan, F. (2004) 'TransTasman Summit: NZ Inc quickly set up', *New Zealand Herald*, 14 May, A7.

Oram, R. (2005a) Business column, *Sunday Star-Times*, 1 May.

Oram, R. (2005b) 'Tough task for our politicians – and us', *Sunday Star-Times*, 21 August, D2.

Porter, M. E. and W. Emmons (2003) 'Institutions for Collaboration, Overview', *Harvard Business School Case*, 9-703-436.

Rai, S. M. (2004) 'Gendering Global Governance', *International Feminist Journal of Politics* 6, 4, 579–601.

Roberts, P. (2005) 'Tertiary education, knowledge, and neoliberalism', in J. Codd and K. Sullivan (eds), *Education Policy Directions in Aotearoa New Zealand*, Southbank, VIC, Thomson Dunmore Press.

Skilling, D. and D. Boven (2005a) *No country is an island: Moving the New Zealand economy forward by taking it to the world*, discussion paper 2005/3, Auckland, New Zealand Institute.

Skilling, D. and D. Boven (2005b) *The international performance of the New Zealand economy*, discussion paper 2005/4, Auckland, New Zealand Institute.

True, J. (2004) 'Country Before Money? Economic Globalization and National Identity in New Zealand', in E. Helleiner and A. Pickel (eds), *Economic Nationalism in a Globalizing World*, Ithaca, Cornell University Press.

World Economic Forum (2005) *Global Competitiveness Report 2005/06*, New York, Palgrave.

FOUR

Populist Roots of Political Leadership in New Zealand

Barry Gustafson

The *vox populi,* the voice of the people, usually referred to today as public opinion, is important in both democratic and non-democratic societies. Throughout history, governments, political parties and individual leaders have sought to legitimise themselves and mobilise support through popular appeals that have often been based on the defining of group identity and shared interest that differentiates those appealed to from others. Not all, however, can be labelled 'populist'.

The terms 'populist' and 'populism' are not easy to define precisely. There are two possible ways of defining those words. One is a strict definition that covers movements of protest against governments or parties seen as entrenched defenders of the existing political, economic and social order. The other is a looser definition covering any political leader or movement able to mobilise popular support on a broad basis.

The essence of populism is a belief in the soundness of the collective values and instincts of the 'ordinary people' within society, as distinct from elites and/or minorities that are perceived and portrayed as being corrupt and a threat to the unity and the welfare of the 'ordinary people'. Virtue resides in the people and in their collective traditions, and the populist politician seeks to identify with, articulate and even personify the people's interests and will against the political and business elites who have usurped power and betrayed the people (Love 1984; Gustafson 1993a; Bennett 2002–3).

Non-democratic leaders of various types, in both opposition and government, have often tried to build popular support by appealing to ethnicity, religion or an ideology such as fascism or communism that stresses the priority of the 'ordinary people' in the nation. Such populist leaders blame society's problems on corrupt and untrustworthy leaders, despised foreigners, religious or ideological nonconformists, or unpopular domestic minorities, who, it is argued, threaten the state's homogeneous identity and unity or conspire against the welfare of the majority. Many of the leaders of post-colonial states in the latter half of the twentieth century were populists.

In democracies also from time to time politicians emerge who are clearly populist. Of course, in an effort to win votes, most democratic politicians seek to persuade voters that they represent the majority and can be trusted more than their rivals. Democracy involves transactions between politicians and voters. At elections, politicians promise to meet voters' specific material wants, such as jobs, heath care, education, housing, tax cuts. The politicians also appeal to the voters' concerns, emotions and prejudices in fields such as external security, law and order, immigration and threats to traditional values and culture.

Characterising Populist Leaders

The term 'populist leader', however, usually refers in a democracy like New Zealand to a politician who goes beyond bargaining for votes, or simply showing a populist tendency, or making a populist appeal, to one who exhibits all or most of the characteristics that were first discerned in a modern democracy in the People's Party, which sprang up in the rural United States in the 1890s (Hofstadter 1960). One can argue that the populist tradition has remained a strand of American politics ever since and has been most recently observable in the unsuccessful presidential campaigns of the minority candidates Ross Perot, Pat Buchanan and Ralph Nader, and also in the campaigns of the Democrats against the influence of big business on the Bush administration, and the Republicans against the influence on the Democrats of liberal social engineers unrepresentative of America's traditional 'moral majority'.

The first characteristic is the populist leader's claim to know what ordinary, decent and commonsense people think and want, and to be able, therefore, to empathise with their frustrations and aspirations, and speak on their behalf. The populist leader blames the established political parties and leaders for having become corrupted and for having deceived, forgotten or ignored the interests of the common man and woman. Such a politician projects understanding, sympathy, certainty and strength to those seeking solace, reassurance and security from a leader who can be trusted. Somewhat ironically, a populist leader will often condemn politicians generally and warn against trusting them, with the exception of course of him- or herself, who only has the good of the people at heart.

Secondly, populists usually draw much of their support from people who feel marginalised, insecure, deprived, threatened, neglected, displaced, frustrated, deceived or betrayed by those currently in power, particularly during times of rapid economic recession, technological modernisation and social change. Struggling small farmers, small business people, the self-employed, and those on relatively low fixed incomes may often respond to their perceived loss of status and/or income, or threat of such loss, by rallying to a populist leader. They often resent what they see as their hard-earned income being taken from them and given to welfare beneficiaries, non-productive civil servants or new immigrants. Often people in rural areas or small towns dislike what they see as their neglect or exploitation by politicians, bureaucrats and businessmen from the large cities. Populist leaders, parties and movements lose much of their saliency and appeal as conditions improve and emotions calm.

Thirdly, populism is anti-elitist. Populists see conspiracies and hidden agendas among urban big business, bankers, politicians, bureaucrats and intellectuals to enrich or advance themselves in ways detrimental to the 'ordinary people' or the 'silent majority'. Often those elites are seen as arrogant, deviant and treacherous cosmopolitan minorities driven not only by selfish greed but also by alien ideas imported from abroad. Populism can be intensely moralistic and despises people who become rich through speculation, monopoly or lending at high interest rates.

A fourth characteristic is an intense nationalism opposed to foreign influence, including that of international organisations, multinational companies and foreign investment. This can become ethnocentric, anti-intellectual, anti-immigrant and even racist. Populists are prone to promote a 'them–us' attitude towards those perceived as not the 'ordinary people' and to scapegoat those who are different and to blame them for unsatisfactory situations. As a result, populists tend to be anti-multicul-turalism and to favour instead a homogeneous society into which minorities become assimilated.

Fifthly, populism usually simplifies and exploits people's nostalgia for a supposedly more certain, secure and moral past and may well be reactionary in promising to rebuild the moral values and social relationships of that past.

Sixthly, a populist leader is not only the dominant operational leader of a movement or party but often comes to personify it publicly and in the minds and hearts of rank and file supporters. This makes it difficult for secondary leaders to disagree with the leader or even succeed that leader when he or she dies or is overthrown.

Populism, in short, involves a deep sense of injustice. It is a romantic, rather than a rational, reactive protest against the decay of the old order, against a perceived loss of national identity and even sovereignty, against the malign influence of elites, and against those who do not fit the national stereotype. Although it is possible to discern what a person favours from what they oppose, one writer has suggested that modern populism simply feeds on a range of negative sentiments. It is anti-big business, anti-the political establishment, anti-union, anti-corruption, anti-intellectual, anti-modern, anti-foreign, anti-minority, even anti-the political system itself (Schedler, 1996, 292–3; Miller 1993). All this is usually articulated by and personified in a dominant leader.

External events outside the control of a government may well create the potential for the emergence of or an upsurge in support for a populist leader, for example: defeat in a war; hyperinflation destroying the savings and pensions of the middle classes; a serious economic recession or depression; dramatic economic restructuring; rapid and radical social and cultural change; or mass immigration perceived as threatening by native-born citizens. These events can provide a context for heightening a politician's situational charisma. The politician assures voters that they are not responsible for their predicament but are innocent victims and promises to fix the problem and prosecute and punish those responsible.

Populists, however, are much better at identifying problems, protesting against them and blaming others than in suggesting comprehensive, specific and practical solutions. Most populist politicians flourish in opposition rather than in government. They appeal to emotion rather than the intellect and are reactionary in looking backwards rather than progressive in looking forward. Many populist politicians can be criticised not only for being negative and emotional but also for being opportunistic, seeking to advance their careers by cynically manipulating public prejudice and resentments.

Populist leaders can of course be either moral or immoral in their appeal. Moral populists seek to bridge sectional interests, propose positive reforms and inspire and lead people toward some common good. On the other hand, immoral or negative populists seek merely to exploit people's, admittedly often understandable and legitimate, fears and frustrations by blaming scapegoats in order to gain personal power as an end in itself (Burns 1978; Clarke 1991).

One significant characteristic of populism is that the populist politician seeks to engage directly with the population by talking to the people over the heads of the political establishment and by reminding the experts, bureaucrats and other politicians that the people know best. This has become much more possible since the development of the electronic media and public opinion polling. Populists can now appeal directly through television and radio to their supporters and potential followers in their homes and monitor that appeal not merely through intuition but through continual polling. The short sound bites used in television in particular lend themselves to the unqualified, dogmatic simplification so suited to populist rhetoric. As the late Labour politician Arthur Faulkner used to like reminding his colleagues, 'There are two truisms in politics: people matter most and KISS – keep it simple, stupid'.[1]

In recent years, there has been some irony in seeing the development of what has been called 'market populism', in which the 'New Right' neo-liberal followers of F. A. Hayek and Milton and Rose Friedman have attacked the state bureaucracy, state regulation and state welfare and stressed the freedom of the market and the individual, in ways and rhetoric reminiscent of earlier, but much more anti-big business, populists (Sawer 2003). 'New Right' populists attack government elites, both politicians and bureaucrats, as special interests. They are seen as a highly educated 'meritocracy', which, it is alleged, holds values different from and views contemptuous of traditional mainstream citizens. This is a new class, happy to tax producers and redistribute wealth through welfare, while at the same time making more and more people dependent on the state and also more controlled by it. The new elite also engages in 'politically correct social engineering' because it is perceived as drawing its membership and core support disproportionately from feminists, homosexuals, ethnic minorities, the irreligious and those employed in managing the public sector.

Populist Politicians in New Zealand

Most significant New Zealand politicians in the last hundred years have exhibited some of the characteristics associated with populist leadership, though many would have resented being called populist. Certainly on the left of the political spectrum, 'King Dick' (Richard John) Seddon, prime minister and Liberal leader from 1893 to 1906, and Michael Joseph Savage, Labour's first prime minister 1935–40, claimed, with some justification, to understand and represent the relative have-nots in a society devastated by the depressions of the 1880s and the 1930s respectively. They also portrayed themselves as the foe of urban bankers and businessmen and large landowners and as the paternalistic defender of the interests of small farmers and manual workers. They both offered strong leadership to create a fairer society for the majority of the population and tried to arouse the 'ordinary people' and transform their basically self-centred aspirations into a transcending moral crusade for righteous collective action. Neither, however, can be simply and clearly labelled a populist when measured against all the characteristics mentioned above (Hamer 1993; Gustafson 1986 and 1999).

On the right of the political spectrum, the Reform Party leader 'Kaiser Bill' (William Ferguson) Massey, prime minister 1912–25, and the National Party's equally forceful Sidney George Holland, prime minister 1949–57, were adept at portraying their parties as the representative of 'ordinary' New Zealanders against alien trade unionists with their foreign Marxist and syndicalist ideologies and their British or Australian accents. But again, neither was really a populist (Gustafson 1993a and 2000a).

The New Zealand prime minister who most closely matches the populist model was undoubtedly Robert David Muldoon. He believed that the majority of New Zealanders wanted a strong, competent leader and he sought, with considerable success for a long time, to cultivate that image. Muldoon was demonstrably and sometimes violently anti-elitist and anti-intellectual and suspicious of the bureaucracy. He distrusted ideology, whether from the extreme left or the extreme right. He saw both unionist officials and bankers as threats to the welfare of the community as a whole, which needed to be protected by the government from their excesses. His goal was always the creation or maintenance of a fair society characterised by equality of opportunity. He disliked foreign interference in New Zealand affairs, demonstrated a very conservative nostalgia for the past, economically and socially, and exalted ordinary people, part of whom he saw as 'Rob's Mob', and their interests and wishes. He was paternalistic in his attitude towards the 'ordinary bloke or blokess' and felt that he instinctively understood and represented them. Socially he stressed conformity and community rather than pluralism or individualism and he valued stability and security above all else. As a result he was equally trenchant in condemning 'left-wing stirrers' and 'right-wing greedies', both of whom threatened the unity or prosperity of the 'ordinary people'. His populism was most evident in opposition between 1972 and 1975 and again after he was ousted as National's leader in 1984. Shortly before becoming prime minister he marked out his populist credentials by asserting that 'Economics is not money, or wealth, or resources, but people; their hopes, their fears, their reactions to stimuli or adversity', and his 1975 election slogan, 'New Zealand the way *you* want it', was quintessential populism (Muldoon 1974, 1977, 1981 and 1986; Gustafson 2000b; Zavos 1978; Templeton 1995; Jones 1997; Moon 1999; Easton 2001; Clark 2004; Johansson 2002 and 2005).

Like most populist leaders, Muldoon was not a particularly good team man but thought he personally knew best. Increasingly, lieutenants in cabinet and caucus became reluctant to challenge him. In time, he came to personify his party. Many of his followers, dismissed by opponents as 'Rob's Mob', felt that their loyalty to him was greater than their loyalty to the party he led and which after 1984 they perceived as rejecting him and them. Muldoon had a strong personality and an obsessive ego. He believed that he not only had more ability and integrity than those in office but that he had a duty to articulate discontent, to defend a somewhat over-romanticised past that was being dismantled, to try to protect those who were being disadvantaged by the upheavals, and to promise justice or revenge against those who were, in his opinion, damaging the 'ordinary bloke'. Certainly, in 1975, if not after 1984, he showed that the more the political, commercial, intellectual and social establishments attack a populist leader, the more likely that person is to be regarded by his or her followers as a hero being persecuted for the courage of their convictions and defence of the views and interests of their followers.

The most populist of New Zealand's political figures, however, never became prime minister but engaged in what one commentator has called 'the politics of victimhood'.[2] They were the leaders of smaller parties, often with a distinctive base of supporters who felt alienated from the political, economic and social establishments and who saw a charismatic personality as their spokesman.

They include, in the 1930s, Tahupotiki Wiremu Ratana, who although never himself a Member of Parliament created a new Maori Christian denomination and social movement and rallied the excluded, dispossessed and powerless among Maori voters. Eventually, recognising that a small group of independent Maori MPs was unlikely to achieve significant political and legislative change without the help of a larger mainstream political party, he established an electoral alliance with Labour. That broke the political power of the traditional and conservative tribal leaders and politicians such as Te Puea and Apirana Ngata and transferred all four Maori seats into the hands of Ratana's supporters, including his son and, subsequently, his daughter-in-law (Ballara 1996). In some ways the defection from Labour of Matiu Rata and his creation of the independent Mana Motuhake Party in the 1980s and the more recent emergence of a new Maori Party under the leadership of Tariana Turia and Dr Pita Sharples have similar populist roots, including a deep sense of betrayal over the Treaty of Waitangi and all that it symbolised to Maori.

John A. Lee was a fiery Labour politician able to whip up emotions with his oratory at mass meetings or in well-crafted novels, pamphlets and articles. A one-armed war hero, Lee was a MP 1922–8 and 1931–43 and certainly exhibited many of the characteristics of a populist politician. He became a trenchant critic of businessmen, bankers, trade union bosses and the Catholic Church but, when Savage thwarted his ambition, Lee responded so viciously that he was expelled from the Labour Party in 1940, though he remained an MP until defeated at the general election three years later. An admirer prior to World War II of the 'strength' of Hitler and Mussolini, Lee formed in 1940 a short-lived and unsuccessful Democratic Soldier Labour Party, which was marked by a distinct cult of the personality (Olssen 1977 and 1999).

Just as Lee split away some of Labour's vote at the 1943 election, polling just over 4 per cent of the vote but winning no seats, so in 1984 Bob Jones's short-lived New Zealand Party, which gained just over 12 per cent of the vote, could partly be seen as a populist revolt and protest against Muldoon and the National Party (Aimer 1985; Gustafson 2002b, 339–42 and 381–2; Jones 1997, 143–53). Jones and his party appealed particularly to disaffected conservative voters, those in business, the professions, farmers and the self-employed, most of whom had previously voted National or Social Credit. Jones, a one-time admirer and supporter of Muldoon, was a self-made millionaire who was never really part of the business establishment. Very much an individualist he was a direct and effective speaker and writer, often abrasive and sometimes arrogantly so. He detested state intervention and control and the interference of bureaucratic regulators, politically correct busybodies, traffic officers and journalists in his life. The principles for which he and his party stood were those of liberal capitalism and indeed leaned towards libertarianism: freedom; private enterprise; individual initiative, rewards and responsibility; private ownership; national self-reliance. In some policy areas, such as education and defence, however, the New Zealand Party adopted modern, even radical, policies. This made it difficult to classify it as simply a conservative or right-wing party, although it won very little support from former Labour voters. Jones himself exuded confidence and authority and the fact that the New Zealand Party was generally referred to as 'the Jones Party' indicates the extent to which he dominated and personified it. He and the party were indistinguishable. Jones was a charismatic leader, he did challenge the political establishment, from which he had become alienated and which he regarded as betraying the best interests of the country, and he did attract supporters who also felt they were oppressed and/or marginalised.

Populist leaders and parties in the United States and elsewhere have often appealed to fundamentalist and evangelical religious voters who not only disliked state interference and control in their economic and social lives but who also despaired of what they saw as a breakdown in conventional morality and family values. The social and moral agendas were seen as having been hijacked by irreligious intellectuals and self-interested deviant minorities in ways that were anathema to the supposedly 'silent majority' of ordinary 'moral' people. In New Zealand, such morally conservative politicians, who have included conservative Catholics as well as Protestants, have been usually accommodated within major parties, for example the anti-abortion leaders Dr Gerald Wall in Labour or Frank Gill in National. In recent decades, however, smaller, morally conservative parties have emerged, seeking to rally voters who feel threatened by what they see as the success of non-religious, if not anti-religious, liberals in increasingly dominating the political agenda on such matters as abortion and homosexuality, in rejecting conventional family values and even the traditional family unit itself, and in facilitating the availability of alcohol and drugs and promoting sexual promiscuity among younger New Zealanders. They see the major parties, Labour and National, as avoiding such issues either because of the inevitable division attention to them causes among their diverse caucuses and constituencies or even because, in the case of Labour, it appears already to have been captured by the social liberals. As a result, a number of Christian-influenced populist leaders and small parties have emerged: the Christian Heritage Party, the Christian Democrats, the Christian Coalition, Future New Zealand, United Future and most recently Destiny New Zealand.

The populist appeals of such parties are illustrated in books written by two of their leaders, Graeme Lee and Peter Dunne. Lee, a former National Party MP and cabinet minister, and subsequently an evangelical pastor, argues that, 'Most people today would say integrity is a joke as it applies to central politics. Indeed, over recent years Parliament has come to represent the very opposite of integrity by its behaviour .... The catchy by-line to the Christian Democrats Political Party was "Pro-Family, Pro-Values, Pro-Life". The "pro" stands for proactive and "strongly for". Consider how much time we spend acting reactively. We find it easier to rage after the event than to work harder to pre-empt the issue' (Lee 2002, 35, 63).

In speech after speech, Dunne, a former Labour MP and minister, has referred to 'the deep cynicism and mistrust most voters have about politicians and political parties ... because they have been lied to and let down too often'. He claimed that 'We have had enough of the disillusionment, the political double-talk, the broken promises, the character assassination and the lack of core values, that have driven politics for too long' and that he was 'fed up with seeing the sensible mainstream of our nation derided, while we pander more and more to every whim of the extremists. Every strike against mainstream families is a strike against the core of our society, and a further triumph for ideology over common sense.' He added that ' Leadership is always a pact between the leader, the followers, and a dream ... leadership is about serving the public; understanding people's needs, and responding to them in a principled and coherent way' (Dunne 2002, 24–6).

Three other New Zealand politicians who emerged in the latter quarter of the twentieth century were undeniably populists. They were Bruce Beetham, Jim Anderton and Winston Peters, all of whom became the undisputed leaders of their parties and personified what those parties stood for, or more correctly against. They were neo-conservatives, not neo-liberals, and led parties that were marked by nostalgia and xenophobia and a distrust of big business, big government, globalisation and the two traditional large parties, National and Labour, from the disillusioned constituencies of which the new smaller parties derived many of their supporters.

Beetham, a teacher and teachers' training college lecturer, who had spent most of his career in the Waikato, became the Social Credit Party's leader in 1972 and was to lead it for the next fourteen years, for six of them as MP for Rangitikei (1978–84). Although Beetham developed something of a personality cult, Social Credit also had a committed core of members who believed fervently in a financial conspiracy against the people. Many had been almost evangelically committed to their cause for many years before Beetham even joined the party, less than three years before he became leader. They were small farmers and small businessmen, self-employed accountants, lawyers, doctors and tradesmen, and tended to come from rural areas and smaller towns that saw themselves as neglected or even exploited by the urban elites, cosmopolitan bankers, an arrogant and expensive bureaucracy and a callous and possibly corrupt government. Many were also religious and socially conservative, despite their commitment to radical monetary reform based on a detestation of usury. Particularly at the 1978 and 1981 elections, when Social Credit polled 16 per cent and almost 21 per cent respectively, Beetham and Social Credit's support was augmented by a larger group of 'protest voters', who expressed their dissatisfaction with what they saw as both Labour's and National's indifference towards them and their interests (Bryant 1981; Miller 1985).

Anderton was at first a mainstream politician as president of the Labour Party and from 1984 to 1989 Labour MP for Sydenham. Denied cabinet office by his caucus colleagues and increasingly critical of the New Right economic policies pursued by David Lange and Roger Douglas after 1984, Anderton resigned from the Labour Party in 1989 and formed a breakaway NewLabour Party. Re-elected for that new party in 1990, he subsequently formed and in 1991 became leader of an Alliance of three minor anti-establishment parties, all of which exhibited populist characteristics: NewLabour, the Democrats (formerly Social Credit) and Mana Motuhake. The Greens and a short-lived Liberal Party, formed by two defecting National Party MPs, Hamish McIntyre and Gilbert Myles, joined the Alliance the following year. As one NewLabour and Alliance member observed, 'It would not be an exaggeration to say that there was a revivalist tone to the early Alliance. Other parties might break their promises, but the Alliance would not' (Jesson 1997).

Probably the most anti-establishment party in the Alliance, although it broke away and stood separately at the 1999 and 2002 elections, was the Green Party. The Greens were populist in many ways, disliking techno-logical modernisation, unfettered consumerism, economic globalisation, multinational corporations, and the influence on New Zealand of for-eign governments, such as the United States, or international economic organisations, such as the International Monetary Fund, the World Trade Organisation, and the Asia Pacific Economic Council. They also showed, however, that populism does not always manifest itself through a disciplined party led by a dominant leader but may be much more a mass movement bringing together, under collective leadership, a number of sometimes related single-issue protest or pressure groups: women's, labour, civil rights, consumer, anti-war, anti-nuclear, ethnic minority, gay and lesbian, as well as environmental.

For a time it was thought that another disaffected National Party MP, Winston Peters, a former minister, might join the Alliance. However, when he finally left National in 1993, he rejected approaches from the Alliance and chose instead to form his own party, New Zealand First. At its launch, with classic populist rhetoric, he declared that he and 'the relegated, denigrated and forgotten' people would hold politicians to account and would restore honest government in the interests of all to New Zealand (Peters 1993).

Peters is undoubtedly the most obvious contemporary populist politi-cal leader in New Zealand. He embodies almost all the characteristics of the model (Hames 1995; Miller 2003). A charming and courageous, if egocentric, politician, Peters over a long period built his personal reputation, political following and eventually independent party, New Zealand First, by exploiting widespread discontent during the 1980s and 1990s and consistently and stridently attacking the political, bureaucratic, business, financial and intellectual elites. He often argued that these elites were sometimes not simply inefficient but corrupt in conspiring against the interests of ordinary citizens and in not protecting them from financial predators, dangerous criminals and excessive numbers of foreign immigrants and refugees.

Peters was originally elected as a National Party Member of Parliament, first for the marginal South Auckland seat of Hunua (1978–81) and then after three years in the wilderness for the very affluent and safe National seat of Tauranga (National MP 1984–93, Independent 1993, NZ First 1993–2005). He was initially regarded as a supporter of economic deregulation but came to regard the privatisation and sale of New Zealand's assets, including land, to foreigners as a loss of national sovereignty. By 1996 Peters was asking, 'Whose country is it? A country fit for the families of ordinary New Zealanders whose votes have placed the politicians in power, or a paradise for foreign take-over merchants looking for cheap gains at our expense?'[3]

He also became the most effective voice of protest for the people who felt themselves, often with justification, to be the casualties of the economic reforms unleashed by Douglas and Ruth Richardson in the 1980s and 1990s. Economic restructuring increased unemployment, ruined many small business people and farmers, and penalised heavily those on low incomes. The elderly also suffered from, and rebelled furiously against, the discriminatory taxation imposed on them by both the Labour and National governments of the late 1980s and early 1990s. All found a champion in Peters. At the same time others in the financial sector, many regarded as insider friends of the politicians, made enormous fortunes from privatised public assets and spent what Peters regarded as their ill-gotten gains very ostentatiously, adding insult to injury.

While Peters waged a number of crusades against businessmen whom he believed were corrupt, and incidentally had to pay large damages for defamation when he could not substantiate some of the charges, his major campaign was that known as 'the Winebox'. Peters charged that a group of New Zealand's leading businessmen, lawyers and bankers, assisted by lax if not corrupt officials in Inland Revenue and the Serious Fraud Office, had conspired to defraud the New Zealand taxpayer by setting up a sham taxation system based in the Cook Islands. Although a Royal Commission did not support Peters's major allegations, many ordinary voters did accept that Peters had been justified in his criticisms.

Peters went beyond economic populism, however, to arguing that New Zealand's national identity was threatened both by the sale of New Zealand assets and land to foreigners and by excessive immigration, particularly from Asia. Immigration from China, South Korea, Taiwan and Hong Kong during the 1990s and the early 2000s provided fertile political ground for Peters to exploit. Peters criticised wealthy Asian immigrants for building ostentatious homes, forcing up property prices generally. He asserted that poorer Asian immigrants and refugees put pressure on state housing and the health and welfare systems. Irrespective of their wealth, such Asian immigrants, many of whom had limited English language skills, put pressure on the education system, and often went back overseas after gaining an education. Many were bad drivers, others ravaged marine life on the foreshore, some were prone to criminal activity, others were unscrupulous employers, and their non-assimilation damaged New Zealanders' national identity. Native-born New Zealanders faced the danger of becoming 'strangers in our own backyard; serfs in our own country'.[4]

Unexpectedly, after the 1996 election, which had given New Zealand First 13.4 per cent of the party vote and the balance of power in parliament, Peters entered a coalition government with National, against whom he had campaigned without quarter. Many of his supporters were astounded if not enraged. He became Deputy Prime Minister and Treasurer but risked losing his populist appeal as the courageous and uncompromising champion of the powerless and those betrayed by previous governments. Indeed many who had voted for him in order to punish and oust the previous National Government felt themselves betrayed. In 1998, however, both the coalition government and Peters's own New Zealand First Party split asunder. His removal from the government enabled him again to project himself as an opposition leader and he and his party, with only 4.3 per cent of the party vote, survived the 1999 election because Peters narrowly retained his own seat of Tauranga.

At the 2002 election, Peters and New Zealand First won 10.4 per cent of the party vote, making it again, as it had been in 1996, clearly the third most popular party in the legislature. This success reflected the populist appeal of three issues that he had used to varying extents at every election he had contested since first becoming an MP in 1978. One was immigration, the second law and order, and the third an attack on the willingness of both Labour and National governments to allow the division of New Zealand into Maori and Pakeha through an increasingly radical interpretation of the Treaty of Waitangi. Peters, himself of Maori and Scottish descent, has never been reticent in attacking other individual Maori, although he believed that much of the problem lay with the misguided and even demeaning paternalism of 'sickly white liberals'. He believed that the unity of New Zealand was being destroyed by manufactured grievances and by corruption arising out of the government provision of services based on ethnicity. Far too much of the money spent on Maori by the government, he argued, went into the corrupt hands of a few rather than being used to help a greater proportion of those of Maori descent to become economically independent. New Zealanders of Maori descent had to take individual responsibility for themselves and their families and stop blaming everyone else and bewailing the injustices of the previous century and a half. He downplayed the complexity of such issues and simply asserted that he and his party could fix these problems.

Although Peters is an excellent platform speaker of almost religious intensity and appeal, he also has the ability, like Muldoon, Lange and Helen Clark, to use television very effectively. Television is a medium that lends itself to a populist politician's simple, clear, unambiguous statements. If the politician also can convey strength, sympathy and a sense of humour, a bond can easily be forged with viewers who either agree with what is being said or are simply left with a favourable overall impression. Peters may be a populist politician but he has also, despite his many vitriolic critics, been genuinely popular with a significant section of voters for over twenty years. His very unsympathetic biographer concluded that Peters was driven almost entirely by public opinion and by a desire to be prime minister (Hames 1995, 76–7). That is too simplistic. Peters did feel genuinely and strongly that the direction the National Government took economically and in regard to the Treaty of Waitangi after 1990 was wrong and chose to align himself with those whom he saw as the victims rather than the beneficiaries of those policies.

In 2004, New Zealand First took strong populist positions on the issues of the ownership of the seashore, the civil union legislation and the rights of would-be refugees in New Zealand. On the first, it argued that the government should simply legislate so that all New Zealanders owned and had a right to use the seashore. On the second, it suggested that the controversial civil union legislation, which in effect legitimised homosexual marriages, should be decided not by a small group of elitist Members of Parliament but by a majority of all ordinary New Zealanders in a referendum. On the third, Peters was the most outspoken politician on the need to reinforce the primacy of the elected parliament over an appointed judiciary, following the Supreme Court's decision to release on bail the Algerian refugee Ahmed Zaoui, whom Peters claimed should have been deported the moment he arrived in New Zealand two years before.

Peters and New Zealand First were unable to sustain the level of popular support that they obtained with these campaigns through to the 2005 election, when Peters lost narrowly the seat of Tauranga that he had held for 21 years and the number of New Zealand First MPs was almost halved to seven. Nevertheless, because of the balance of parties in the new parliament, he became the key to whether New Zealand would be governed by a Labour-led or a National-led coalition government. He chose to support Labour, becoming in the process Minister of Foreign Affairs, although he and his party remained outside cabinet and the formal government. Peters, therefore, continues to be a force in New Zealand politics, although the party would struggle to hold its vote without its leader.

While they criticise Peters and New Zealand First for their populism, the leaders of other parties are not averse to themselves using populist appeals. Both of ACT's leaders, Richard Prebble and Rodney Hide, have tried, with less success than Peters, to build support by campaigning on the high tax, big and intrusive government, law and order, and one-nation issues.

So has National's most recent leader Dr Don Brash. For example, in early 2004 Brash doubled National's support in the polls with his 'Orewa speech', in which he attacked the Labour Government's policies for dividing New Zealand into Maori and non-Maori and giving the former special rights based on the Treaty of Waitangi. In the 2005 election Brash ran an unashamedly populist campaign that even upstaged Peters, Dunne and Hide. Brash largely collapsed the vote of the smaller centre-right parties back into National with promises to cut tax, roll back the government bureaucracy, and stop what he saw as the preferential treatment of Maori compared to other New Zealanders. He was helped by very effective though oversimplified billboards and television advertisements that ridiculed Labour's dancing, tax-gathering cabinet ministers. He did not seem to see anything wrong with religious fundamentalists such as the Exclusive Brethren spending large sums of money surreptitiously to damage his Labour and Green opponents. Brash claimed to represent New Zealand's more normal, moral and deserving 'mainstream' but, whenever he was asked who was not 'mainstream', he had some trouble explaining precisely. Indeed in the last leaders' debate on television he ended up saying that it was anyone who supported the Labour Party, by implication anyone who didn't agree with or support him.

Labour's Clark has also shown some populist tendencies in stressing her strong leadership, by invoking New Zealand nationalism through her anti-nuclear stance and by continually recognising and honouring New Zealand's military history. She and her colleagues also used a populist tactic in suggesting that their National and ACT opponents were influenced, if not controlled, by avaricious big businessmen or by American interests behind the scenes, to the potential detriment of ordinary New Zealanders or New Zealand's independent foreign policy.

Because of their general support and, in some cases, responsibility for the economic reforms of the last twenty years, however, no National, Labour or ACT politician is as able to adopt an as unequivocally populist position on economic, social and racial matters as Peters has been able to do and he remains the clearest example of a populist politician in New Zealand's recent history.

1   Comments made to the author on many occasions.
2   John Pagani *cit*. John Armstrong, 'To the victim go the spoils', *Weekend Herald*, 27–28 November 2004.
3   Reported in *New Zealand Herald*, 2 February 1996, cited in Miller 2003, 266.
4   Reported in *Dominion*, 22 July 1993, cited in Miller 2003, 266.

Aimer, P. (1985) 'The New Zealand Party', in H. Gold (ed.), *New Zealand Politics in Perspective*, Auckland, Longman Paul, 189–203.

Ballara, A. (1996) 'Tahupotiki Wiremu Ratana', in *The Dictionary of New Zealand Biography, Volume Three*, Auckland and Wellington, Auckland University Press with Bridget Williams Books and Department of Internal Affairs, 414–18.

Bennett, S. (2002–03) 'Populism in Australian National Politics', in *Research Note 8*, Canberra, Parliament of Australia Parliamentary Library.

Bryant, G. (1981) *Beetham*, Palmerston North, Dunmore.

Burns, J. M. (1978) *Leadership*, New York, Harper and Row.

Dunne, P. (2002) *Home is where My Heart is*, Wellington, United Future New Zealand.

Easton, B. (2001) *The Nationbuilders*, Auckland, Auckland University Press.

Clark, M. (ed.) (2004) *Muldoon Revisited*, Palmerston North, Dunmore.

Clarke, P. (1991) *A Question of Leadership: From Gladstone to Thatcher*, London, Penguin.

Gustafson, B. (1986) *From the Cradle to the Grave: A Biography of Michael Joseph Savage*, Auckland, Reed Methuen.

Gustafson, B. (1993a) 'Regeneration, Rejection or Realignment', in G. R. Hawke (ed.), *Changing Politics*, Wellington, Institute of Policy Studies, 68–102.

Gustafson, B. (1993b) 'William Ferguson Massey', in *The Dictionary of New Zealand Biography, Volume Two*, Auckland and Wellington, Bridget Williams Books and Department of Internal Affairs, 447–51.

Gustafson, B. (1999) 'Michael Joseph Savage', in *The Dictionary of New Zealand Biography, Volume Four*, Auckland and Wellington, Auckland University Press with Bridget Williams Books and Department of Internal Affairs, 445–8.

Gustafson, B. (2000a) 'Sidney George Holland', in *The Dictionary of New Zealand Biography, Volume Five*, Auckland and Wellington, Auckland University Press with Bridget Williams Books and Department of Internal Affairs, 229–31.

Gustafson, B. (2000b) *His Way: A Biography of Robert Muldoon*, Auckland, Auckland University Press.

Hamer, D. (1993) 'Richard John Seddon', in *The Dictionary of New Zealand Biography, Volume Two*, Wellington, Bridget Williams Books and Department of Internal Affairs, 447–51.

Hames, M. (1995) *Winston First: The Unauthorised Account of Winston Peter's Career*, Auckland, Random House.

Hofstadter, R. (1960) *The Age of Reform: From Bryan to F. D. R.*, New York, Vintage Books.

Jesson, B. (1997) 'The Alliance', in R. Miller (ed.), *New Zealand Politics in Transition*, Auckland, Oxford University Press, 156–64.

Johansson, J. (2002) 'Political Leadership: New Zealand Theory and Practice', unpublished PhD thesis, Wellington, Victoria University of Wellington.

Johansson, J. (2005) *Two Titans: Muldoon, Lange and Leadership*, Palmerston North, Dunmore.

Jones, B. (1997) *Memories of Muldoon*, Christchurch, Canterbury University Press.

Lee, G. (2002) *Faith, Politics and Servant Leadership*, Auckland, Castle Publishing.

Love, P. (1984) *Labor and the Money Power: Australian Labor Populism 1890–1950*, Melbourne, Melbourne University Press.

Miller, R. (1985) 'Social Credit/The Democratic Party', in H. Gold (ed.), *New Zealand Politics in Perspective*, Auckland, Longman Paul, 205–15.

Miller, R. (1997) 'The New Zealand First Party', in R. Miller (ed.), *New Zealand Politics in Transition*, Auckland, Oxford University Press, 165–76.

Miller, R. (2003) 'New Zealand First', in R. Miller (ed.), *New Zealand Government and Politics*, Melbourne, Oxford University Press, 261–73.

Miller, W. R. (1993) 'A Centennial Historiography of Populism', in *Kansas History: A Journal of the Central Plains*, 16:1, 54–69.

Moon, P. (1999) *Muldoon: A Study in Public Leadership*, Wellington, Pacific Press Ltd.

Muldoon, R. D. (1974) *The Rise of a Young Turk*, Auckland, A. H. and A.W. Reed.

Muldoon, R. D. (1977) *Muldoon*, Wellington, A. H. and A. W. Reed.

Muldoon, R. D. (1981) *My Way*, Wellington, A. H. and A. W. Reed.

Muldoon, R. D. (1986) *Number 38*, Auckland, Reed Methuen.

Olssen, E. (1977) *John A. Lee*, Dunedin, University of Otago Press.

Olssen, E. (1999) 'John Alfred Alexander Lee', in *The Dictionary of New Zealand Biography, Volume Four*, Auckland and Wellington, Auckland University Press with Bridget Williams Books and Department of Internal Affairs, 284–6.

Peters, W. (1993) 'New Zealand First – A New Beginning', speech at the launch of the New Zealand First Party, Auckland, 18 July.

Sawer, M. (2003) 'Down with elites and up with inequality: Market populism in Australia', in *Australian Review of Public Affairs*, 27 October, available at: http://www.australianreview.net/digest/2003/10/sawer.html

Schedler, A. (1996) 'Anti-Political-Establishment Parties', in *Party Politics*, 2/3, 291–312.

Templeton, H. (1995) *All Honourable Men: Inside the Muldoon Cabinet 1975–84*, Auckland, Auckland University Press.

Zavos, S. (1978) *The Real Muldoon*, Wellington, Fourth Estate Books.

Leading Political and Cultural Change

FIVE

The Leadership Styles of Helen Clark and Don Brash

John Henderson
and Seishi Gomibuchi

One approach to the study of leadership has been described as the 'operational code analysis'. It is based on the assumption that leadership is a product of two important motivations: *philosophical beliefs*, which shape the leader's evaluation of the nature of politics and other actors, and *instrumental beliefs*, which prescribe the leader's preferred strategies, tactics and actions for achieving desired objectives. In short, the focus is on, firstly, what the leader believes and, secondly, what he or she should do about these beliefs. The approach assumes that these beliefs can be discerned through an analysis of a leader's past rhetoric, behaviour and biographical information. It further assumes that the beliefs remain relatively stable over time. As a result, operational codes can be used as a reliable reference point in explaining a leader's behaviour, both past, present and future.

The operational code analysis can be applied to any type of leadership, whether it be political, business or religious, as well as to any organisational setting. In this chapter we choose to study two prominent New Zealand political leaders, the Prime Minister, Helen Clark, and the leader of the Opposition, Donald Brash. Why select these particular Leaders? Despite some realignment in power dynamics induced by the introduction of MMP in 1996, prime ministers still remain the most powerful political figures in New Zealand. The magnitude of the power they enjoy makes them a necessary topic for consideration in this volume.

In the following sections, Clark and Brash's operational codes are analysed using ten diagnostic questions drawn from their philosophical and instrumental beliefs. The analysis draws inferences about their operational codes from the public record of their rhetoric, such as interviews, speeches and other statements, as well as from available biographical information.

Firstly, a point of explanation about the selection and use in this chapter of direct quotations. The quotations, which are illustrative only, have been selected for their relevance to the operational code. The actual number of quotations and when they were made is not as important as what they reveal about the pattern of beliefs which emerges. If correctly assessed, this pattern should remain fairly constant over time and provide clues regarding future behaviour. The challenge is to reveal the patterns over time between rhetoric and political actions. The supporting evidence is selected because it illustrates these patterns. Of course, as with all academic research, the analysis must stand or fall on the evidence presented.

As we well know, political leaders are prone to presenting themselves in the most favourable light. Frequent use is made of public opinion polls and focus groups to slant their rhetoric with a view to maximising political gain. But the operational code approach considers this to be a short-term issue. Over time, congruence is bound to emerge between behaviour and belief (Walker et al. 2003, 223–4). Indeed the code, once established, will help reveal when the 'manipulation' is taking place. The important point here is that the operational code analysis is not about testing the 'correctness' of a quote, but rather what it reveals about the leader's belief system. Even 'lies' can provide important clues. Leites's work, which led to the establishment of the operational code approach, drew on the pronouncements of the Soviet Politburo in the early Cold War years. Leites (1951) did not, of course, believe the propaganda he analysed was factually correct. What interested him was what it revealed about the Politburo's belief system and how this could influence future actions.

Helen Clark and Don Brash – Similarities and Differences

Before examining Clark and Brash's philosophical and instrumental beliefs, some biographical information helps set the scene. Clark and

Brash share a number of similarities as well as notable differences. The first similarity has to do with their upbringing and concerns the extent to which their ideological beliefs differed from those of their parents. Don Brash, who was born in Wanganui in 1940, grew up as the youngest child in a household dominated by his father, a leading Presbyterian minister and supporter of left-wing causes. Helen Clark, who was born in 1950, was the first child of Waikato farmers, George and Margaret Clark. Although Clark's parents had a 'liberal' streak in their views, their natural political instinct was conservative, with George playing a prominent role in the local National Party organisation. The second commonality between the two leaders is their high level of intelligence. Brash gained a first-class degree in economics at the University of Canterbury and a PhD from the Australian National University. Clark's first-class MA was gained in political science at the University of Auckland and she was working on a doctorate when political activity interrupted her academic career.

The third similarity rests with their ambitions and lifelong interest in politics. Clark has devoted her life to politics. After joining the Labour Party in 1972, Clark quickly established herself as a prominent party member, steadily climbing up the ranks. While working as a lecturer in Political Studies at the University of Auckland (her first and only full-time job prior to becoming a parliamentarian), she harboured ambitions of pursuing a political career. She stood unsuccessfully for parliament in 1975 (in the National stronghold of Piako) before winning the seat of Mt Albert in 1981.

Brash considered a career in the church, and then developed a strong ambition to work for the New Zealand Ministry of Foreign Affairs, before joining the World Bank in 1966. His motivation was essentially political in the broad sense of the term; he wanted to play a part in creating a better world. In 1980, by which time he was a successful merchant banker, Brash unsuccessfully contested the East Coast Bays by-election as a National candidate. He tried again, without success, in the 1981 general election. He then carved out a successful business career and served for fourteen years as Governor of the Reserve Bank – ironically originally appointed by the Labour Government in 1988. He unexpectedly relinquished the Reserve Bank governorship to stand as a National list candidate for the 2002 election, and became National Party leader the following year.

The most notable difference between Brash and Clark can be found in their ideologies, although each claims to hold views representing the traditional, mainstream values held by New Zealanders (Brash 2005a; Edwards 2001, 323). Brash is known to have been a strong right-wing supporter of the free market. Clark, in contrast, has identified herself as a social democrat, acknowledging a positive, albeit somewhat limited, role played by government in a modern society and economy.

The second point of difference concerns their paths to leadership. Whereas Clark served a twelve-year apprenticeship as a backbench MP, cabinet minister and deputy leader before assuming the party leadership, it took only one year for Brash to reach the same position.

Philosophical Beliefs

What are Brash and Clark's world views? According to their beliefs, how does the political world function? What are their political goals and objectives? Philosophical beliefs provide us with insight into the two leaders' understanding of the world of politics.

What is the 'essential' nature of political life?
This question seeks to establish the leader's beliefs about how the political world operates. It also reveals the leader's policy and political leanings. While agreeing that political life is about public service, philosophically Clark and Brash are very different politicians:

CLARK BELIEF (1): THE SOCIAL DEMOCRATIC APPROACH CAN PROVIDE
OPPORTUNITY, SECURITY AND FAIR PLAY FOR ALL.
Clark's view of the ideal society embodies centre-left, social democratic values. She believes in a cohesive (bound by a unique national identity and pride) yet tolerant and inclusive society in which every citizen can enjoy 'opportunity, security, and fair play' (Clark 2003c), as well as decent access to public services and infrastructure (such as education and health). Government should play a crucial role in creating such a society, but it can only do so with a strong and prosperous economy (Clark 2004b), in partnership with business, the community and local government (Clark 2002; 2003a). Although Clark's view on economics has become somewhat more orthodox (Munro, 1989), her overall philosophical beliefs have remained largely intact over the years (Young 2003).

BRASH BELIEF (1): PHILOSOPHICAL DIFFERENCES ARE ABOUT MEANS, NOT ENDS. IT IS POSSIBLE FOR A FREE MARKETER TO HAVE A SOCIAL CONSCIENCE.

Like Clark, Brash also has well-established philosophical beliefs. There is no doubt that Brash belongs to the economic right and is a committed free marketer. He extols the virtues of small government, self-reliance, enterprise, low taxation and freedom of choice. He remains an enthusiastic supporter of the free market economic reforms of the 1980s introduced by Labour's finance minister Roger Douglas and continued by National's Ruth Richardson in the early 1990s. But Brash also insists that he has a strong social conscience, which he traces to the influence of his church-minister father. He, however, admits to having difficulty revealing the compassion he feels. In 1980 he reflected: 'The assumption I grew up with was that only the left wing cared about people. That is a lot of hogwash. There is a difference in the understanding of the means, but not of the ends' (Ashton 1980). These means include a major role for the private sector in delivering social services.

Like his father, Brash once held strong socialist views, until they were replaced by economic liberalism during his study at ANU. While Brash has described this conversion as a 'road to Damascus experience' (Brash 1995), he stresses that it was based on experience, not theory: 'My own abandonment of Keynesian economics and Fabian socialism was not the result . . . of reading Hayek, Popper or even Friedman, but of a gradual recognition that neither Keynesian economics nor Fabian socialism actually worked . . . .' (Brash 1996). Nevertheless, there seems little doubt that Brash became as much a true believer of the right as he had once been of the left.

Is the political universe one of harmony or conflict?

CLARK BELIEF (2): POLITICS CAN BE BRUTAL, PERSONAL AND UNFAIR. WHEN CHALLENGED POLITICAL LEADERS SHOULD NOT SHY AWAY FROM CONFRONTATION.

Despite her belief that politics ought to be a 'contest of ideas' (Light 1988) and a professed dislike for the conflictual nature of politics, Clark believes a leader under attack must respond: 'I will hit back very, very hard if I think the government has been unfairly criticised' (Edwards 2001, 332). She considers shying away from confrontation to be a political mistake, saying, 'I would rather have the abuse that comes from being strong than the abuse that comes from being weak' (Edwards 2001, 330).

BRASH BELIEF (2): IDEALLY, THE POLITICAL UNIVERSE SHOULD REFLECT HARMONY, NOT CONFLICT.

Recalling his Christian upbringing, Brash has claimed that 'the most fundamental principle of Christianity ... is love' and that is 'absolutely right' (Roger 2004, 37). Brash has an intense dislike for what he calls 'nastiness' in politics. 'New Zealanders like strong leaders, they like decisive leaders, but I don't think they like nastiness' (Tunnah 2004).

Brash's lack of political aggression runs the risk of being seen as weakness. He is particularly vulnerable in parliament's debating chamber where, as a journalist has noted, 'a certain ability at verbal all-in wrestling is required' (Hosking 2004). Brash is clearly not comfortable in the parliamentary arena of political confrontation. However his controversial 2004 and 2005 'State of the Nation' speeches, delivered at Orewa on the potentially explosive topics of race relations and welfare benefit reform respectively, reveal that he is not afraid of provoking divisive public debate (Brash 2004a; 2005b).

What is the fundamental nature of one's opponents?

CLARK BELIEF (3): POLITICAL OPPONENTS PROPOSE VALUES THAT ARE DETRIMENTAL TO SOCIETY.

Clark essentially sees her political opponents as proponents of values different from her own. Her primary political enemies are the supporters of New Right economic policies, which she holds responsible for the creation, through the 1980s and 1990s, of 'growing inequality, social fragmentation, and despair in many quarters' (Clark 2003b). Clark understands that, in order to advance their views, political opponents will employ both fair means and foul: 'I've no doubt our opponents will scrape the bottom of the barrel for every bit of mud they can throw' (Clark 2004b).

BRASH BELIEF (3): POLITICS SHOULD NOT BE PERSONALISED.

Brash's 'gentlemanly' approach to politics does not allow him to see his opponents as evil. 'I have good friends, and people I respect on both sides of parliament' (Brash 2002a). Political debate, for Brash, should be about policy, not personality. In his maiden speech to parliament he pledged that he would 'continue to be willing to acknowledge good policy from whichever party it emerges' (Brash 2002c).

What are the prospects for the eventual realisation of one's fundamental values and aspirations?
CLARK BELIEF (4): THERE ARE NO SHORTCUTS, YET THROUGH CAREFUL AND NUMEROUS STEPS, VALUES AND ASPIRATIONS CAN BE REALISED.
While Clark stresses that there is no 'magic wand', she believes values can be achieved by taking careful and incremental steps in cooperation with other key actors in society (Clark 2003a). Regarding the progress that her government has made towards reaching its political goals, and the prospect of fully realising them, she has commented that 'Every reasonable person knows that the path is a long one. Half a century's decline isn't reversed over night, but reversed it can be and is being' (Clark 2003b).

BRASH BELIEF (4): PROSPECTS FOR REALISING POLITICAL AMBITIONS ARE GOOD PROVIDING THE POLICY SETTINGS ARE SOUND.
Brash was attracted to politics, he says, by a concern for the need to alleviate poverty. He has cited Singapore and South Korea as examples of what can be achieved through sound economic policies (Clifton 2004, 18). He believes that, in the case of New Zealand, inherent disadvantages such as small size and distance are less important than the quality of the policy settings. In this sense, Brash sees himself as a technocrat. But he is also 'a fifth generation New Zealander who yields to nobody when it comes to loyalty to New Zealand' (Brash 1995).

Can one be optimistic?
CLARK BELIEF (5): CAUTIOUS OPTIMISM IS CALLED FOR.
While generally optimistic, Clark warns against complacency. If political damage can be undone, so can positive accomplishments: 'We've made a lot of progress and a lot of changes. But none of what is happening can be taken for granted.' Achievements can be 'quickly shattered by a change of government' (Clark 2004a). Clark warns: 'No matter how good our record is, we can never rest on our laurels and think we've done enough for our country because there will always be more to do' (Clark 2005).

BRASH BELIEF (5): OPTIMISTIC YES, BUT BEWARE OF MOOD SWINGS.
Brash believes that 'we have plenty of reasons for being optimistic' (Brash 2001) regarding New Zealand's future. He is, however, concerned about the 'wild swings' in mood between optimism and pessimism displayed by the New Zealand public towards the outcomes of economic reform (Brash 1999). He remains worried about the consequences of failing to continue with the economic reforms initiated by Labour in the 1980s and continued by the National government in the early 1990s. But he continues to be optimistic about the future for New Zealand 'if we get policy and attitudes right' (Goldsmith 2005, 285).

Is the political future predictable? In what sense and to what extent?
CLARK BELIEF (6): UNPREDICTABILITY IS PART OF POLITICS. NEVERTHELESS PREDICTABILITY CAN BE ENHANCED THROUGH CAREFUL PLANNING AND MANAGEMENT.
Clark likens the prime minister's job to her favourite pastime: 'It's like climbing: one mountain is conquered, there are always more standing behind it. And in government, the mountains don't always show up early on the radar, and may not even be drawn on the map!' (Clark 2003c). Nevertheless, sound government not only requires predictability but also provides it: 'I like to see things set up so that nothing is entirely unanticipated. And that requires management' (Smith 1994, 29). Campaign pledges must be made carefully and sparingly, and once made, every effort should be made to honour them.

BRASH BELIEF (6): WHILE THE FUTURE IS NOT PREDICTABLE, THE ROLE OF GOVERNMENT IS TO MAKE THE GOVERNMENT POLICY AND BUSINESS ENVIRONMENTS AS PREDICTABLE AS POSSIBLE.
In an interview Brash reflected: 'Life is like that. You often have to make decisions never knowing what the outcome will be' (Roger 2004, 38). He is particularly concerned about the increased uncertainty that has resulted from the introduction of the proportional MMP electoral system. Important policy and political implications flow from the unpredictable nature of politics. Brash has commented: 'The reality is that governments have a right, indeed a duty, to give a lead. Sometimes they face situations not contemplated when they are campaigning for office. Sometimes they are simply unaware of existing reality when they are formulating their

campaign pledges ...' (Brash 1998) In other words, changed circumstances can justify a failure to implement campaign pledges, or excuse actions taken without an electoral mandate. This could provide the rationale for a future Brash-led government to reactivate radical economic reforms, despite soothing comments to the contrary.

How much 'control' or 'mastery' can one have over historical development? What is one's role in 'moving' and 'shaping' history in the desired direction?

CLARK BELIEF (7): WHILE COMPLETE CONTROL OVER HISTORICAL DEVELOPMENT IS BEYOND ONE'S ABILITY, AFFECTING IT IN A SIGNIFICANT WAY IS NOT.

Clark believes that in a limited, yet considerable, way, she can influence the direction and the shape of the future and that she already has (Venter 2002). 'You have to believe that you can make a difference and once you stop believing that it's time to move on to something else' (Light 1998, 23). She has observed that with her position as prime minister comes 'enormous' power to oversee the direction of government policies (Edwards 2001, 328), although 'you wouldn't want to push your luck too much' (Edwards 2001, 329).

BRASH BELIEF (7): THE INDIVIDUAL CAN MAKE A DIFFERENCE.

Brash believes individuals who are willing to challenge the status quo can make a difference. Reflecting on his father's courage as a conscientious objector in World War II, he says, 'That willingness to be a lone voice was quite important in my childhood' (Roger 2004, 36).

What is the role of 'chance' in human affairs and historical development?

CLARK BELIEF (8): THROUGH GOOD MANAGEMENT THE ROLE OF CHANCE IN HISTORICAL DEVELOPMENT CAN BE REDUCED.

Clark believes good leadership does not leave things to chance: 'I like my moves planned. I like to know what the consequences are. You won't find me throwing the balls up in the air' (Campbell, 2001, 17). Through good management and leadership, she believes that 'you've got to make your luck' (Laws 2003, 62). If, however, the unexpected happens, there is no point in dwelling over it. Instead, one should use it as a learning opportunity and move on: '[N]ever look back. There is no point. You learn from the experience' (Young 2003).

BRASH BELIEF (8): CHANCE TAKES SECOND PLACE TO HARD WORK.
For Brash 'there is no silver bullet' (Brash 2002a). Chance in the form of miracle cures will not happen. There is no substitute for hard work. His biographer concludes: 'His entire life has been about setting himself difficult targets and striving night and day to achieve them' (Goldsmith 2005, 281).

The Instrumental Beliefs

Philosophical beliefs reflect leaders' personal, intrinsic values and relate to their ideological orientation. Instrumental beliefs, on the other hand, provide an indication of what these leaders might do in order to realise goals set in motion by their philosophical beliefs. Such *modus operandi* is likely to be shaped by one's past political experience (both successes and failures). The vast difference between the two leaders in this regard may have profound implications. Clark, an astute learner from history, has constructed her instrumental beliefs by using positive as well as negative lessons from past politicians and governments. In addition, she has had more than eleven years as a party leader to practise and adjust these beliefs. Consequently, there is strong coherence and consistency in her instrumental beliefs, formed around the philosophy that trust given by the public is the most crucial asset in achieving political objectives. The acquisition and retention of trust must therefore be of utmost priority for a government, and, as the leader, Clark assumes the ultimate responsibility for this task.

Brash, on the other hand, lacks Clark's political experience. Although as Reserve Bank governor he may have had plenty of opportunities to observe politics at close range, he is nonetheless still a novice politician, at times seemingly naively so. He may have had a lifetime to formulate his philosophical beliefs, but as to how to enact them, his beliefs are less solid. His newness to the role of political leader may in part explain the contradictions between caution and decisiveness, and between principle and pragmatism.

What is the best approach for selecting goals or objectives for political action?

CLARK BELIEF (9): LEADERS NEED TO BE INCLUSIVE WHILE GATHERING INFORMATION, FORMING IDEAS, AND CONSIDERING STRATEGIES AND OPTIONS. HOWEVER, IT IS THE LEADER'S JOB TO MAKE DECISIONS.

In order to formulate goals and objectives, Clark believes wide and inclusive consultation to be vital. Alienation of key constituents is likely to result in resentment and failure. Similarly, she finds little advantage in setting objectives and goals that are unlikely to be popular. She says, 'In our change agenda, we will be looking to work with people, not against them, and to build the maximum possible consensus around vision and goals' (Clark 2003b). Nevertheless, consultation should not go on endlessly and leaders must make final decisions authoritatively: 'I operate on the basis that it is important to be fair, it is important to consult people. But in the end, decisions have to be made by leaders' (recorded in TVNZ 2004b).

CLARK BELIEF (10): SET ACHIEVABLE AND PRACTICAL OBJECTIVES INVOLVING DETAILED STEPS. ONCE OBJECTIVES ARE DETERMINED, STATE THEM CLEARLY.

Clark believes that delivering on promises previously made is a fundamental way by which her government can build and maintain public trust (Clark 2005). For this to occur, however, the government must be certain that its promises are modest, pragmatic and achievable. Clark says, 'Watching the last thirty years of New Zealand politics has taught me a few lessons. Of them all, the most important is to promise only what you can deliver and then to keep your word. That has been a guiding principle for Labour in government' (Clark 2000). Realisable objectives demand careful planning and financial prudence: 'The art of governing . . . rests on the balance struck between head and heart' (Clark 2003b). She prefers a mid- to long-term approach: 'I am working to a long-term vision and set of beliefs about what should happen in New Zealand and I see each three years [an electoral cycle] as part of that journey' (Young 2003). Equally important to Clark is the view that once objectives and goals are set, they should be stated clearly and accompanied by specific strategies, initiatives and programmes so that 'what you see is what you will get' (Campbell 2001, 17).

BRASH BELIEF (9): GOALS AND OBJECTIVES SHOULD BE SELECTED ON THE BASIS OF RATIONAL ANALYSIS.

Brash is fond of calling for 'rational and level-headed debate' and 'principled and rigorous' policy analysis (Brash 2003b). Unlike Clark, he dismisses the role of emotion (heart). Brash claims he 'never gets in rages and never shouts' (Brash 2004b). Rational analysis involves hearing all points of view. 'I think it is fundamentally important, if you are going to be the boss, to have people who are willing to say: I am sorry, that won't work' (Brash 2003c). But it is also important not to be seen as a puppet in the hands of advisers, especially in areas where the leader has special expertise (finance in the case of Brash). Ultimately Brash accepts that the leader must lead and this can result in sharp differences with colleagues. For example, his failure to consult key party members regarding the 2005 Orewa speech, and the demotion of the welfare spokeswoman, Katherine Rich, who disagreed with aspects of the speech, led to criticisms that Brash's leadership was 'divisive' (Milne 2005).

BRASH BELIEF (10): GOVERNMENT POLICY-MAKING SHOULD TAKE ACCOUNT OF POLITICAL REALITY.

Brash concedes that his enthusiasm for the free market is not universally accepted by the public, especially in the areas of social policy. Reflecting on the economic reforms of the 1980s, Brash commented: 'As someone who is strongly committed to the democratic process, I certainly worry about the extent to which the reform process got ahead of the democratic process' (Brash 1998). Brash is concerned that this democratic deficit could result in the erosion of public confidence in the process of government. This creates a dilemma for Brash: on the one hand, 'political parties can only do what they can sell to the public at large' (Perigo 2004); on the other hand, failure to act because of political considerations could have serious economic consequences for the nation's future.

The need to take into account political considerations has already affected Brash's leadership. While he might act differently as prime minister, so far Brash has preferred a more cautious, 'democratic' approach. He likes to test the political waters first. As the political journalist Vernon Small has observed, he likes to 'avoid, downplay, or defuse issues for which the public have no stomach, even if the party and MPs think they are desirable' (Small 2004). This has left Brash open to 'Dithering Don' and 'flip-flop' accusations on such issues such as, for example, superannuation, nuclear ship visits and taxation reform.

How are goals most effectively pursued?

CLARK BELIEF (11): THOROUGH PREPARATION, DECISIVE EXECUTION AND LEADERSHIP IS NECESSARY TO ACHIEVE GOALS.

Clark believes that meticulous preparation and hard work is crucial for successful realisation of her goals and objectives (Clark 2000, 127). In order to ensure success, leaders have to take charge: 'I do like to be in control of what I do. I do like to know what is going on' (Edwards 2001, 342). This belief may necessitate occasional intervention in other ministers' responsibilities so as to protect the administration's integrity. Clark says, 'My basic desire is for everyone to get on and do the job well, but if I think anyone is falling by the wayside I will get involved . . .' (Roger 2000, 98).

CLARK BELIEF (12): IT IS IMPORTANT TO MONITOR PUBLIC REACTION TO GOVERNMENT PROGRAMMES CLOSELY TO ENSURE THAT THEY ARE WELL SUPPORTED.

Clark believes that when executing policies, the government must closely monitor public reactions and remain open to making any changes or compromises necessary, including the occasional abandonment of programmes: 'We . . . have a responsibility to remain open and alert to new trends, new ideas and new forces in society, and to keep listening' (Clark 2003c). The short-term, 'crash through' approach against public wishes will not work (Clark 2003b), and will only result in 'the inevitable voting out' of the government (Campbell 2001, 17).

BRASH BELIEF (11): LEADERSHIP IS THE CRUCIAL ELEMENT IN ACHIEVING DESIRED GOALS.

Brash strongly believes governments have a right and a duty to lead from the front (Roger 2004, 42). This is especially the case in economic policy, where the general public does not have a good understanding of 'crucial issues'. Leaders in the political and business communities must educate the public on 'necessary' economic reforms (Brash 1999). Brash also continues to believe that governments must govern and should not have to wait for majority support before taking essential economic reforms (Brash 1998).

BRASH BELIEF (12): GOALS ARE BEST PURSUED THROUGH DETERMINATION AND HARD WORK.

Once a decision has been made, hard work is essential to ensure its implementation. Brash readily admits to having been a workaholic since high school (Roger 2004, 42).

How are the risks of political action calculated, controlled and accepted?

CLARK BELIEF (13): RISKS CAN BE MINIMISED THROUGH CAREFUL RESEARCH, CONSULTATION, PLANNING AND EXECUTION.

Although political leaders cannot foresee all the potential risks lying ahead, some are more detectable and controllable than others. Wherever possible, it is their duty to take only calculated – thus manageable – risks. Clark uses various means to monitor and manipulate public perception of government actions and to anticipate opponents' moves (O'Leary 2002), including the effective use of opinion polls. Also, by stating its policy initiatives and programmes clearly, thereby generating certainty, the government is able to reduce potential political fall-out, by not taking any serious risks itself.

CLARK BELIEF (14): IF MISTAKES ARE MADE, DEAL WITH THEM OPENLY, FAIRLY AND PROMPTLY. IT IS NOT WORTH DEFENDING THE INDEFENSIBLE.

Although risks can be minimised, mistakes are bound to happen. Once they do, Clark believes they should be dealt with openly and promptly. The worst crisis management is to leave the issue unresolved. 'You deal with them [problems] as quickly as you can and move on. Don't let it [*sic*] drag on. If you let it drag on, it will' (Edwards 2001, 322). Tackling problems in a transparent manner is vital for retaining her government's credibility: 'Sometimes people let you down. And they let you down to a point where, if you don't say something, people think, well maybe that's acceptable. And it isn't' (Edwards 2001, 329). Clark may protect her colleagues against unfair criticisms, but has no time for the helpless cause: 'I won't cover for witless things that people have done' (Edwards 2001, 330). Such an attempt can backfire: 'I think the electorate has a pretty acute bullshit detector' (Ansley 2002, 21). Those responsible for political transgressions discover that often accountability is sought publicly by Clark, and accompanied by harsh reprimands, regardless of their status or personal relationship with her.

BRASH BELIEF (13): RISKS MUST BE ACCEPTED AS PART OF THE POLITI-
CAL PROCESS. THERE ARE NO CERTAINTIES, ALTHOUGH RISKS MAY BE
MINIMISED BY CAREFUL ANALYSIS.

Brash portrays himself as a politician who is prepared to take political
risks. He recalls that his return to active party politics was fraught with
risks. He had to give up the prestigious and highly paid job of Reserve
Bank governor for an uncertain future (Roger 2004, 38). His bid for party
leadership after just two years in parliament was certainly risky. So too
were the Orewa speeches on the delicate topics of race relations and welfare reform.

BRASH BELIEF (14): SPEED OF IMPLEMENTING POLICY DECISIONS CAN
HELP MINIMISE THE RISK THAT POLICY WILL BE WATERED DOWN,
ALTHOUGH THIS MAY INCREASE THE POLITICAL RISK.

Brash has high praise for the 'suicidally courageous politicians' of the
fourth Labour Government who backed finance minister Roger Douglas
(Brash 1998), believing that their actions show that sometimes it may be
necessary to take extreme political risks to achieve crucial policy goals. Yet
Brash has promised that a future Brash-led government will not deliver
a 'thunderbolt of reform . . . . Rather we simply have to patiently build on
and improve . . .' (*NZ Herald*, 18 May 2004).

What is the best 'timing' of action to advance one's interests?

CLARK BELIEF (15): THE MOST OPPORTUNE TIME TO TAKE ACTION IS
WHEN THERE IS SUFFICIENT SUPPORT FOR IT.

There is no point in fighting a losing battle. In 1993, when Clark was
approached by her supporters to challenge Mike Moore, then leader of
the Labour Party, her reply was: 'I'm not going to stand unless I know
I'm going to win' (Edwards 2001, 227). She explains that prime ministers
can be decisive and strong only if 'you've got very strong backing' from
caucus colleagues (O'Sullivan 2005). Likewise, sufficient public support is
vital for her actions' success: '[W]hile the public's got a lot of faith in your
judgement, you've got a lot of leeway' (Edwards, 2001, 330).

BRASH BELIEF (15): WHILE IT IS GENERALLY BETTER TO ACT THAN PRO-
CRASTINATE, THE LONG TERM IS MORE IMPORTANT THAN THE SHORT
TERM.

Brash recognises that timing is all-important. He recalls his mother's advice to take up opportunities as they became available (Roger 2004, 36). Reflecting on his time as Reserve Bank governor, he commented on 'Monetary policy, like many other aspects of life, in which a single stitch in time saves . . .' (Brash 2002b).

In politics, there is constant tension between caution and decisiveness. Yet, former Labour Prime Minister David Lange has observed that philosophically Brash has a long-term approach to life. 'Don Brash was not a six o'clock news man, not a monthly poll man, nor even a triennial election man, but he is looking ahead . . .' (Clifton 2004, 16). Brash lends support to this assessment with the comment: 'Most New Zealanders would . . . be prepared to make sacrifices in the short term for a better future in the long term' (Brash 1981, 40). It is better to 'take some tough decisions, with less gravy now, but the prospects of plenty later' (Brash 2003a).

What is the utility and role of different means for advancing one's interests?

CLARK BELIEF (16): BE FLEXIBLE AND USE APPROPRIATE ALTERNATIVE MEANS FOR DIFFERENT SITUATIONS.

Throughout her political experience, Clark 'learnt the hard way as I went along about what worked and what didn't' (Venter 2003). While her normal leadership style is consensual and inclusive, under certain circumstances, she has readily abandoned it, especially when she judges that the public calls for 'decisive' and 'authoritative' actions. For instance, when Clark was faced with potential caucus dissent over her administration's handling of the seabed and foreshore issue in early 2004, she sternly stated: 'I judge that the present situation requires leadership and I will give it, and my message to my colleagues is "If you want to get on board for the ride, get on, because this train is moving"' (TVNZ 2004a).

BRASH BELIEF (16): DIFFERENT TIMES AND ISSUES CALL FOR DIFFERENT STRATEGIES.

While Brash considers that he has a positive approach, his Orewa speeches have showed an awareness that negatives often work better in advancing political interests. However, the milder tone of his 2005 Orewa speech revealed a further important feature of the Brash approach, which is to avoid being overly provocative. The speech was short on detail and avoided restating Brash's earlier, more radical, views such as putting time limits on benefits, and requiring those seeking work to congregate each morning at the local post office.

Conclusion

Political leaders' options may be restricted – or even pre-determined – by contextual factors. However, there is often room for their unique individualities, such as their world view or style, to play a part in deciding on their move in the given circumstances. The operational code analysis reveals patterns in the leaders' behaviour. These patterns, or operational codes, can serve not only as a useful tool in understanding leaders' past behaviour but also provide clues for predicting future political behaviour.

Our analysis of Clark has supported the commonly held view of the Labour prime minister as a pragmatist with values that can be broadly defined as social democratic. The guiding principle of her operational code is the belief that the acquisition and retention of public trust is vital for successful governance. It appears that although Clark knows the direction in which she wishes to lead New Zealand, the content of government programmes and preferred means of implementation are determined by this principle. Consensual or decisive (in decision-making), prudent or opportunistic (when taking political actions), conciliatory or aggressive (towards oppositions), protective or punitive (towards subordinates in trouble) – Clark flexibly adapts her leadership style in accordance with the circumstances so as to maximise the chance of her programmes' success while minimising the risk of public alienation. This may seem like a basic axiom which every political leader attempts to follow. What separates Clark from many of her contemporaries, however, is her pertinacious determination to constantly vary her style as she sees fit. Furthermore, with her strong managerial skills (Nichols 2004) and considerable power (O'Sullivan 2005), Clark has remained firmly in charge of government business and ensured her administration also observes her pragmatism.

What do the operational codes tell us about the future? Given her predictability and risk-averse management style, it is most likely that Clark and her government will continue pursuing the present course in terms of both policy direction and style of governance. Any radical policy lurch or political action, especially against public opinion, would be most unlikely under her leadership.

While for Clark the prediction of more of the same can be made with some confidence, this is not the case with Brash. He is still a relative newcomer to the leadership role. Two questions warrant attention. Firstly, is he a pragmatist or man of principle? Secondly, on the question of economic reform, is Brash an incrementalist or a revolutionary? Brash's relative newness to parliamentary politics after years of unblemished service as Reserve Bank governor equipped him well for the anti-politician role: he was a man of principle who was able to portray himself as above politics. Much of this was sacrificed when Brash delivered his Orewa speeches and joined the company of those opportunist politicians who ceaselessly play the race and welfare cards. For Brash, it worked incredibly well in 2004 – at least in the short term – because he was seen to be such a man of principle and integrity. This remains true with respect to his philosophical beliefs. But in terms of political actions that are guided by instrumental beliefs, Brash is a pragmatist who is willing to follow the political strategists' goal of maximising political advantage.

Gradual or 'crash-through' economic reform? Would Don Brash turn out to be another Roger Douglas? As this analysis has shown, philosophically Brash strongly identifies with the 'Rogernomics' monetarist reforms. He also gives Douglas credit for 'cogently' arguing the case for comprehensive as opposed to piecemeal economic reform. But, in terms of what Brash says he will do, the pragmatist again wins out – at least for now. There will, he promises, be no reform 'thunderbolts'. But what if New Zealand's economic circumstances should change for the worse? Then, seeing himself as a man of principle, Brash as prime minister may feel compelled to prescribe the tough Rogernomics medicine, regardless of the political consequences. His biographer, Paul Goldsmith, does not directly address this issue. However, he recalls how, soon after taking the leadership, Brash warned parliament about the need for urgency in addressing New Zealand's 'worrying' economic and social prospects. He portrays Brash as a leader who will take up this challenge. He is, according to Goldsmith, a leader of 'clear moral vision and lack of self doubt', and 'instinctively a reformer' determined to make a 'quantum leap forward' (Goldsmith 2005, 265, 280, 285).

How much difference, if any, would it make to New Zealand if Brash, rather than Clark, were prime minister? In the end it is their respective philosophical beliefs that take precedence, and there are notable differences between the two leaders in that respect, although both have moved towards the political centre ground. In terms of 'instrumental' beliefs on how to play the game of politics, both appear to be pragmatists. However, whereas Clark constantly balances the pursuit of her political goals with an understanding of the need for public trust in the government, Brash is still feeling his way. His pragmatism may be short-lived, and a radical shift back to the economic right is a distinct possibility under a future Brash-led government.

John Henderson wishes to acknowledge the research assistance provided by Greg Watson, a graduate student at the University of Canterbury. Seishi Gomibuchi wishes to thank Liz Chisholm, Christine Crampton and Janet Anderson for their help.

Ansley, B. (2002) 'Prime Mover', *New Zealand Listener*, 27 July, 18–21.
Ashton, L. (1980) 'Countdown for the Bays team', *Auckland Star*, 5 September, 5.
Brash, D. (1981) 'Economy', in G. Bryant, *New Zealand 2001*, Auckland, Cassell, 32–40.
Brash, D. (1995) 'Foreign Investment in New Zealand', speech to Wellington Rotary Club, 20 November.
Brash, D. (1996) 'New Zealand's Remarkable Reforms', speech to Institute of Economic Affairs, London, 4 June.
Brash, D. (1998) 'New Zealand's Economic Reforms: A Model for Change?', speech at Chatham House, London, 3 June.
Brash, D. (1999) 'Comments on accepting the NZIER Economic Award', 18 August.
Brash, D. (2001) 'Faster Growth? If We Want It', Address to the Knowledge Wave Conference, Auckland, 2 August.
Brash, D. (2002a) 'We Can Do So Much Better', Address to Albany business people, Auckland, 17 May.
Brash, D. (2002b) 'Monetary Policy and Growth', speech to the Auckland Rotary Club, Auckland, 27 May.
Brash, D. (2002c) Maiden speech in Parliament, 3 September.
Brash, D. (2003a) 'Where to from here?', speech to Orewa Rotary Club, Auckland 28 January.
Brash, D. (2003b) 'The Potential Pitfalls of the New Zealand Superannuation Fund', Auckland, 7 March.
Brash, D. (2003c) Speech to the annual conference of the New Zealand Road Transport Forum, 14 September.
Brash, D. (2004a) 'Nationhood', Address to the Orewa Rotary Club, Auckland, 27 January.
Brash, D. (2004b) 'Don Brash Responds to his Critics', speech to the Northern Club, Auckland, 4 March.

Brash, D. (2005a) 'Tax systems rewards idleness and mediocrity', *Dominion Post*, 18 January, B5.

Brash, D. (2005b) Address to the Orewa Rotary Club, 25 January, reproduced in the *Dominion Post*, 26 January, B5.

Campbell, G. (2001) 'How to Run the Country, Part One', *New Zealand Listener*, 24 November, 15–17.

Clark, H. (2000) Address to Labour Party Conference 2000, Wellington Town Hall, 18 November.

Clark, H. (2002) Address at Labour's Campaign Launch, Aotea Centre, Auckland, 18 June.

Clark, H. (2003a) Prime Minister's Statement to Parliament, Parliament Buildings, Wellington, 11 February.

Clark. H. (2003b) Address to Knowledge Wave Conference, Auckland, 19 February.

Clark, H. (2003c) Address to NZ Labour Party Conference, Christchurch, 8 November.

Clark, H. (2004a) 'The Hikoi of Hope – five years on', Address to the Inner City Churches Lent Programme, Christchurch, 4 March.

Clark, H. (2004b) 'Labour: Moving Ahead', Address to the 2004 Labour Party Conference, Auckland, 13 November.

Clark, H. (2005) Address to Labour Party Congress, Wellington, 2 April.

Clifton, J. (2004) 'Man of the Moment', *New Zealand Listener*, 28 February, 16–21.

Edwards, B. (2001) *Helen: Portrait of a Prime Minister*, Auckland, Exisle.

George, A. (1969) 'The "Operational Code": A Neglected Approach to the Study of Political Leaders and Decision Making', *International Studies Quarterly*, 13, 190–222.

Goldsmith, P. (2005), *Brash: A Biography*, Auckland, Penguin.

Henderson, J. T. (1978) 'The "Operational Code" of Robert David Muldoon', in S. Levine (ed.), *Politics in New Zealand*, Auckland, Allen & Unwin.

Hewitson, M. (2003) 'Don Brash, boring ahead with confidence', *New Zealand Herald*, 22 November, A28.

Holsti, O. (1970) 'The Operational Code Approach to the Study of Political Leaders: John Foster Dulles' Philosophical and Instrumental Beliefs', *Canadian Journal of Political Science*, 3, 123–57.

Hosking, R. (2004) 'How Don Brash has Shaken up Politics', *National Business Review*, 13 October, 14.

Laws, M. (2003) 'Face to Face with the Prime Minister', *North & South*, September, 60–65.

Leites, N. (1951) *The Operational Code of the Politburo*, New York, McGraw-Hill.

Light, E. (1998) 'A Career in Politics', *Her Business*, July/August, 20–23.

Marfleet, G. (2000) 'The Operational Code of John F. Kennedy During the Cuban Missile Crisis: A Comparison of Public and Private Rhetoric', *Political Psychology*, 21, 545–58.

Milne, J. (2005) 'Brash's divisive leadership splitting National Party', *New Zealand Herald*, 6 February 2005, retrieved 14 May 2005, from: http://www.nzherald.co.nz/index.cfm?ObjectID=10009701

Munro, M. (1989) 'Helen Clark: misunderstood Ms?' *Sunday Magazine*, 10 December, 28–34.

Nichols, J. (2004) 'Helen Clark: A Pragmatic-Strong Prime Minister', *Political Science*, 56/2, 99–109.

O'Leary, E. (2002) 'Political Spin', in J. McGregor and M. Comrie (eds), *What's News?: Reclaiming journalism in New Zealand*, Palmerston North, Dunmore.

O'Sullivan, F. (2005) 'The presidential predilections of Helen Clark', *New Zealand Herald*, 29 March, retrieved 29 March 2005, from: http://www.nzherald.co.nz/index.cfm?ObjectID=10117545

Perigo, L. (2004) 'Interview with Don Brash', *Solo HQ*, 20 April, retrieved 10 December 2004, from: http://www.solohq.com/Articles/Brash/The_Right_Stuff.shtml

Roger, W. (2000) 'Face to Face', *North & South*, September, 94–101.

Roger, W. (2004) 'The Rise and Rise of Don Brash', *North & South*, April, 34–43.

Schafer, M. and S. Crichlow (2000) 'Bill Clinton's Operational Code: Assessing Source Material Bias', *Political Psychology*, 21, 559–71.

Small, V. (2004) 'Sidestepping the "third rail"', *Press*, 14 May, B15.
Smith, A. (1994) 'Helen Clark: Crisis Manager', *Management*, October, 28–29.
Tunnah, H. (2004) 'Looking Down at a Year in Charge', *New Zealand Herald*, 23 October, B5.
TVNZ (2004a) *Face to Face*, interview with Kim Hill, 25 February, TV One.
TVNZ (2004b) *One Network News Insights: Bring It On*, 14 June, TV One.
Venter, N. (2002) 'The Political Prime of Miss Helen Clark', *Dominion Post*, 8 July, A4.
Venter, N. (2003) 'Enjoying the Buzz as Beehive's Queen Bee', *Press*, 29 November, 15.
Walker, S., M. Schafer and M. D. Young (1998) 'Systematic Procedures for Operational Code
    Analysis: Measuring and Modeling Jimmy Carter's Operational Code', *International
    Studies Quarterly*, 42, 175–90.
Walker, S., M. Schafer and M. D. Young (1999) 'Presidential Operational Codes and Foreign
    Conflicts in the Post-Cold War World', *Journal of Conflict Resolution*, 43, 610–25.
Walker, S., M. Schafer and M. D. Young (2003) 'Profiling the Operational Codes of Political
    Leaders', in J. M. Post (ed.), *The Psychological Assessment of Political Leaders: With
    Profiles of Saddam Hussein and Bill Clinton*, Ann Arbor, University of Michigan Press.
Walker, S., M. Schafer and M. D. Young (2003b) 'Operational Code Beliefs and Object
    Appraisal [of Saddam Hussein]', in J. M. Post (ed.), *The Psychological Assessment of
    Political Leaders: With Profiles of Saddam Hussein and Bill Clinton*.
Young, A. (2003) 'Helen Clark Looks Back at 10 years as Labour Leader', *New Zealand
    Herald*, 29 November, retrieved 27 December 2004, from: http://www.nzherald.co.nz/
    index.cfm?ObjectID=3536718.

SIX

Leadership in Cabinet Under MMP

Elizabeth McLeay

Without an understanding of the institutional context, political leadership cannot be fully understood: the analysis of personality alone cannot tell the full story. This chapter focuses primarily on the formal and informal institutional structure within which New Zealand political leaders operate. It does not argue that personality and leadership style are entirely contingent on institutional factors. Rather, it maintains that constitutional form and structural and normative contexts provide both constraints and opportunities. A leader's personal characteristics are tested within those institutional parameters.

Institutions obviously matter a great deal in leadership studies. Compare the political resources of a military dictatorship with those of a prime minister in a liberal democracy, for example. Or, within democratic systems, contrast the political resources of elected presidents in presidential systems with those of prime ministers in parliamentary systems. Despite what has been labelled the 'presidentialism' of the office of prime minister, there remain significant differences between leaders in different political structures (Heffernan 2005; McAllister 1996). But are leaders in majoritarian parliamentary systems different in any way from those in non-majoritarian ones? Here we enter into more subtle sets of institutional dynamics. More particularly, did New Zealand's shift to a proportional electoral system, with the associated transformation of parliament, have any bearing on the exercise of leadership within cabinet? New Zealand continues to be a unitary, unicameral, parliamentary system. Because the main features of the political system remain intact, it is possible to test the impact of proportionality on political leadership.

This does not mean that disentangling the significant variables is easy. For example, very soon after MMP was introduced, New Zealand had its first woman prime minister, Jenny Shipley, and she was succeeded by the first elected woman prime minister, Helen Clark. One of the parties with which Labour negotiated was co-led by a woman, Jeanette Fitzsimons of the Green Party. So it may be that differences in leadership style since the advent of MMP are at least partly the product of gender difference.

Another confusing variable is the role played by international affairs, which always throw prime ministers into the forefront of public attention. The years after 1996 saw a couple of major trade rounds, the attacks on the USA on 11 September 2001 and the subsequent invasions of Afghanistan and Iraq, crises that challenged leadership capacity in the same way that leaders elected under the previous electoral rules were tested.

Nevertheless, despite the difficulties in analysing the various factors at work, the political science literature contains enough evidence that institutions matter to justify analysing the institutional differences that MMP brought about. Thus I am arguing that understanding political actors involves knowing about their environment, the informal rules and norms that are embedded in the formal set of roles that embody political structures.[1] New Zealand provides a fascinating opportunity to test out these ideas, since electoral reform radically altered the immediate context in which prime ministers operated.[2]

I adopt several analytical frameworks to help understand political leadership, focusing on each of these in turn. Firstly, I discuss the political resources (constitutional and political) that are available to leaders. This concept is more helpful than that of power because,

> [I]t is impossible, and indeed fruitless, to try and identify a single site of power within the core executive, because power is everywhere. The structures of dependency and the distribution of resources mean that all actors can have some success. No single actor can achieve what he or she wants without exchanging resources, and therefore compromise is built into the structure of government (Smith 1999, 6–7).[3]

Political scientists have borrowed the idea of exchange relationships from sociologists, conceiving political actors interacting in ways that benefit everyone.

Secondly, I show how the key players – especially prime ministers – are linked into policy networks, using their political resources to pursue their goals through resource exchange (Smith 1999, 4). The notion of policy network generally refers to the relationship between government agencies and interest groups, and the ways in which resources are interdependent. Policy networks can be conceived in primarily structural or, alternatively, personal terms (see especially Marsh 1998, 3–16). Here I am primarily confining the term to prime ministers' networks within central government and parliament.

The third section analyses how the new electoral system introduced new veto players into the policy networks – individual or collective political actors whose consent is necessary before changes can be made. The concept of veto players supplements the notion of political actors with resources because it helps pinpoint how institutional change can affect actors' resources through altering their exchange networks. Tsebelis usefully distinguishes between institutional veto players and partisan veto players (1995 and 2000). In New Zealand's case, while the introduction of the Mixed Member Proportional (MMP) electoral system did not add institutional veto players (adding an upper house or a constitutional court, for example), it did add partisan veto players by representing more parties in parliament. Thus, leading a government involved leaders using more transactional skills than in the past, where the crafts of persuasion, negotiation, including offering penalties and rewards, and compromise have heightened importance (and see Hayward 2001).

Before concluding with some reflections on the evolution of political leadership, briefly arguing that transactional skills are not the only ones needed in today's world, I place prime ministers in a wider, cultural perspective, by discussing expectations about their representative roles.

Leaders and their Political Resources

Because neither the office of prime minister nor cabinet itself is defined in statute, MMP leaders, like their predecessors, could build on tradition while redefining their roles (Alley 1992; McLeay 1995). After the advent of MMP, however, the circumstances of coalition and minority government reduced the extent of leaders' policy initiatives. Before these new constraints are discussed in the next section, however, I analyse some aspects of New Zealand's political institutions that affect the political resources of prime ministers.

Prime-ministerial authority: succession issues
MMP appeared to have brought governmental instability to New Zealand. Between the 1996 and 2005 general elections there were three prime ministers: Jim Bolger, Jenny Shipley and Helen Clark.[4] Bolger led a majority coalition, as did his successor, Shipley, until mid-1998, but from then on all governments were minority administrations. Two junior coalition parties split up as a direct consequence of the problems of being in government (New Zealand First and the Alliance). But these difficulties also provided some important challenges for political leaders and tested the durability of certain constitutional conventions.

The post-MMP multi-party parliaments might well have reduced the authority of prime ministers through creating periods of uncertainty and instability after general elections that failed to produce a single party that was the clear majority winner. Crises may also develop when governments lose their majorities or, alternatively, when uncertainty is created through leadership changes.

Contrary to some anxieties concerning the possible politicisation of the governor-general's role in appointing a new prime minister and government, even before the 1996 election the then Governor-General, Sir Michael Hardie Boys, made it clear that the choice of government was for parliament and the parties to decide, not the Governor-General. Subsequently he stressed that 'The formation of a Government is a political decision and must be arrived at by politicians' (Hardie Boys 1998, 2–3). This comment affirmed the continuity of an important constitutional principle of political succession in New Zealand: governments are determined by voters and elected representatives, not by appointed governors-general.

The post-election succession processes developed piecemeal. After the long weeks of negotiation with both major parties after the 1996 election, Winston Peters, the New Zealand First leader, chose National as preferred coalition partner. Bolger, prime minister since 1990, continued in that position, albeit with a mere one-seat majority for the new coalition government (Boston and McLeay 1997). After the 1999 election, because Labour and the Alliance had already been negotiating in preparation to form a new government, they were able to announce immediately their coalition arrangements (Boston and Church 2000). It had become imperative for Jim Anderton (Alliance) and Clark (Labour) to patch up their past differences,[5] and to demonstrate to voters before the election that, if they chose to support either of their parties, the two leaders, with their parties, were committed to govern together if they had the parliamentary numbers. After the coalition was announced immediately after the election, it became clear that the Greens had also won seats and that Labour, even with the Alliance, lacked a parliamentary majority. Labour then negotiated an informal agreement with the Greens on confidence and supply (Boston 2000). After the 2002 election, the negotiations again left the Governor-General in no doubt that the new Labour–Progressive coalition government was secure with its formal agreement with United Future on issues of confidence and supply and its further policy agreement with the Greens on certain other matters (Boston and Church 2003). In 2005, because the election night result was so evenly balanced between the Labour and National parties and the allocation of seats among the parties depended on the distribution of special votes, firm inter-party negotiations were delayed until the final results were declared. On all four occasions (1996, 1999, 2002 and 2005) it was clear that the party leaders, assisted by key advisers, made the decisions and that the Governor-General played the traditional role of confirming those decisions. In that sense there was no change to the relative powers of the Governor-General and party leaders respectively.

Skilled leadership was required to create governments, on the other hand, requiring inter-party negotiating skills that leaders had to develop, since they had not been required when one party was a clear winner on its own under the two-party system that had existed since 1935. The exception was Bolger, who had had some experience of negotiating with other leaders during the 1993–96 parliamentary term, as the two main parties lost supporters and the National Government lost its majority. Clearly, Clark and Anderton learned new leadership skills by watching the unpopularity of the protracted game played by New Zealand First after 1996 as it negotiated with both Labour and National and then went against its previous public pronouncements that had been critical of the latter party. So the first four elections not only showed the limitations of the authority of governors-general but also showed that leaders had to adopt new sorts of negotiating tactics if they wished to be in power. Further, the art of compromise became a key skill – not only to know when to give in to the demands of other parties but also when not to give way.

The 1999, 2002 and 2005 post-election discussions, although not those in 1996 when New Zealand First set out the rules of the game, indicated that the major party leaders had the authority to take the lead in government formation discussions simply because they had the most seats. If this becomes the norm in government formation bargaining, then it is the leaders of these two parties who will remain the dominant players. Note, though, that it was the smaller party leaders who held the primary bargaining resource – the parliamentary votes necessary to create majorities – in each of those circumstances (for example, New Zealand First in 1996, the Alliance and the Greens in 1999 and the Progressives and United Future in 2002). Subsequently, what those smaller party leaders who chose to take their seats in cabinet rather than remaining outside the government had to learn was that the post-election negotiations represented the zenith of their powers: once the deals were done, their political capital immediately diminished because flexing their muscles through driving hard bargains once in government was to risk losing public support. Their political resources had to be carefully protected, not squandered.

There was one mid-term change of prime minister that might have tested both the Governor-General's reserve powers and the political management skills of the leaders. In late 1997 Shipley challenged Bolger's leadership and prime-ministership. Realising that he had lost his basic political resource, the majority support of National's parliamentary party, Bolger announced that he would resign at the end of November. After some vacillation and expressions of annoyance that he had not been consulted about the leadership change, Peters, Deputy Prime Minister and New Zealand First leader, announced that his party would remain in the coalition government. The Governor-General wrote,

> In appointing Mrs Shipley, I observed the established convention that the Governor-General appoints as Prime Minister the person who appears to command the confidence of the House. In this case, I was satisfied (on the

basis of public statements in the media and Mrs Shipley's own assurances)
that she did command that confidence, and I appointed her accordingly
(Hardie Boys 1998, 4).

These events reaffirmed the traditional constitutional conventions regarding the mid-term transfer of prime-ministerial power. The Governor-
General accepted the right of a party to replace its leader even though that
leader was a prime minister who headed a coalition government and who
had been jointly responsible for its formation.

Prime ministers only rarely lose the confidence of their caucuses
having won, rather than lost, the preceding election. But apart from
Bolger there were other post-1935 examples, all leaders of single-party
majority governments who resigned their prime-ministerial warrants
some months before a general election. Each succumbed to pressure from
those who accurately forecast that under the incumbents' leadership their
parties would lose. Bolger's National predecessors were Sidney Holland
(1957) and Keith Holyoake (1972). In Labour, Geoffrey Palmer and Mike
Moore successively lost their positions during 1990. In all these cases, their
successors actually lost the next general election (and see Hayward 2005;
and Massicote 1998). Leadership succession in Labour and National has
always been in the hands of the parliamentary parties and MMP made no
difference to this situation. When a prime minister, or any other leader, no
longer represents the party in the ways that the caucus followers expect,
then they withdraw their support. That support is a leader's fundamental
political resource in a parliamentary system (and see Heffernan 2005, esp.
62–4). What was different after MMP compared with the earlier episodes
was a direct consequence of electoral system change: the difficulty experienced by many National MPs in accepting the role of partisan veto players
(New Zealand First) in the policy-making network. In a sense Bolger was
the victim of a culture clash between his party colleagues' expectations
that their party's priorities and policies should be paramount, even in a
coalition government, and the reality of the new negotiation and compromises that had to be worked through.

In the case of several of the smaller parties (including ACT, the Greens
and the Maori Party), their leadership selection rules conform more to
Canadian and British practices by involving party members beyond the
narrow confines of caucus. Were leadership spills to occur within any of

these parties while in government, then a protracted period of uncertainty might ensue. Also, if Labour and/or National were to expand the constituency for voting for their leaders, the situation would be similar. On the other side of the argument, however, because it is much more difficult to unseat leaders who are elected from party conventions or from constituent groups of the party, then leadership spills would almost certainly become less frequent. Party rules and processes make a good deal of difference to leadership selection, and this key process interacts with constitutional requirements, political circumstances and incumbent and aspirant personality. Leaders who are elected from a wider constituency than their parliamentary caucuses have a more unequivocal support base, and a more unconditional political resource, than do leaders who are elected by their immediate colleagues.

Leadership patronage

All prime ministers in parliamentary systems have the formal authority to choose and to dismiss their ministers, one of their most important political resources. In practice, within Labour the parliamentary party elects the cabinet ministers, while the prime minister allocates portfolios and appoints ministers outside cabinet and, also, under-secretaries (McLeay 1995). Thus for Labour leaders the scope of this particular political resource is constrained, potentially affecting their personal authority, as David Lange discovered when he dismissed Roger Douglas only to have that MP re-elected to cabinet. National prime ministers, in comparison, retained the power to appoint and dismiss, although they frequently consulted widely, even on occasion taking a 'straw poll' of caucus colleagues.

In coalition governments, leaders negotiate over the number of ministers each party has and how portfolios are allocated. This has been the case in New Zealand although the 1996 agreement spelled out all the details, including the allocation of a new position, Treasurer, to New Zealand First; while the subsequent agreements were shorter, meaning that the actual patronage deals were not as publicly expressed. The fact that the sizes and structures of cabinets have not been constitutionally defined and restricted meant that the patronage resources of prime ministers and coalition leaders were in formal terms unlimited, although all ministers have to be MPs. The real growth to the size of ministries (including ministers inside and outside cabinet) had occurred during the 1980s. This flexibility had been a useful resource for prime ministers because it allowed them to expand their patronage by appointing more MPs to executive office, rewarding the able and loyal (not necessarily the same people) and dominating their caucuses by sheer weight of numbers. The flexibility of the cabinet system proved useful to MMP prime ministers who needed to make room in their ministries for representatives of the smaller coalition parties.

But with two leaders in coalition cabinets, who would dismiss ministers who had not performed satisfactorily? The question of dismissal is altogether trickier than that of appointment, posing a possible conflict of authority between the prime minister and the coalition partner leader, were they to disagree on the fortunes of a minister. In fact, there have been more dismissals of ministers since 1996 than before, with most occurring under Clark's prime-ministership. If anything, the power to dismiss had been strengthened because after MMP it was much more difficult for collective cabinet responsibility to surmount individual ministerial responsibility. Prime ministers and other party leaders within cabinet had to forestall possible criticisms of erring ministers by partisan veto players within the legislative policy networks. It became more imperative to preserve the cohesion of the coalition government than to preserve the position of a minister who had offended.

What would happen if the leaders of the two coalition partners disagreed over a policy issue? Would the patronage powers of the prime minister trump those of the leaders of coalition partners? The relationship between Peters and Shipley was plainly less compatible than that between Peters and Bolger. After a dispute between the governing parties over the sale of Wellington Airport, Peters publicly criticised Shipley's actions and leadership. She promptly dismissed him from his positions as Treasurer and Deputy Prime Minister (McLeay 1999). This incident reaffirmed the continued authority of the prime minister as the governor-general's chief adviser as against all other ministers, including coalition party leaders.

The consequential disintegration of New Zealand First after Peters's dismissal left some of its ministers in office with Shipley, a potentially unstable arrangement that actually lasted until the 1999 election. But the next coalition government also found itself in difficulties when Labour's junior partner, the Alliance, split over its leader's decision to support

Labour in sending military aid to Afghanistan after the USA invaded that country. Policy differences were interwoven with criticisms of Anderton's leadership style and tactics. He appeared to some Alliance MPs and members to be too accommodating to Labour's priorities. Nevertheless, the situation this time was different because, even though Anderton had fallen out with his own party, Clark and Anderton continued to get along, a relationship that was still apparently strong well into Labour's second term as senior coalition partner (with Anderton by then leading the Progressives). After the 2002 Alliance split, the government limped along for some months before the prime minister called an early election, perhaps learning from Shipley's failure to act similarly in 1998.

Dissolving parliament

A prime minister's authority to determine the timing of a general election (within the limit of the parliamentary term) is often depicted as an important political resource, arming a leader with the threat to curtail awkward MPs' parliamentary careers, especially worrying for those in marginal seats and for parties with low support in the opinion polls.[6] The Governor-General's assent to Clark's recommendation that an election be held in July 2002 confirmed the constitutional convention that the prime minister could indeed act thus, as long as she or he still retained the confidence of the House. Clearly, that a prime minister was not running a majority government did not affect the constitutional situation so long as there was no immediate risk of losing a vote of confidence (see Church 2003). The above events demonstrated that calling an early election remained a useful political resource in the hands of a prime minister, a resource that could be used to threaten discontented coalition parties but which had to be employed cautiously because of possible voter backlash.

The prime-ministerial agency support system

The support system of the post-MMP leaders was substantially the same as that of their predecessors, but could be stretched and re-interpreted to suit the new demands of coalition and minority government. The basic design and the bureaucratisation of the prime-ministerial and cabinet support systems were established during the 1980s (McLeay 1995). The Cabinet Office, which developed from the late 1940s onwards, had become the neutral secretariat of the prime minister, although prime ministers needed rather more help, especially on constitutional issues, as MMP loomed and then was implemented. The Department of Prime Minister and Cabinet provided policy support and there was the Prime Minister's Office, designed for the more political activities. These organisations, somewhat expanded in numbers, continued to be important political resources for prime ministers after MMP. One significant development was the growth of the office of Deputy Prime Minister. This was particularly important for the first two MMP governments, when the leader of the junior coalition partner held that position.

Thus a system that could cope with the complexities of new policy networks was already in existence and could be adapted for inter-party negotiations. New key players in these processes, such as Heather Simpson (Clark's adviser, 1999–) and Andrew Ladley (Anderton's adviser, 1999–2002) could be plugged into the existing system and play an effective role in running the new networks. The key change after MMP was the increased number of political advisers rather than the actual shape of the institutional support system (James 2002, 65; Wintringham 2002, 6–7). And many were employed to work the new policy network.

New Zealand prime ministers have historically been expected to play the major leadership role in shaping the policy agenda both internally, through chairing cabinet and its key committees, and externally, in parliament and in public. This aspect is far too broad to be discussed here. Instead, I focus on how the new veto players affected the immediate environment within which prime ministers must lead.

Prime Ministers, Veto Players and Policy Networks

With the exception of the period between August 1998 and the 1999 election, when Shipley headed a minority government comprising National plus a mixture of former New Zealand First ministers, between 1996 and 2005 two party leaders sat at the cabinet table. There was the larger party leader, who took the prime-ministership, and the smaller party leader, who either took the position of deputy prime minister, as happened in the first two coalition governments, or another senior portfolio, as happened after the 2002 election.

The immediate impact of MMP therefore was the institutionalisation of an authoritative alternative voice inside government that was qualitatively different from any other arrangement in recent history. Even a very strong minister with his or her own power base, someone like Tom Shand from the Holyoake years, for example, or Roger Douglas from the Lange period, lacked the authority derived from being a party leader, chosen by parliamentary colleagues and, furthermore, possessing the invaluable resource of parliamentary votes. It is worth noting, however, that this might not have been the case had New Zealand experienced single-party minority governments between 1996 and 2004, rather than coalitions. As it was, habits of negotiation and compromise had to be developed within the core political executive itself, with consequences for managing the policy process, inter-party relationships, and communications with key public servants, as well as for leaders themselves. In short, prime ministers were faced with veto players who sat with them around the cabinet table.

Managing government business was yet more complex. With minority administrations, negotiations took place with non-governing parties, either for official support to maintain the government in office or to create legislative coalitions, bargaining on an issue-by-issue basis to get government bills through the select committees (often lacking government majorities) and parliament itself. MMP had changed the network of roles and personalities in which prime ministers operated, inserting parliamentary partisan veto players into the core decision-making system. Prime ministers have always had to develop bilateral relationships with other ministers, and these can be a political resource. Under MMP, these relationships were more complicated.

As well as the new tasks of ensuring that consultation and bargaining took place so that prime ministers and governments could count on their budgets being approved by parliament and their bills becoming law, the traditional tasks remained to be performed. Prime ministers shaped the cabinet committee system, although now this was done in conjunction with the junior coalition partner leader. The only prime minister to depart from the conventional committee design was Shipley, who decided to have fewer, larger committees (McLeay 2003, 100) that met fortnightly rather than weekly. Prime ministers chaired cabinet meetings, although the situation was no longer quite as Holyoake had described it earlier: 'The final responsibility for determining the consensus of opinion expressed rests with the chairman' (Holyoake, 1972, 75). In the first place, after MMP, major agreements had already been hammered out in a series of bi-party meetings. Secondly, the chair, although holding the majority numbers in cabinet, had also to heed the views of the other party leader. Third, the relationship between prime ministers and ministers of finance, always the crucial nexus within cabinet dynamics, altered during the National–New Zealand First administration when the Treasurer was also the leader of the junior coalition party. This changed again after 1999 when Clark managed to keep all the major spending portfolios, including Finance, in Labour hands, an interesting exercise in bargaining success and patronage distribution.

FIGURE 1: Leadership Networks, 1996–2004

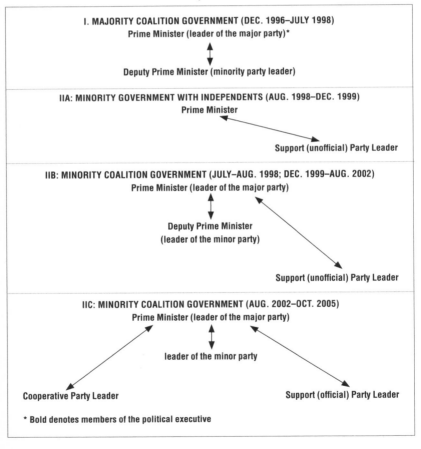

I. MAJORITY COALITION GOVERNMENT (DEC. 1996–JULY 1998)
Prime Minister (leader of the major party)*

Deputy Prime Minister (minority party leader)

IIA: MINORITY GOVERNMENT WITH INDEPENDENTS (AUG. 1998–DEC. 1999)
Prime Minister

Support (unofficial) Party Leader

IIB: MINORITY COALITION GOVERNMENT (JULY–AUG. 1998; DEC. 1999–AUG. 2002)
Prime Minister (leader of the major party)

Deputy Prime Minister
(leader of the minor party)

Support (unofficial) Party Leader

IIC: MINORITY COALITION GOVERNMENT (AUG. 2002–OCT. 2005)
Prime Minister (leader of the major party)

leader of the minor party

Cooperative Party Leader

Support (official) Party Leader

* Bold denotes members of the political executive

The minority coalition governments meant that the new, partisan veto players were of two varieties: those internal to government, who held ministerial warrants, and those external to government, the support parties.

Each had its own political resources. The internal veto players had the support of their party colleagues (as long as they could retain their loyalty), electoral support and the authority that came with their portfolio responsibilities. The external players lacked the last source of authority but had a compensating gain of freedom of action, freedom from being bound by collective cabinet responsibility. In the end, though, parliamentary numbers, and the ideological spread of the parliamentary parties, counted a great deal when assessing prime-ministerial and leadership authority. Bolger had a simpler leadership network to build up exchange relationships with than had Clark, for example, but his policy options were more constrained. The New Zealand First contingent was large and held within its power that of the majority of parliamentary votes. Clark, on the other hand, although leading a minority government, could seek support from more than one external veto player, depending on the issue being legislated. She could use two different networks. Not that this was ever an easy task because to please one might antagonise the other irrevocably. Such manoeuvring required skilled leadership, the help of key staff and the trust of party colleagues: a new type of leadership style.

As can be seen, it is not only the existence of partisan veto players that matters when assessing leadership in cabinet in a proportionally elected parliamentary system. It is also the extent of their particular political resources, both in terms of the parliamentary votes they can command and their ideological positions. Different exchange networks have different consequences for political leadership. But traditional institutional norms also are important, as the following section argues.

Leadership and the Question of Representation

Even before the advent of television and the personalisation of politics, leaders came to represent their parties and, in the case of prime ministers, assumed the authority to represent their governments. Thus, using the notion of representation in a very broad sense, effective prime ministers are expected to play both classical roles: delegate (representing the interests of supporters) and trustee (representing the public interest). For example, Keith Holyoake expressed his dual role as follows:

> There are constant pressures right throughout the country that are brought to bear upon Ministers, and the Prime Minister in particular . . . . As leader of the team he has the task of summing up the direction and thinking of his Government and, ultimately, of Parliament (Holyoake 1972, 72).

And,

> [T]he Prime Minister carries special responsibility as the leader of the Government, chairman of Cabinet and as the person who will be held primarily responsible by the people for any decision by a Minister or what happens in any field of government activity (Holyoake 1972, 74).

Although their tasks of representing their governments in particular and the people in general can be in conflict with one another, prime ministers are the only politicians who can reconcile them. If they can turn the representative roles into widespread support, they are powerful political resources. But support only comes with trust, and trust relies on leaders voicing the views of the group they are leading, as well as performing successfully through winning elections and implementing policies.

The representation of party is perhaps a prime minister's most problematical task under MMP, as Bolger's resignation demonstrated. It is also a role that became more complex as a result of the increased heterogeneity of parliament that was a direct consequence of the new electoral rules, with more Maori and women (a trend begun under plurality rules), among other examples. Clark discovered the difficulties of her role during the debate over the seabed and foreshore issue (see chapter 11). Her government's decision on this resulted in a ministerial resignation (Tariana Turia) and, at the next general election in 2005, cost the Labour Party four Maori seats, which went to the new Maori Party. Prime ministers, unlike opposition leaders, have the added problem of not only having to express the policy expectations of their parties' various groups and factions but also having to realise them. Representing party also extends beyond caucus to members in the extra-parliamentary party (Holyoake 1972) although perhaps extra-parliamentary parties are less important today than when Holyoake was prime minister. This is not however a consequence of MMP but of the decline in party membership in New Zealand since the 1960s and the increase in the resources (financial and support personnel) of elected representatives.

It can be argued that prime ministers' representative roles actually became wider after 1996, given that they represented coalition governments. So not only did they acquire partisan veto players but also, somehow or other, prime ministers had to represent the government as a whole to the people. This is essential to present the required image of stable, collective government, characteristics that have long been part of the New Zealand political culture. Yet, while representing the policies and goals of their government, prime ministers had also to allow coalition partner leaders to share that representative role, a difficult and inherently contradictory task. Bolger did it fairly successfully, but in sharing the embodiment of government with Peters lost the confidence of his own team. Shipley found it easier to operate on her own, without the distraction of Peters at her side, but lost the confidence of the electors in the 1999 election. Clark managed to represent the government while still allowing Anderton to be authoritative publicly, but this was insufficient for his own party that split under the tension of shared power. And after the 2002 election, with only two seats won by the dissidents that left the Alliance, Clark made Labour's deputy leader, Michael Cullen, deputy prime minister, thus effectively creating a triumvirate with herself unequivocally at the head of the team. Successive opinion polls that chose Clark as most preferred prime minister, well ahead of the opposition leader and anyone else, cemented this position (and see Vowles and Aimer 2004, 173–83).

Thus it might be the case that prime ministers in proportionally elected parliaments can accrue political resources in terms of strong public support every bit as much as did their predecessors. To a large extent this depends on personality and perceived strength. It might be related to gender difference, too, but there have been too few women leaders historically to be able to generalise reliably about this factor. It also depends on the characteristics of those who oppose the prime minister from the opposition benches, as it always did. But the leader of the opposition under MMP has to struggle for attention in a highly competitive situation, as Bill English, National leader between 2001 and 2003, when he lost that position to Don Brash, discovered. There are not nearly as many incentives for the opposition parties to present a united front as there are for the parties in office, which must retain cohesion to retain political power itself. In this way, a prime minister who has proved a degree of effectiveness has the advantage over a leader of the opposition whose role in a proportionally elected parliament is by no means as clear as it was previously. Simply put, it became unclear as to whom or what a leader of the opposition represented, apart from his or her own party. The implications are that, in future, leaders of the opposition will use divisive tactics in order to carve out support bases, as did the leader of the National Party, Don Brash, early in 2004 when he spoke against what he labelled special treatment of Maori, a theme that continued throughout the 2005 general election campaign when he argued that his party stood for 'mainstream' New Zealanders.

The resources of political leaders are contingent on many factors. Prime ministers, however, have authority (see Smith 1999) that no other leaders possess, a unique political resource even in coalition governments.

Prime-ministerial Leadership in the 21st Century: an Evolving Role

I have argued that institutional change made a difference to leadership in cabinet. Within cabinet, the presence of the leader of the minority coalition partner provided an authoritative representative voice with whom the prime minister must consult and negotiate. That there were minority governments for most of the post-1996 period made other parties significant players in the parliamentary policy process. From a situation of having no partisan veto players under FPP, prime ministers had to learn to cope with one or more.

Thus different skills and new 'negotiation norms' were needed. These fit well with New Zealanders' values concerning leadership style. A survey carried out in the late 1990s found that 65 per cent of respondents agreed with the statement that 'A party leader should be prepared to cooperate with other groups, even if it means compromising some important beliefs', while 28 per cent agreed that 'A party leader should stand firm for what he or she believes, even if others disagree' (Perry and Webster 1999, 545). Transactional skills are essential for leaders, and voters approve of them.

But effective leadership is not only a matter of adding negotiation skills to the traditional roles and tasks. First, leaders must project an image that encompasses their own party interests. Prime ministers, however, must also represent their governments, coalition or otherwise. Especially in the age of mass media, it is the prime minister who is the face of government. Prime ministers possess the authority that makes this an imperative and that strengthens their position in relation to other leaders. There is a new, unifying role to be played. This is particularly important when a country is divided over significant policy issues, the problem of the ownership of the seabed and foreshore, for example, or over key foreign policy and defence decisions, such as whether to wage war on Iraq along with New Zealand's traditional partners, the USA, Britain and Australia. In circumstances such as these, when government itself is divided, leaders need to call on rhetorical skills that were demanded less frequently in the past.

Secondly, MMP has meant that effective leaders must develop longer time horizons than previously (and see Pierson 2000, 261–2). Relationships with other leaders and parties must be nursed carefully, with regard to discussions on government formation and policy implementation. Clark learned this lesson, first by noting what happened in 1996, and then by carefully remedying her relationship with the Green leaders after the very public disagreement between the two parties over genetic engineering during the 2002 election campaign.

The task of the prime minister is larger than it was. And if prime ministers can manage authority effectively, they can be as strong as their predecessors who led single-party majority governments, not necessarily in getting policies through parliament but in terms of creating a nationwide personal following (and see Henderson 2003). In an odd sense, MMP has meant that an effective prime minister can transcend party allegiance in a way that was not possible when leaders and followers were either inside or outside government, and politics was entirely a zero-sum game. A group of us wrote before the first MMP general election at the end of 1996:

> Prime Ministers generally have less power in a multi-party government. Consequently, prime ministerial dominance of the kind associated with the Muldoon years is unlikely. Against this, the Prime Minister's role as a mediator, conciliator, and final arbiter of inter-party and intra-party disputes will doubtless be more important (Boston et al. 1996, 127–8).

But to see leadership of cabinet under MMP as *solely* requiring new sorts of negotiation skills has proved to be a misleading interpretation of the new leadership role; and we cannot arbitrarily state that prime ministers have become less powerful, because much depends on the personality of the leaders involved (prime minister and others), the distribution of seats among the parliamentary parties – the partisan veto players and policy networks part of the argument – and the established norms and values of how leaders represent their governments to citizens. Although inter-party negotiations certainly required leaders to put in place new processes and to lead negotiations by example, the skills actually required to weather the changes are as much public as private ones. Further, the very fact of institutional change required prime ministers to take a vitally important part in establishing public trust in the new processes. Electoral system change itself provided the opportunity for prime ministers to show their leadership capacities and failings.

Thus, leading in a transactional manner through the use of negotiation and consultation was a necessary condition for effective leadership after MMP was introduced but it certainly was not a sufficient one. Crises abroad and rapid and radical economic and social change at home, the need for the reassertion of traditional representative roles in the new policy environment, as well as the novel skills required to negotiate policy decisions and shape the political agenda, all have called for the reinvention of leadership by prime ministers in Aotearoa New Zealand.

---

1   There is now an extensive literature on institutionalism, old and new. For a good overview see Lowndes 2003.
2   I would like to thank Margaret Hayward for giving me the opportunity to learn from her research into prime-ministerial leadership in changing times (Hayward 2005).
3   Martin Smith identifies British prime ministers' resources as patronage (the right to appoint and dismiss), authority, political support/party, political support/electorate, the Prime Minister's Office and bilateral policymaking (Smith 1999, 32, table 2.1).
4   After MMP, Bolger (National Party) was prime minister between December 1996 and December 1997, when Shipley defeated him for the leadership and became prime minister. She lost that position in the December 1999 general election when Helen Clark (Labour Party) became prime minister. Clark retained that position after the July 2002 general election.

5   Clark and Anderton fell out with one another during the fourth Labour Government when Clark chose to remain within Labour and Anderton to depart from it, forming NewLabour.
6   New Zealand's triennial term (although not Australia's) appears to have acted as a constraint on a frequent use of this prime-ministerial resource.

Alley, R. (1992) 'The Powers of the Prime Minister', in H. Gold (ed.), *New Zealand Politics in Perspective*, 3rd edn, Auckland, Longman Paul.
Boston, J. (2000) 'Forming the Coalition between Labour and the Alliance', in J. Boston, S. Church, S. Levine, E. McLeay and N. S. Roberts (eds), *Left Turn: The New Zealand General Election of 1999*, Wellington, Victoria University Press.
Boston, J. and S. Church (2000) 'Pre-election Wheeling and Dealing: The New Zealand Experience', in J. Boston, S. Church, S. Levine, E. McLeay and N. S. Roberts (eds), *Left Turn: The New Zealand General Election of 1999*, Wellington, Victoria University Press.
Boston, J. and S. Church (2003) 'Government Formation after the 2002 General Election', in J. Boston, S. Church, S. Levine, E. McLeay and N. S. Roberts (eds), *New Zealand Votes: The General Election of 2002*, Wellington, Victoria University Press.
Boston, J., S. Levine, E. McLeay and N. S. Roberts (1996) *New Zealand under MMP: A New Politics?* Auckland, Auckland University Press with Bridget Williams Books.
Boston, J. and E. McLeay (1997) 'Forming the First MMP Government: Theory, Practice and Prospects', in J. Boston, S. Levine, E. McLeay and N. S. Roberts (eds), *From Campaign to Coalition: The 1996 MMP Election*, Palmerston North, Dunmore.
Church, S. (2003) 'Going Early', in J. Boston, S. Church, S. Levine, E. McLeay, and N. S. Roberts (eds), *New Zealand Votes: The General Election of 2002*, Wellington, Victoria University Press.
Hardie Boys, M. (1998) 'The Constitutional Challenges of MMP: A Magical Demystification Tour', speech presented at the conference on Governing Under MMP: the Constitutional and Policy Challenges, Wellington, Institute of Policy Studies, 3 December.
Hayward, M. (2001) 'A Comparison of the Leadership and Change Management Styles of Four New Zealand Prime Ministers: 1984–1997', in K. W. Parry (ed.), *Leadership in the Antipodes: Findings, Implications and a Leader Profile*, Wellington, Institute of Policy Studies and Centre for the Study of Leadership.
Hayward, M. (2005) 'Prime Ministerial Leadership in New Zealand During a Time of Change – 1984 to 2002: A Comparison of Leadership Styles', PhD thesis, Victoria University of Wellington.
Heffernan, R. (2005) 'Why the Prime Minister cannot be a President: Comparing Institutional Imperatives in Britain and America', *Parliamentary Affairs*, 58, 53–70.
Henderson, J. (2003) 'The Prime Minister: Powers and Personality', in R. Miller (ed.), *New Zealand Government and Politics*, 3rd edn, Melbourne, Oxford University Press.
Holyoake, K. (1972) 'The Task of Prime Minister', in L. Cleveland and A. D. Robinson (eds), *Readings in New Zealand Government*, Wellington, A. H. and A. W. Reed.
Lowndes, V. (2003) 'Institutionalism', in D. Marsh and G. Stoker (eds), *Theory and Methods in Political Science*, 2nd edn, Houndmills, Basingstoke, Palgrave Macmillan.
James, C. (2002) *The Tie that Binds: The Relationship Between Ministers and Chief Executives*, Wellington, Institute of Policy Studies and New Zealand Centre for Public Law.
McAllister, I. (1996) 'Leaders', in L. LeDuc, R. G. Niemi and P. Norris (eds), *Comparing Democracies: Elections and Voting in Global Perspective*, Thousand Oaks, CA, and London, Sage.
McLeay, E. (1995) *Cabinet and Political Power in New Zealand*, Auckland, Oxford University Press.

McLeay, E. (1999) 'What is the Constitutional Status of the New Zealand Cabinet Office Manual?' *Public Law Review*, 10, 11–17.

McLeay, E. (2003) 'Cabinet', in R. Miller (ed.), *New Zealand Government and Politics*, 3rd edn, Melbourne, Oxford University Press.

Marsh, D. (1998) 'The Development of the Policy Network Approach', in D. Marsh (ed.), *Comparative Policy Networks*, Buckingham, Oxford University Press.

Massicote, L. (1998) 'Can Successors Succeed? Assessing the Odds for Prime Ministerial Re-election in Old Commonwealth Countries since 1945', *Commonwealth and Comparative Studies*, 36, 96–109.

Perry, P. and A. Webster (1999) *New Zealand Politics at the Turn of the Millennium: Attitudes and Values about Politics and Government*, Auckland, Alpha.

Pierson, P. (2000) 'Increasing Returns, Path Dependence, and the Study of Politics', *American Political Science Review*, 94, 251–67.

Smith, M. H. (1999) *The Core Executive in Britain*, Houndmills, Basingstoke, Macmillan.

Tsebelis, G. (1995) 'Veto Players and Law Production in Parliamentary Democracies', in H. Doring (ed.), *Parliaments and Majority Rule in Western Europe*, New York, St Martins Press.

Tsebelis, G. (2000) 'Veto Players and Institutional Analysis', *Governance*, 13, 441–74.

Vowles, J. and P. Aimer (2004) 'Political Leadership, Representation and Trust', in J. Vowles, P. Aimer, S. Banducci, J. Karp and R. Miller (eds), *Voters' Veto: The 2002 Election in New Zealand and the Consolidation of Minority Government*, Auckland, Auckland University Press.

Wintringham, M. (2002) 'Annual Report of the State Services Commissioner', in *Annual Report of the State Services Commission for the year ended 30 June 2002*, Wellington, State Services Commission, available at: http:www.ssc.govt.nz/ar2002/

SEVEN

Minor Party Leadership Under Proportional Representation

Raymond Miller

Fascinating people, folks with values and personalities sometimes very unlike those dominating the political mainstream, have been tempted out to the periphery to organize, become active in, or lead third parties.[1]

For much of the last century, the leaders of New Zealand's minor parties were relegated to a cameo appearance at each election. Outside of the election campaign, the absence of parliamentary seats prevented them from either influencing the legislative process or curbing the excesses of governmental power. By the 1980s there were signs that the era of two-party dominance was coming to an end. Buoyed by a rapid rise in their share of the vote, followed by the introduction of proportional representation (PR), the minor parties began to multiply and move towards the political mainstream. Today, their combined strength ensures a prominent role in parliament and government, thereby justifying their inclusion in this volume on political leadership in New Zealand.

This chapter will assess the proposition that minor party leaders are their movement's greatest potential weakness, as well as its greatest strength. Minor parties can be divided into two basic categories: those established before and those after the 1993 electoral referendum. The latter group, which includes the ACT and United (now United Future) parties, was formed for largely opportunistic motives, notably to exploit the opportunities for participation in government under PR. The pre-referendum minor parties, on the other hand, are products of conflict, either as a result of doctrinal disagreement with a major party or from frustrated personal ambition.

Most of the parties formed before the advent of PR remain personality-based and follow the leadership model of party organisation, distinguishing features of which include: a strong, sometimes even charismatic, leader; weak organisation; and a small nucleus of followers, whose identification with the party is centred on their personal attachment to the leader (Whiteley and Seyd 2002, 212). Past exponents of the leadership model include John A. Lee (Democratic Soldier Labour), Bruce Beetham (Social Credit), Matiu Rata (Mana Motuhake), Robert (Bob) Jones (New Zealand Party), as well as the leaders of several micro-parties on the extreme left and right. Overseas examples of minor parties based on the leadership model include Ross Perot's Reform Party (United States), Lucien Bouchard's Bloc Québécois (Canada), Jean-Marie Pen's National Front (France), James Goldsmith's Referendum Party (Britain), and Pauline Hanson's One Nation Party (Australia).

In the introductory chapter to this volume, political leadership was described as 'creating certainty in uncertain' times. Whereas a number of the post-referendum party leaders have adopted a generally constructive role, the pre-referendum parties are led by political outsiders, whose temperaments are better attuned to the role of 'agitator' or 'motivator' than to that of an 'organiser', 'manager' or 'administrator'. Reflecting an ability to exploit and perpetuate feelings of rejection, powerlessness and distrust, such leaders are better known for their expressive rather than their instrumental or skills-based qualities of leadership As one comparative study found, 'small parties mobilize those voters whose grievances have been ignored by the larger parties' (Muller-Rommel 1991, 13).

This potential mismatch between the exploitation of dissent through the polarising rhetoric of the mobilising leader and the responsibilities associated with the exercise of political power is best exemplified by the case of the New Zealand First leader, Winston Peters. Following the 2005 election, Peters requested and received the position of Minister of Foreign Affairs while remaining outside of government. From this dual insider–outsider position, he might hope to enjoy the 'baubles of office' without jeopardising the anti-establishment, anti-government sentiment that is the life blood of his movement.

In discussing the importance of context, especially any differences in the role, influence and status of minor party leaders under pre-referendum and post-referendum conditions, this chapter will assess the role of followers, a scarce resource in any small party, but especially one that is associated with either a polarising leader or an unpopular cause. As we will see, the loyalty of followers can also be sorely tested by the inevitable trade-offs their leaders must make on deciding to be part of a coalition government. Finally, we will attempt to identify the particular qualities required of minor party leaders within a Mixed Member Proportional (MMP) parliament and government, focusing on the ways in which they differ from those of a major party leader.

Models of Minor Party Leadership

It is possible to identify two distinct types of minor party leader: the *rebel* leader and the *reconciling* leader. Rebel leaders tend to be products of the adversarial two-party system, whereas reconciling leaders came into prominence with the advent of MMP and coalition government. As we will see, this is not to suggest that rebel leaders cannot emerge and prosper under MMP, or that leaders are not capable of displaying characteristics of both types, either simultaneously or at different points in their political careers. Indeed, one of the dilemmas faced by minor party leaders today is the need to be both a rebel leader to their followers and a reconciling leader to the other parties with whom they share a legislative or executive role.

Although the notion of rebel leaders is primarily attached to radical and revolutionary leaders, with Nelson Mandela and Sinn Fein's Gerry Adams being contemporary examples, elements of the rebel leadership model can be found in a number of the minor parties, especially those splinter or breakaway movements created from the two major parties. In a study of rebel leaders that includes Mahatma Gandhi and Fidel Castro, James Downton identifies several characteristics that we can apply to our study of minor party leadership. These include, firstly, the personal devotion of followers to the leader rather than to the organisation; secondly, an ability to win 'converts' among those made anxious by economic, social or political change; thirdly, an uncompromising message of transformation that exploits dissatisfaction with the regime and offers the promise of enhanced social and political arrangements; and, finally, the stigmatisation of rebel leaders and their followers by the ruling elite as 'outcasts' and 'deviants' (1973, 57–74).

Rebel leaders tend to be political agitators, who thrive on conflict, are often narcissistic and possess an unbending belief in the virtue of their cause (Lasswell 1977). But such leaders also tend to be both conspiratorial and deeply distrustful of their political opponents, traits that help to explain the difficult transition made by minor party leaders and followers to the demands of coalition government. While their behaviour can be largely accommodated within the acceptable bounds of inter-party competition, there are times when it spills over into more radical action. As we will see, over the years this has taken a number of different forms, including a staged walkout of parliament (the Greens in protest at the government's policy on genetic engineering) or cabinet (Peters and his New Zealand First ministerial colleagues); an unauthorised occupation of Parliament Buildings (Garry Knapp and the Democrats); and a hikoi or march (Tariana Turia and her nascent Maori Party from Northland to Wellington, and the 'Enough is Enough' rallies by Bishop Brian Tamaki and Destiny New Zealand). While some have been inclined to dismiss such actions as the work of political malcontents and rabble-rousers, they reflect a legitimate sense of powerlessness and mission that is widely experienced by the leaders and followers of small parties (Gillespie 1993, 277).

Reconciling leaders, on the other hand, are motivated less by principle and policy than by personal ambition, tempered by an aptitude for consultation and compromise. While reconciling leaders may lack a devoted following, and perhaps even a grassroots party organisation, their strength lies in an ability to forge alliances with the leaders of other parties, even including their fiercest election rivals. Unlike rebel leaders, who are prone to adopting bottom-line or non-negotiable positions, reconciling leaders are generally prepared to forego the bulk of their policy priorities in the interests of a direct, if subordinate, role in government. An early example of a reconciling post-MMP leader is Peter Dunne, whose Future New Zealand Party (formed 1994) initially had no organisation, no members and no policies. Rather, the party's sole *raison d'être* was to occupy the political centre ground, whence it promised to provide stable coalition government with either major party. While Dunne's goal was entirely consistent with the role of small parties under MMP, before the 2002 election campaign it failed to spark any discernible public attention or support. Indeed, since the advent of MMP a succession of reconciling minor party leaders have failed at the ballot box. These include Clive Matthewson (United), Graeme Lee (Christian Democrats), Ross Meurant (Right of Centre/Conservatives) and Tau Henare (Mauri Pacific).

The characteristics of the rebel leader fit most closely with the experiences of the Alliance and New Zealand First, although they can also be found in a number of micro-parties, including Christian Heritage and, more recently, the Maori and Destiny New Zealand parties. Rebel leadership in New Zealand has its roots in one of the purest and most enduring two-party systems in the developed world. For much of the pre-war and early post-war period, combined electoral support for the two major parties averaged over 90 per cent. This reflected a broad two-party consensus over such matters as universal welfare, the protection of small businesses and domestic producers through a complex array of government regulations and subsidies, limited immigration and the use of taxation to maintain New Zealand's reputedly egalitarian society. This broad-based agreement was reinforced by an unrelenting conformity among New Zealand's small, predominantly mono-cultural immigrant population. Any attempt to challenge the prevailing consensus of opinion or to break the two-party monolith was treated with contempt by the two major parties and their followers, as illustrated by the plight of the only minor party of any consequence, Social Credit. Despite contesting every general election from 1954 on, it failed to gain any public respectability and was stigmatised as a party of monetary-reform zealots and social misfits.

Beginning in the 1980s, prolonged economic recession and the radical reform agendas of successive governments had a profound impact on public opinion, as well as on morale within the two major parties. The first rebel leader to emerge from this growing mood of popular discontent was Jim Anderton, a former president of the Labour Party, who was expelled from the Labour caucus in 1988 for opposing the government's privatisation agenda. Having won the 1990 election in a landslide, National accelerated the process of free market reform, a decision that provoked the same voter and party activist backlash that had beset Labour. In 1993, a second rebel leader, deposed Maori Affairs minister Winston Peters, resigned from National and forced a by-election in the seat of Tauranga.

His New Zealand First Party soon became a catalyst for other disaffected MPs, as well as former National Party members and activists. At first it was known as the 'Peters party', an unintended marketing ploy that helped to brand it as a rebel movement and compensated for the inevitable lack of organisation and resources.

Changing Context

Despite the growing support of voters, not to mention the devotion of their followers, before the advent of MMP the minor parties and their leaders remained on the margins of the political system. Denied any meaningful representation under the first-past-the-post (FPP) electoral system, there were few opportunities to engage with the political process or to exercise leadership outside the traditional functions of small parties in two-party systems. One such function was to represent non-mainstream opinion on a range of single issues deemed to be inadequately covered by the major parties, examples of which included constitutional reform, the environment, alternative medicine, anti-fluoridation, animal rights and monetary reform. Yet another historic function of minor parties in two-party systems was that of safety valve for voter discontent. Despite their forlorn chances of winning parliamentary seats, small parties provided an alternative to voting for National and Labour. Such roles were necessarily limited, however. According to Giovanni Sartori's test of relevance, parties are only relevant if they exercise either 'coalition' or 'blackmail' potential (1976, 122–3). Because the minor parties failed this test of relevance on both counts, having neither forced their way into government nor exercised the balance of power, they were treated as little more than a distraction, only to be taken seriously when their vote was likely to influence the outcome of a closely fought contest between the two main parties.

It is hard to exaggerate the impact of electoral reform on the influence and longevity of the growing array of small parties formed during the 1980s and 1990s. At the 1993 election, the last under FPP, despite a combined vote of 31 per cent, the minor parties picked up only four of the available 99 seats. Had the 1993 referendum resulted in the retention of FPP (the final vote for MMP was 53 per cent), there is every prospect that, within a short space of time, several of the minor parties would have repeated the all-too-familiar pattern of either collapsing back into one of the major parties or disbanding. As supporters of the Values Party and Bob Jones's New Zealand Party had found some years earlier, sustaining a competitive organisation under the disproportional rules of FPP posed an almost insurmountable challenge to all small parties and their leaders. Hence, one of the most visible results of the referendum was a redoubling of enthusiasm and effort by the existing small parties. As we have seen, they were joined by a number of new, largely opportunistic movements. While this proliferation of parties was largely a product of MMP, it also reflected what voting trends had been suggesting for some time, namely the emergence of a more volatile and pluralistic electorate.

In assuming the role of 'institutional actors' for the first time, minor party leaders were forced to make a number of operational and behavioural adjustments. As discussed in chapter 1, the political outcomes of MMP, particularly the advent of coalition government, demanded a less partisan and combative style of leadership on all sides. While features of the former adversarial system persist, stable coalition government is conditional upon a willingness to consult and trust all partners to the agreement. Inevitably, this requires a measure of openness and an ability to listen to opposing arguments with a view to reaching decisions that meet with universal acceptance, if not support. To this end, some of the behavioural traits of the rebel leader have had to be modified or suppressed, a requirement that has had a number of implications for the symbiotic relationship that exists between leaders and followers, as we will see from the following case studies. While the interplay between leadership and following varies from one minor party to the next, there are some common elements that can be applied to the questions raised in chapter 1: What does the political leadership involve? How does context matter? And how significant are followers?

Winston Peters and New Zealand First (1996–98)
The inter-dependence of leaders and followers is best illustrated with reference to Peters's role in the decline and collapse of the National–New Zealand First coalition between 1996 and 1998. Although Peters's immediate reputation as a rebel leader was largely derived from his stridently nationalistic views on foreign investment, immigration and race relations, challenging the prevailing orthodoxy had been a hallmark of his

political career. As a National minister, he had engaged in bitter disputes with a number of cabinet colleagues, including the Prime Minister, Jim Bolger, the finance minister, Bill Birch, and the social welfare minister, Jenny Shipley, over the direction of government reform. This personal animosity continued long after Peters's departure from National, causing the New Zealand First's deputy leader, Tau Henare, to predict that his leader would never join a government in which Bolger, Birch and Shipley retained their ministerial responsibilities. During the 1996 election campaign Peters went even further in assuring electors that the only way to get rid of the National Government was to cast their vote for New Zealand First. Under the glare of publicity, the coalition negotiations process assumed a carnival atmosphere, with encouragement from Peters, who conducted parallel negotiations with the two major parties in an atmosphere of mutual secrecy, suspicion and distrust. In this way he was able to exploit the role of political rebel until the very moment the decision was announced.

Few could have been prepared for Peters's transformation from political rebel to government spokesman and political insider. In addition to his party receiving a disproportionate share of the seats in cabinet, Peters was given the plum positions of Treasurer and Deputy Prime Minister, making him, as acting prime minister, the official spokesman for the government whenever the prime minister was absent overseas. Despite showing some aptitude for the administrative requirements of this new role, Peters appeared to have overlooked the electoral costs. Having forged an unlikely electoral alliance of elderly non-Maori and low-income Maori on the basis of their mutual antipathy to National, Peters's preference for a National-led government resulted in an immediate collapse of the New Zealand First vote. In the three-month period immediately following the election, party support dropped from 13 per cent to 2 per cent, where it remained for most of the next three years. The greatest losses occurred in the Maori electorates, all of which had been Labour strongholds from the 1930s until the arrival of Winston Peters and New Zealand First. All five Maori seats returned to the Labour fold at the following election.

But opposition to the coalition was not limited to supporters of New Zealand First. Immediately after the 1996 election, in which National had won a mere third of all the seats, some senior National party officials warned of the dangers of negotiating with Peters – in addition to having been an outspoken critic of government policy as a National MP, Peters had been closely associated with a rebel clique within the caucus, including Sir Robert Muldoon, Hamish McIntyre, Michael Laws, Gilbert Myles and Peter McCardle, the latter three of whom went on to become New Zealand First MPs. Peters's critics argued that National should rebuild its electoral base in opposition with a view to returning to power at the 1999 election. Their concerns were confirmed by the terms of the 72-page coalition agreement, which, in addition to a generous allocation of ministerial portfolios to the small party, acceded to most of its policy demands. The sheer scale of these concessions simply confirmed the suspicion of a number of National MPs that their party's chief negotiators, notably the prime minister, had been out-foxed.

Over the course of the next year there were rumours of an increasingly close working relationship between Bolger and Peters. Concerned at the corrosive effect of the coalition partnership on popular support for National,[2] in November 1997 Bolger's caucus colleagues replaced him as prime minister with Jenny Shipley, a politician with a reputation for toughness and a demonstrated willingness to 'deal to' Peters and his small band of backbench MPs and ministers.

In addition to a small and shrinking support base, New Zealand First suffered from two further weaknesses common among rebel-led parties, namely lack of organisational structure and political inexperience. When combined, these two characteristics resulted in a lack of internal discipline, as illustrated by several breaches of collective cabinet responsibility and allegations of financial mismanagement and other irregularities against some New Zealand First MPs.[3] With public confidence in the coalition crumbling and the party in disarray, in July 1998 Peters reverted to the familiar role of rebel leader by staging a cabinet walkout in protest at the government's decision to privatise its investment in Wellington Airport. Shipley promptly dismissed him from the executive, a decision that resulted in the collapse of the coalition and precipitated a major schism within New Zealand First, with six MPs remaining with Peters and nine continuing to support the Shipley-led government. The electoral toll resulting from these events was severe, with support dropping from a peak of 28 per cent[4] at the height of Peters's anti-immigration campaign in mid-1996 to 4.3 per cent at the 1999 election.

Jim Anderton and the Alliance (1999–2002)

The leadership styles of Peters and Anderton show similarities, as well as differences. Anderton's reputation as a rebel leader was forged during the first half of the 1990s, when his five-party Alliance movement and Labour engaged in a bitter struggle for the support of traditional Labour voters. Following the 1993 election, at which the Alliance secured 18 per cent of the vote, there was growing speculation that the minor party was poised to replace Labour as the dominant force on the centre-left. Although Anderton and Clark were long-time friends, with Clark having served as Anderton's campaign manager in 1980 during his unsuccessful bid for the Auckland mayoralty, the split with Labour precipitated a marked deterioration in their relationship, to a point where the two barely spoke. Before the 1996 election, Anderton stipulated that a coalition with Labour was conditional upon the two agreeing to the terms of an agreement before polling day. Clark replied that she would only contemplate a deal between the two parties once the results of the election were known. This standoff effectively precluded the possibility of a centre-left government between 1996 and 1999.

While personal ambition dictated that a compromise be reached before the 1999 election, relations between the two parties remained strained, especially at the grassroots level. Alliance members were particularly wary of any post-election coalition agreement, on the grounds that Labour could not be trusted and that policy concessions would be unfairly shared between the two parties. However, by 1998 Anderton's instinct for a more reconciling style of leadership was becoming apparent. Clark was invited to address the Alliance's annual conference. During the following year's election campaign, Anderton modified the party's position on a number of radical policies that were likely to cause embarrassment to the Labour leadership, especially on welfare spending and taxation. After the election, the coalition agreement was settled within a week, and without any reference to policy, a decision that sparked concern among the Alliance's left-wing supporters.

The implications of this omission became apparent within a matter of months. Opposition to government policy from sections of the business community, especially over Labour's commitment to the re-nationalisation of Accident Compensation and repeal of the Employment Contracts Act, resulted in a softening of those Alliance policies the government deemed to be business-unfriendly. This included the postponement of plans for a government-owned bank and substantial modifications to funding and entitlement provisions of the proposed parental leave legislation. While Labour appeared to be the major beneficiary of this repositioning of policy towards the middle ground, with poll results over the next three years substantially exceeding the 39 per cent of the vote received at the 1999 election, support for the Alliance languished, sparking complaints within the Alliance that it was not being adequately compensated for Anderton's cooperation (having secured 8 per cent of the vote at the 1999 election, support for the party trended downwards before levelling out at between 3.4 and 4.5 per cent).[5]

Unlike Peters, Anderton refused to be recast as a rebel leader, even in the face of growing party pressure and declining voter support. Internal tensions reached breaking point in the wake of the government's decision in October 2001 to commit troops to the invasion of Afghanistan. At the Alliance's annual conference, delegates accused Anderton and his parliamentary colleagues of acquiescence in the face of both external pressure from President George W. Bush and domestic pressure from the Labour-dominated cabinet. The Alliance leader replied that he was constrained by the doctrine of collective cabinet responsibility. Arguments can be mounted within cabinet, he explained, but once a collective decision has been made, ministers must either accept the outcome or resign from cabinet. A majority of delegates were clearly of the opinion that resignation would have been the appropriate course of action, a view either overtly or covertly endorsed by some senior party officials. While anti-war sentiment runs deep among the movement's left-wing members, there were other influences on this decision, including a deep and abiding distrust of Labour; growing concern that, as the second ranking member of the government, Anderton had lost touch with his grassroots support; and a power struggle between the extra-parliamentary leadership, led by the president, Matt McCarten, and the party's parliamentary wing, notably Anderton, Matt Robson and the former deputy leader, Sandra Lee. Having lost his battle within the Alliance, Anderton and a small band of supporters broke away to form the 'Jim Anderton Progressive Coalition' on the eve of the 2002 election campaign. In recognition of his loyalty to her government and its policies, Clark guaranteed Anderton a cabinet post in the next Labour-led government.

The Greens and GE (2002)

Consistent with the grassroots nature of the international environmental movement, Green party members hold starkly different views on leaders and followers from those of their counterparts in the other minor parties. The party's first election campaign was fought without a recognised leader, and various strategies were devised to thwart the development of a personality cult. These included placing strong emphasis on a consensual style of decision-making and the introduction of dual leaders. As a result, the notion of following has virtually no connection with leadership, but rather with the radical values and principles of the movement. Indeed, so inherently suspicious are some members of the motives and *modus operandi* of politicians, they would prefer that their party serve in permanent opposition than become a partner in government. This scepticism of political power places the Green Party in the forefront of New Zealand's rebel movements.

Despite a generally satisfactory working relationship between the Green Party leaders and the government during Labour's first term, any hopes of a Labour–Green coalition were dashed over the Greens' stance on genetic engineering. In May 2002 the Green MPs staged a parliamentary walkout without giving the prime minister the agreed advance warning of their decision. During the subsequent election campaign, the Green leaders threatened to bring down the government in the event that it proceeded with its plan to lift the moratorium on the growth of genetically modified plants in late 2003. Their decision dealt a mortal blow to any suggestion that the Greens might be part of the next government. Despite continuing to support the bulk of the government's legislative agenda, especially its initiatives on individual and human rights, the Green MPs voted with the Opposition on all confidence motions. However, in the lead-up to the 2005 election their attitude towards Labour appeared to soften. In contrast to their position in 2002, the Greens would set no pre-conditions or bottom line to a coalition arrangement with Labour.

Peters, Dunne and the Greens (2005)

More than at any other election since the advent of MMP, the results of the 2005 election presented several party leaders with a strategic dilemma. Given the dramatic decline in the minor party vote (from almost 40 per cent in 2002 to 19 per cent), and also, somewhat paradoxically, increased opportunity for influence in a finely balanced parliament, would the call to rebel leadership in opposition be stronger than the lure of reconciling leadership in government? During the campaign, most of the speculation had centred on the pivotal role likely to be played by Winston Peters in the event of a hung parliament. Given his reputation for hubris and obfuscation, it was hardly surprising that Peters came under intense media pressure during the campaign to announce his coalition preferences before polling day. The resulting announcement seemed straightforward enough. New Zealand First, he promised, would stay out of government but abstain from voting on confidence and supply, thereby assisting in the survival of the party with the most seats.

The faulty logic of the subsequent assertion that New Zealand First remained a party of opposition, despite Peters's decision to accept a senior ministerial post, was not lost on National. It fought successfully to prevent the New Zealand First MPs from being seated with the opposition parties in parliament. That Peters's broken promise would have electoral costs, as it had in 1996, became evident within a matter of days. The resignation in protest of the party's long-time president, Doug Woolerton, indicated significant internal party opposition to the decision. Moreover, a TV3/TNS poll released shortly after the terms of the Labour–New Zealand First agreement were announced revealed an immediate drop in the party's popular support from 5.7 per cent on election day to a mere 3.5 per cent, its poorest poll result in several years.[6]

A feature of the coalition negotiations was the seemingly non-negotiable ultimatum from Peters and Dunne that they would not support a government that included the Greens. While their view that the small environmental party was extreme hardly squared with its mildly leftist policies, it is more likely to have had its roots in the non-conformist lifestyles and liberal social values of some Green MPs and activists. While Dunne's views on the issue were of little consequence, his party's three seats being surplus to Labour's requirements for a 58-vote majority on confidence and supply, the support of New Zealand First's seven MPs was essential to the government's long-term survival. However, Clark's decision to leave the Greens out in the cold for a third time was not simply about numbers, but also the perceived need to re-establish Labour's credentials as a government of middle New Zealand.

To summarise the foregoing discussion on the four elections under MMP, while the changing political and electoral context has provided the leaders of the small parties with unprecedented opportunities for influence, there have been significant costs. As the contrasting experiences of Peters and Anderton show, while a reconciling style of leadership is a pre-condition for stable coalition government, it can have a corrosive effect on internal party unity and electoral support. Having successfully built their electoral mandate around feelings of rejection, powerlessness and distrust, the two leaders experienced ebbing electoral and party support, which worsened the longer they were in government. Peters's failure to earn the respect of key National Party leaders, including Shipley, helps explain his defiant exit from cabinet in 1998 over the Wellington Airport decision. In contrast, Anderton's reputation as a team player was never in question and stood him in good stead during his dispute with the Alliance, with the prime minister declaring well before the 2002 election that there would be a place for Anderton in the next cabinet. The Greens, on the other hand, having raised ideology to the level of religious doctrine during the GE debate, faced rejection by Labour in 2002, and New Zealand First and United Future in 2005, on the basis that their views were misguided and extreme.

Functions of Minor Party Leaders

The skills required of minor party leaders are more instinctive and expressive than those generally associated with the leaders of the major parties. While the emphasis will vary from leader to leader, it is possible to identify five functions of minor party leaders:

Agitator

A characteristic found in many minor party leaders, especially those who have either broken away from a major party or adopted a populist style of leadership (see chapter 3), is that of political agitator. Such leaders relish the role of political outsiders and have an unquestioning faith in the virtue of their cause. But agitators are also adept at exploiting feelings of rejection and victimisation, with prime targets being members of the political, bureaucratic, business and media elites. As a result, minor party leaders and their followers can be difficult partners in government.

While their behaviour sits acceptably within the bounds of inter-party competition, if not restrained, it can frustrate the goals of stable and effective coalition government.

Organiser

Unlike the leaders of the major parties, who are able to draw on a large pool of administrative and organisational talent, the small party leaders are frequently called upon to be organisers. This involves a wide range of activities associated with the creation and nurturing of a party organisation, including the recruitment of new members, direct involvement in fundraising activities, and even copy-writing and designing the party's advertising campaign. Because their active supporters are thinly and unevenly spread across the country's 69 geographical electorates, the party's organisational structure tends to be highly centralised, often operating directly out of the leader's parliamentary office. As a result, the leader's professional advisers, paid researchers, and administrative and secretarial staff are frequently drawn into the party's regular and campaign activities.

Until recently, the United Future party organisation was centred in the parliamentary office of its leader. As well as attending to his constituency and parliamentary business, Peter Dunne carried out a number of the most mundane duties of a party organiser, such as directly responding to email and telephone enquiries from party officials and members of the public, including students. Although less attentive to routine organisational matters, the leaders of the New Zealand First and Progressive parties maintain a much more hands-on approach to administrative matters than do their counterparts in the larger parties. During its final years as a parliamentary party, the Alliance operated its Electoral Liaison Unit within parliament. The party president and general secretary even maintained a parliamentary office and were employed by Parliamentary Services (Miller 2005, 83). While less is known about the organisation of the fledgling Maori Party, it is safe to assume that it is centrally managed in the parliamentary office of its co-leader, Tariana Turia.

Campaigner

As well as retaining the support of their core followers, the leaders of the minor parties face the recurring task of rebuilding their electoral constituency at each and every general election. Whereas identification with the two major parties is strong, voter identification with the minor parties remains weak and unstable. As Peter Aimer has observed, while 'substantial majorities of Labour and National voters [are] fervent voters', relatively small minorities of voters claim any identification with the minor parties (Vowles et al. 1998, 62). One obvious problem is the increasing vulnerability of minor parties to the whims of strategic voters, that is, 'choosing a party on the day which attracted their support, but which was not the one they "most liked"' (Vowles et al. 2002, 30). This can be illustrated with reference to the high level of voter volatility evident during the 2002 election campaign, when voters were clearly weighing up how best to veto Labour's plan to govern alone. A poll conducted shortly before the campaign found that, whereas some 82 per cent of voters supported one or other of the two major parties, support for the minor parties totalled a mere 18 per cent. By polling day some four weeks later the combined minor party vote had more than doubled to 39 per cent. Together with the perennial problems associated with scarce resources and lack of media attention, the absence of a stable core of support places huge demands on the mobilising capacity of the party leader.

For an example of a mobilising leader it is hard to go past the campaigning skills of Winston Peters. Although a deeply polarising figure, no other politician of his generation has commanded from his core following such intense personal loyalty and respect. 'Charisma' is an elusive term, and one that is used grudgingly when applied to the subject of leadership in New Zealand.[7] This said, Peters displays shades of the charismatic style of leadership, including self-belief, a flamboyant and attractive personality, the ability to speak with clarity and conviction, and an instinctive understanding of the theatrical nature of politics. There is more than a touch of the authoritarian politician in his populist principles and policies, and his popularity with Maori evokes images of a warrior prophet. Perhaps more important than any of these qualities, however, is his keen sense of timing. Peters understands the rhythm of an election campaign like no other minor party leader. As he demonstrated in 1996, and again in 2002, he had the ability not only to retain a highly marginal seat, but also to lift the party vote higher than that of any other small party. Despite losing Tauranga, in 2005 New Zealand First managed to preserve its reputation as the third party in New Zealand politics.

Legislator

Historically, parliament has not been a particularly congenial or productive environment for small parties. Before the introduction of MMP, the few minor party MPs who managed to win parliamentary seats were treated with indifference bordering on contempt. However, the advent of coalition government, especially minority government, ensured that all future governments would be required to seek the small parties' legislative support. In 2002, Peter Dunne provided a model of what small parties can achieve outside of government with his 'good faith and no surprises' agreement with the Labour-led government. Despite his post-election claim that all options were on the table, it was clear that the United Future leader would prefer to stay out of government – apart from concerns about the electoral costs of being too closely associated with a centre-left administration, he wanted to give his seven novice MPs time to adjust to the rigours of parliamentary life. During the campaign, Dunne's pledge to help restore stable government was clearly directed at the capricious legislative behaviour of the Greens and New Zealand First, including the latter party's failure to participate in some key debates and parliamentary enquiries, most significantly the multi-party Superannuation Accord. As well as promising confidence and supply for the next three years, Dunne could be expected to support the bulk of the government's economic and social policy agenda. However, he was also able to create distance from the government by opposing some landmark social and constitutional legislation, including the Prostitution (2003), Civil Union (2004) and Relationships (2005) bills, as well as the creation of a New Zealand Supreme Court (2003) and passage of the Foreshore and Seabed (2004) legislation. As a reward for United Future's 'good faith and no surprises' support, the government agreed to the creation of a Commission for the Family. In 2005, Dunne was put in charge of the potentially important Constitutional Review committee, which, among other things, was asked to report on whether or not New Zealand should become a republic. While Dunne's record of success between 2002 and 2005 may not be sufficient to dissuade other leaders from pursuing the coalition option, at the very least it demonstrates that minor parties do have a measure of choice.

Administrator

The most unfamiliar, and perhaps demanding, function of minor party leaders concerns the executive skills required of those who decide to take their parties into government. As we have seen, the early termination of successive MMP governments serves as a warning of the costs of coalition. Because coalitions involve trade-offs, they tend to demand levels of executive experience and hard-nosed pragmatism seldom found among small party leaders. In contrast, the leaders of the major parties are generally able to draw on considerable institutional experience, both personally and from within the senior ranks of their party. In 1996, while Winston Peters appeared to have set the agenda for the National–New Zealand First government with his comprehensive list of policy and portfolio demands, National proved more than capable at outmanoeuvring the small party on the issues that really mattered. As McLeay has pointed out elsewhere in this volume, small parties are at their most influential when they are negotiating the terms of a coalition agreement. Once agreement has been reached, making further demands on an issue-by-issue basis is likely to incur a loss of public support. This risk was not widely understood by those senior Alliance officials who exhorted their leader to publicly oppose his Labour cabinet colleagues on a range of domestic and foreign policy. Anderton refused on the grounds that, while this might have short-term electoral benefits, it would inevitably compromise the Alliance's commitment to collective cabinet responsibility, a principle that is at the heart of effective and stable government.

Conclusion

This chapter has discussed two very different styles of minor party leadership in New Zealand. While rebel leadership tended to be associated with the adversarial two-party system, its influence continues to the present time, impacting on the relationship between leaders and their followers in both the legislative and executive arenas, as illustrated by the premature collapse of both the National–New Zealand First and Labour–Alliance governments. Reconciling leaders, on the other hand, came into prominence with the advent of MMP and coalition government. Unlike rebel leaders, who are prone to manipulation, domination and control, reconciling leaders are prepared to forego the bulk of their policy priorities in the interests of a constructive, if subordinate, role in government.

Is the continuing influence of rebel leaders simply a product of the transitional nature of the party and electoral systems, or does it reflect deeper, more systemic needs on the part of the New Zealand electorate? The recent political influence of the Progressive and United Future parties would tend to suggest that our understanding of multi-party politics and coalition government is maturing. This is likely to result in a growing recognition of the legislative and executive functions of minor party leadership. On the other hand, an equally credible argument can be advanced for the view that minor parties and their leaders continue to pose a threat to stable government, as well as to the future of MMP. In the short term, interest is likely to focus on how Winston Peters is able to juggle the insider/outsider role of being a senior minister and an opposition party leader at one and the same time. By reverting to the role of rebel leader part way through his previous term in government, Peters helped bring about the National–New Zealand First government's collapse. Will he be tempted to repeat the same behaviour and, if so, will Clark's Labour-led government survive its three-year term? Time alone will tell.

---

1   Gillespie 1993, 267.
2   During 1997, public support for National declined from a high of 47 per cent to 30 per cent. In contrast, support for Labour rose steadily to over 50 per cent (*One Network News*/Colmar Brunton Poll, Auckland, February–October 1997).
3   After several public disagreements between the health minister, Bill English (National), and the associate health minister, Neil Kirton (New Zealand First), Peters in 1997 dismissed Kirton from the executive. The main target of the Opposition's allegations of financial mismanagement and over-spending was Tukuroirangi Morgan, who, during his previous career as a Maori television journalist and executive, was accused of having maintained an extravagant lifestyle at the taxpayers' expense.
4   *One Network News*/Colmar Brunton Poll, Auckland, May 1996.
5   *National Business Review*/UMR Research Poll, Auckland, January 2000–November 2001.
6   *New Zealand Herald*, 4 November 2005, A6.
7   For a discussion on the meaning of 'charisma', see Bryman 1992.

Bryman, A. (1992) *Charisma and Leadership in Organisations*, London, Sage.
Downton, J. V. (1973) *Rebel Leadership: Commitment and Charisma in the Revolutionary Process*, New York, The Free Press.

Gillespie, J. D. (1993) *Politics at the Periphery: Third Parties in Two-Party America*, Columbia, SC, University of South Carolina Press.

Lasswell, H. D. (1977) *Psychopathology and Politics*, Chicago, University of Chicago Press.

Miller, R. (2005) *Party Politics in New Zealand*, Melbourne, Oxford University Press.

Muller-Rommel, F. and G. Pridham (1991) *Small Parties in Western Europe: Comparative and National Perspectives*, London, Sage.

Sartori, G. (1976) *Parties and Party Systems: A Framework for Analysis*, Cambridge, Cambridge University Press.

Vowles, J., P. Aimer, S. Banducci and J. Karp (eds) (1998) *Voters' Victory? New Zealand's First Election Under Proportional Representation*, Auckland, Auckland University Press.

Vowles, J., P. Aimer, J. Karp, S. Banducci, R. Miller and A. Sullivan (2002) *Proportional Representation on Trial: The 1999 New Zealand General Election and the fate of MMP*, Auckland, Auckland University Press.

Whiteley, P. and P. Seyd (2002) *High-Intensity Participation: The Dynamics of Party Activism in Britain*, Ann Arbor, MI, University of Michigan Press.

Leadership in the Broader Society

EIGHT

Maori Conceptions of Leadership and Self Determination

Ranginui Walker

Since the beginning of European settlement, the relationship between Maori leaders and the ruling elite has taken a number of different forms. In the nineteenth century, the external forces of European capitalism, evangelism and British imperialism impinged either directly or indirectly on traditional Maori leadership structures. These forces progressively undermined the mana of tribal chiefs. While those Maori chiefs who resisted colonisation were put down by armed force and excluded from the power structure of the state, compliant chiefs were co-opted into the ruling class of metropolitan society. They filled auxiliary roles as soldiers, court assessors, public servants and politicians.

In the twentieth century the structural relationship of dominance and subjection between the governing elite and those Maori who were co-opted as 'subalterns' became entrenched.[1] Some subaltern leaders, through training or association with the elite, were infected with an appetite for bourgeois success. They seized the opportunity to achieve economic power by championing Maori rights under the Treaty of Waitangi in the courts and the corridors of political power. But in pursuit of this agenda they unwittingly maintained the hegemony of the ruling class by accepting their definition of how Maori social and economic aspirations should be expressed. On the other hand, those Maori leaders who were aligned more with the disenfranchised majority, engaged in critical discourse against the rulers and their subalterns in the hope of ameliorating the effects of the policies generated by the ruling class.

This chapter proposes four constructions of Maori leadership: the tribal chiefs; the new prophets; the intellectuals; and the organic leaders. All four involve linkages between the leaders and their followers, as well as being contingent upon the different historical and material contexts within which they have been placed, especially in relation to the changing circumstances of Pakeha domination.

Tribal Chiefs and the Destruction of Mana

Chiefly leaders were created by birthright and maintained through mana. Belief in tapu was the all-pervasive spiritual force that controlled Maori behaviour and underpinned the mana of chiefs. Yet at the beginning of the nineteenth century, the sailors who visited New Zealand shores on whaling and sealing ships breached the laws of tapu with impunity. They 'defied the tapu, stole crops, filched weapons or mats for sale as "curiosities" and kidnapped men without scruple' (Sinclair 1969, 35). With the introduction of the musket into the tribal wars of the 1820s, aristocratic breeding and training in weaponry counted for nothing. A rangitira could be felled by a commoner armed with a musket. The mana, ihi and wehi, the awesome power of chiefs of the Stone Age, were unable to withstand leaders, such as Hongi Hika and Te Rauparaha, who possessed muskets. Their bloodletting precipitated an arms race, which further weakened chiefly leadership within the tribes (Sinclair 1969, 84). After ten years of fighting, the chiefs turned to the missionaries, who acted as peacemakers. Whole tribes converted to Christianity because it was thought the Pakeha God provided his followers with greater power and wealth than the Maori in the form of ships, weapons and an amazing quantity of goods (Elsmore 2000, 14).

Conversion to Christianity eliminated the tapu of chiefs, thereby weakening their authority. Their mana was eroded even further by the missionaries' demand to free their slaves and put aside their extra wives as a pre-condition for baptism (Sinclair 1969, 43). The ability to command wealth was one of the pillars that buttressed the authority of chiefs (Firth 1959, 299). With no slaves and only one wife, chiefs no longer had the capacity to produce goods in sufficient quantity to keep up their exchange relationships and maintain the loyalty of their followers. With a 40 per cent reduction of the population by European diseases and musket wars, combined with the progressive erosion of chiefly mana, New Zealand was ripe for a takeover by the British Empire.

Under missionary influence, 41 chiefs signed the Treaty of Waitangi in 1840 for the benefits of British protection, government, law and order (Ross 1958, 27). The Treaty was subsequently hawked around the country and a total of 540 chiefs signed. It mattered not that the paramount chiefs Te Wherowhero, Te Heuheu and Te Kani a Takirau did not sign. The once awesome power of ariki was undermined by the introduction of the European convention of the majority holding sway over the power of paramount chiefs under the colonising ideology of democracy.

On taking office in 1845, Governor Grey neutralised the warrior chief Hone Heke by massing enough soldiers and firepower against him to pacify the north. The governor then made a pre-emptive move against Te Rauparaha by arresting him and detaining him without trial on HMS *Calliope*. The political effect was the assertion of mana by Grey over Te Rauparaha and the spreading of the Crown's sovereignty over the southern half of the North Island (Walker 2004, 103–5). In the South Island, Grey eliminated the mana whenua of the chiefs by extinguishing their title to the land by coercion and threatening military invasion under the guise of 'fair purchase'. Between 1846 and 1863, the entire South Island, including Stewart Island, was bought by the Crown (Evison 1987, 17–32). All that remained of chiefly mana in the south was their whakapapa, the descent lines from noble ancestors of a time past.

In the North Island, the chiefs organised to resist colonisation by holding a series of inter-tribal meetings to discuss kotahitanga. This unity movement, which began in 1854, was already too late. When parliament met for the first time that year, there were no Maori representatives. In an attempt to assert their mana, the chiefs of Kotahitanga formulated the 'pupuri whenua' policy of suspending land sales as a means of controlling Pakeha immigration. In the Waikato the unity movement culminated in the election of Te Wherowhero as the first Maori King. At the final anointing of Te Wherowhero at Ngaruawahia in 1859, Wiremu Tamehana proclaimed that the purpose of the King was to hold the mana whenua and mana tangata of the people (Pei 1960, 223). Governor Grey made war on the King to put him down. He debilitated the King and his supporters by confiscating three million acres of tribal lands in Waikato, Taranaki and the Bay of Plenty.

The New Prophet Leaders

The eclipse of chiefly mana by Grey led to the emergence of new prophet leaders whose mandate derived from Jehovah and the angels of the Christian religion. The founder of the Pai Marire cult, Te Ua Haumene, promised his followers support from legions of angels and immunity to Pakeha bullets if they went into battle against the invaders crying 'Hapa Pai Marire Hau! Hau!' (Greenwood 1980, 1–80). The Hauhau began a guerilla campaign in Taranaki against government troops in April 1864. The campaign spread across the North Island into the Bay of Plenty and to the East Coast. There, the mantle of leadership was thrust on Te Kooti Arikirangi when he was arrested as a rebel and detained without trial on the Chatham Islands. Te Kooti escaped back to the mainland and conducted a hit and run guerilla campaign from the rugged interior of the Urewera. While he managed to elude his pursuers for four years, Te Kooti was not a military strategist, as illustrated by his loss of two set-piece battles at Ngatapa in 1869 and at Te Porere. Consequently neither the ariki Te Heuheu nor King Tawhiao would support him. In 1872, Te Kooti retired from the field of battle behind the aukati, the boundary line of the King Country. His legacy is the Ringatu Church.

The most successful Hauhau leader was Titokowaru of Ngati Ruanui. He resisted the confiscation of Taranaki lands and defeated the government forces at the Battle of Te Ngutu o te Manu in 1868. In his last stand at Taurangaika, Titokowaru's allies deserted him and he became a hunted man. Indicating that mana was as integral to the new style of leadership as it was to the tribal chiefs, it is thought the people left Titokowaru on the eve of battle because he defiled his mana by committing adultery with the wife of one of his allies (Belich 1999, 242–6).

With the failure of these prophets of war to liberate the people from the invaders, other prophets arose preaching pacifism and separation of the races. The leaders of the movement, Te Whiti and Tohu, established a peaceful and prosperous commune at Parihaka. But Te Whiti's active demonstration of resistance to the building of the West Coast Road and the survey of Taranaki land for settlers drew the ire of the Minister of

Native Affairs, John Bryce. In 1881 the prophets were arrested and Parihaka was destroyed. Tohu and Te Whiti were detained without trial in the South Island for a time and eventually released.

In the aftermath of the Land Wars, chiefly leaders organised a series of inter-tribal hui to generate a political response to their subjection by parliament, and the alienation of tribal land through confiscation and the operations of the Native Land Court. In 1892, these assemblies culminated in the establishment of Kotahitanga Mo Te Tiriti o Waitangi, otherwise known as the Maori Parliament. The attempt to integrate the Kingitanga into the movement was opposed by Ngapuhi because Tawhiao refused to give up the title of King. Consequently the Maori political response was bifurcated when Tawhiao formed his own Kauhanganui (Walker 2004, 152–72). The submissions of both the Kotahitanga and the Kauhanganui to New Zealand's House of Representatives sought devolution of control over their own land and resources. The Maori Rights Bill, which was tabled by the member for Northern Maori on behalf of Kotahitanga, was rejected in 1895.

From Prophets to Politics: Intellectuals and Organic Leaders

By 1900, the Maori Parliament, the last forum of chiefly leaders, was moribund. Only two ariki lines survived into the twentieth century. The Te Heuheu dynasty averted confiscation of Tuwharetoa lands in the central North Island by donating the three mountains, Ngaruahoe, Ruapehu and Tongariro, to the Crown for a National Park. The King movement, which had all its lands confiscated, remained loyal to its ariki. That loyalty was rewarded under the ariki Dame Te Atairangikaahu with the $170 million settlement of the Tainui claim in 1995. As for the rest, without mana whenua there were no chiefs and the leadership initiative passed to the new educated elite. Apirana Ngata, the first Maori graduate, entered parliament in the Eastern Maori electorate in 1905. He was followed by Dr Peter Buck for Northern Maori in 1909 and Dr Maui Pomare for Western Maori in 1911. These men, as intellectuals, were subalterns to the power-brokers of metropolitan society. They worked within the power structure of the ruling class essentially as reformists, because they were more concerned with the physical and cultural survival of the Maori than the issue of sovereignty pursued by the chiefs in the previous century. To this end they instituted health reforms, promoted a revival of Maori arts and crafts and started Maori land development schemes using state loans.

Over the issue of Maori land, the intellectual leaders proved powerless. At the time that Sir Apirana Ngata was approaching the height of his political career, the remaining five million acres of Maori land was being alienated at the rate of 72,728 acres per annum (McClean 1950, 61). Ngata's initiative of establishing Maori land incorporations for development purposes provided a limited kind of tribal leadership in the form of management committees elected by shareholders. But the real power in these new structures, like public companies, was in the hands of the major shareholders. The next stage in the evolution of Maori leadership had nothing to do with land ownership, but rather the widespread poverty of the Great Depression. As conditions worsened, the people turned away from the academics to the charismatic prophet leader Tahupotiki Wiremu Ratana.

Ratana, like previous prophets, had his role legitimated by God. He was the mangai, the mouthpiece of God, sent to attend to the spiritual well being of his people. He began his mission in 1918 by performing a number of faith-based healings. His followers signed a covenant professing faith in Jehovah and belief in the Trinity of the Father, Son and Holy Ghost. Ratana renounced tapu and superstitious practices of the past. The pan-Maori ideology of the Ratana Church was signified by the term 'morehu', the survivors of all tribes from the colonial experience. In 1921, when Ratana's followers numbered 19,000, he turned his attention to ture tangata, the physical needs of the people. Ratana turned his movement into a political force by selecting candidates from his church to contest the four Maori seats. His aim was to unify the seats under Maori control. Although Ratana was not an intellectual by profession, he was, in Gramsci's terms, an 'organic intellectual', the thinking and organising element of an oppressed people (Gramsci 1971, 1).

Ratana aligned the three seats won by his candidates in the 1935 election with the Labour Party. He delivered the Eastern Maori seat into the Labour camp in 1943 (Henderson 1972, 83–96). However, the 40-year liaison he initiated with Labour brought little benefit to Maori. The only minor achievement was the passing of the Treaty of Waitangi Act 1975 that established the Waitangi Tribunal. The power of the tribunal was limited to hear grievances after the act came into the force. The reason for this poor outcome of Ratana's efforts was the position of the Maori MPs as subalterns within both the Labour Party and the overall political structure. Their presence in parliament merely legitimated the hegemony of the ruling class.

A former Minister of Maori Affairs, Matiu Rata, realised the true nature of his subaltern role in the Labour Party in 1979, when he was relegated to the backbench and displaced by the leader, Bill Rowling, as the spokesperson on Maori Affairs. Rata subsequently resigned from parliament and founded the Mana Motuhake Party. Rata's defection from Labour weakened the Ratana alliance with the party. Although Mana Motuhake, after a decade of contesting elections, did not succeed in winning one of the four Maori seats, it displaced the National candidates from second to third place. As a result, Mana Motuhake was able to steer Labour in the direction of a more equitable treaty policy. The granting of retrospective power to the Waitangi Tribunal in 1985 and the inclusion of the Treaty in 21 statutes forced both the Labour and National governments to give greater attention to Maori grievances under the treaty.[2]

The first wave of intellectuals having been elected to parliament in the early 1900s, a second wave followed in the 1960s, although on this occasion operating largely outside the parliamentary process. This second group of intellectuals was responsible for developing and expanding Maori studies programmes in the universities, teachers' colleges and polytechnic schools. Besides being instrumental in the development of Maori scholarship, its members began to assume leadership roles in their own tribal trust boards, the Maori Women's Welfare League, incorporations, the Maori Council and the National Congress of Tribes. As 'organic intellectuals', they performed the difficult balancing act of serving their people while meeting their professional obligations as subalterns in the state system. But only those working within the universities have the luxury of academic freedom to challenge the legitimacy of the state and condemn its oppressive policies. Although most graduates, like the leaders that came out of the Maori Battalion, can claim descent from chiefly forebears, their leadership roles are derived from personal achievement rather than ascription.

For an example of the contribution of organic intellectuals one need go no further than the 1984 claim before the Waitangi Tribunal seeking official recognition for the use of Maori in parliament, courts, government departments, local bodies and public bodies. The claimants argued that because the Maori language was not spoken, heard, taught or broadcast, they were prejudiced by a number of statutes, including the Broadcasting Act 1976, Health Act 1956, Hospitals Act 1957, Education Act 1864 and the Maori Affairs Act 1953. The case turned on the Tribunal's acceptance that the Crown's guarantee of 'taonga' in the Treaty of Waitangi embraced the Maori language (Waitangi Tribunal 1989). It recommended that government introduce legislation for the use of Maori in courts and by government departments; that the State Services Act make provision for bilingualism; and that a body be established to foster the language. The outcome was the Maori Language Act 1987, which declared Maori an official language of New Zealand, conferred the right to use Maori in certain legal proceedings and established the office of Maori Language Commissioner. Huirangi Waikerepuru is an example of an organic leader initiating action that transforms oppressive state policies. As an organic intellectual, working within the state system of education, Waikerepuru operated from the non-traditional base of a voluntary association established to promote the Maori language.

The Significance of Context

Far from being exercised in a vacuum, Maori leadership is a product of New Zealand's unique social, historical and cultural context. In this part of the discussion I will examine the importance of context by focusing on four major influences: urbanisation; the Maori institutions; the media; and the Maori renaissance.

Urbanisation and radicalisation

The rural urban shift of over 70 per cent of the Maori population in the second half of the twentieth century had a profound effect on Maori leadership. Urbanisation increased Maori knowledge of metropolitan society, its political structures and its techniques of domination and social control. The crucible of the urban milieu threw up a new generation of organic, activist, Maori leaders who created their own platforms, political networks and supporters. Their overt counter-hegemonic struggle in the form of demonstrations and protest actions had the effect of politicising many Maori and welding them into a potent force for emancipation.

In the vanguard of radical Maori politics in the 1970s was Nga Tamatoa challenging infractions of the Crown against the Treaty of Waitangi. In the next decade the Waitangi Action Committee took up the cause. Tamatoa's activism spurred on the birth of the Maori land rights movement Matakite, which marched on parliament in 1975 under the slogan of 'not one more acre of Maori land' to be alienated. In 1978 the Bastion Point Action Committee added impetus to the movement by the defiant 506-day occupation of disputed Crown land at Orakei. In the 1980s the Waitangi action committee led protest activity against the Waitangi celebrations. Their efforts culminated in the 3000 strong pan-tribal Hikoi ki Waitangi on 6 February 1984. The incoming Labour Government took cognisance of Maori unrest by suspending the celebration of Waitangi Day. Te Runanga Whakawhanaunga i Nga Haahi took up the cause. This ecumenical, pan-tribal organisation was formed out of the Maori sections of the orthodox churches. The runanga organised a national hui at Ngaruawahia on the Treaty of Waitangi. This hui, attended by over a thousand people, sent a resolution to the government demanding that the powers of the Waitangi Tribunal to hear land grievances under the Treaty of Waitangi be made retrospective to 1840.

The thrust of radical Maori politics throughout the 1970s empowered Maori working in a subaltern role within the Department of Maori Affairs to adopt a more pro-active Maori position in the formulation and implementation of programmes. In 1971, Tamatoa's demonstration against the appointment of a non-Maori as district officer for Auckland gave an unequivocal message to the power elite that Maori wanted co-equal leadership roles in the power structure of the state. Tamatoa made the point that, on a pro rata basis, at least one Maori should have achieved district officer status in a department where knowledge of Maori language, marae protocol and customary usages should have been an advantage. Instead, district officers had always to be accompanied by Maori subalterns to interpret for them. Tamatoa signalled that the era of paternalism was over.

Institutions enabling leadership

Among the organisations that played an instrumental role in fostering Maori leadership were the various trust boards and district councils, the Maori Women's Welfare League, the Ministry of Maori Affairs and the Maori Development Corporation. In 1925, Sir Apirana Ngata helped negotiate the Arawa Lakes agreement that culminated in the establishment of the Arawa Trust Board to receive and administer an annuity from the Crown of £6000 on behalf of Te Arawa beneficiaries in settlement of the tribes' claim to the Rotorua lakes. The Tuwharetoa Trust Board was established soon after with the signing of the Taupo Lake agreement. Other trust boards were subsequently established to settle land claims in the Waikato, Taranaki, the Bay of Plenty and the South Island. Although trust boards serve as a mechanism for the election of Maori leaders to replace the chiefs of the past, they are hegemonic constructs of the state for economic and social management. Trust boards are answerable to the Minister of Maori Affairs for the expenditure of funds on scholarships, health, marae grants and economic development.

A new kind of government-fostered leadership emerged in the post-war years, with the establishment of new bureaucratic structures. In 1945, the Maori Social and Economic Advancement Act gave statutory recognition to the tribal committees for their work in the Maori War Effort Organisation. The committees had power to appoint wardens, prevent drunkenness, maintain order on the marae and in public places, and adjudicate on petty offences. The Maori Welfare Act 1962 changed the designation of the tribal committees to Maori committees in recognition of the population shift from tribal to urban areas. It also created an elective four-tier structure of Maori committees, executives, district councils and the Maori council. Responsibility for the new structure was given to the welfare officers of the Department of Maori Affairs. It left out of account authentic Maori leadership structures such as kaumatua and marae committees. In rural areas the members of Maori committees and district councils tended to be tribal leaders, but they could also include people from other tribes. In urban centres Maori committees and district councils tended to be pan-tribal. Overall, the constitution of the Maori Council allowed for the emergence of Maori leaders living outside their tribal areas.

The Maori Women's Welfare League, which was formed by the Department of Maori Affairs in 1951, was the first national pan-Maori organisation. It preceded the Maori Council by ten years. The League also had a four-tier structure of branch committees, executives, district councils and dominion council. Unlike the Maori Council, the League is not underpinned by statute. Its *raison d'être* is the care and nurture of children and families. Consequently, the main focus of the League is family care, health and early childhood education in play-centres and kohanga reo. As state-fostered institutions, the Maori Council and the League provided legitimating bases for organic leaders both within and outside tribal territories. But as subalterns within the power structure of the state, they are expected to cooperate with its bureaucratic systems of control and management of the population in the interests of integration and ultimate assimilation. Any leader who deviates from the role is likely to be perceived as a dangerous subversive and even radical. Those who conform to the role defined by the rulers are rewarded with additional but limited powers and, until recently, imperial honours. The latter operated as buffers between the state and organic leaders outside the power structures who challenged the legitimacy of the Crown on the basis of clause two in the Treaty of Waitangi. Organic leaders, by mounting protest action against the Crown, enabled subalterns to wring concessions from their masters to defuse embarrassing protest activity.

Maori disaffection with the Department of Maori Affairs, as well as the Maori Trustee, grew throughout the 1970s, prompting the minister Duncan McIntyre to conduct an inquiry into the department. He appointed Ihakara Puketapu to do the inquiry. Hitherto, Puketapu had been a career public servant, serving in the London High Commission and the State Services Commission. After Puketapu delivered his report, he was appointed Secretary of Maori Affairs in 1977. Puketapu, like Ngata before him, was not prepared to play a subaltern role to the power elite. He used his position as head of a government bureaucracy to promote Maori emancipation. He and his senior officers conducted district consultations with Maori people to help formulate policy. Puketapu also instituted Hui Whakatauira, where a hundred or so Maori leaders from around the country helped formulate development programmes. Thereafter the department's programme was based on the ideology of 'Tu Tangata', the 'stance of the people' (Puketapu 1982, 4). Puketapu established kokiri management groups at the district level to determine priorities for expenditure in community development. The department went outside established groups such as the Maori Council and the Women's Welfare League to promote the emergence of new leaders in the kokiri units. Puketapu promoted Maori language learning through kohanga reo and job skills training in Maori communities. Kokiri centres gave training in panel-beating, mechanics, carving, furniture remaking, sewing and soft-toy making. By 1965, there were 66 kokiri training centres around New Zealand.

Other programmes generated by the Hui Whakatauira included rapu mahi, women's wananga (learning groups), matua whangai (foster care) and business wananga. The matua whangai programme, initiated by the department in 1983, necessitated the departments of Justice and Maori Affairs entering into negotiations with whanau, hapu and iwi authorities for the placement of children under welfare in the care of their own people. The effectiveness of this programme virtually emptied social welfare homes of their Maori inmates.

In 1981, the department, still under Puketapu's leadership, instituted its most innovative and dynamic programme for language recovery, the kohanga reo. Since its inception over two decades ago, kohanga reo has become one of the most dynamic programmes in the development of young women as leaders. In the struggle for buildings and resources to establish the 700 or so kohanga reo, women have had to learn to deal with bureaucracy. They also put pressure on primary schools to establish bilingual programmes to ensure language continuity for their children after kohanga reo. In March 1984, the organiser of the Maori Educational Development Conference at Turangawaewae Marae made a submission to the Minister of Education, Mr Wellington, which resulted in a grant of $13 million for kohanga reo education. The cost of $25 a child to sustain kohanga reo had become so burdensome on family budgets that the whole system had been in danger of insolvency. The Kohanga Reo Trust, chaired by John Bennett, was established to receive and administer the money for Maori pre-school education. The establishment of the Kohanga Reo Trust provided a model for a dual, bicultural system of education provision and management within the state.

When Labour won the snap election in 1984, the government called an Economic Summit meeting in Wellington. Because those invited were predominantly Pakeha businessmen and captains of industry, the Maori Affairs Department organised its own economic summit, the Hui Taumata. This hui recommended the establishment of a Maori Economic Development Commission and a Maori Development Bank to help close the employment and economic gap between Maori and Pakeha. In response, the Department of Maori Affairs launched its Mana Enterprise scheme in 1985 to fund Maori into businesses such as kiwifruit and marine farming. District committees vetted business proposals at the local level and recommended them to Wira Gardiner, head of Mana Enterprises, for funding. The budget for the first year of operation was $13.5 million (Puketapu 1982, 19).

Maori were not satisfied with the budget for Mana Enterprises. With no move from the government to establish a Maori bank as recommended by the hui taumata, Dr Tamati Reedy, the new Secretary of Maori Affairs, took the initiative by entering into negotiations with Hawaiian business men to obtain an offshore loan of $600 million. Because Treasury and the Minister of Finance had not given approval, Reedy's negotiations triggered the row in parliament over the so-called 'Maori Loans Affair'. The inquiry in 1987 by the State Services Commission into the loan spelt the death knell of the Department of Maori Affairs. The commission recommended the establishment of a new Ministry of Maori Development.[3] Early in 1988 the government circulated the discussion document He Tirohanga Rangapu. The document portended the abolition of Maori Affairs and its replacement by a slimmed-down Ministry of Maori Policy. This new ministry's function was to make policy recommendations only to government. It would not have any responsibility for the delivery of programmes to the people. When the Department of Maori Affairs was phased out late in 1988, it was replaced by Te Tai, the Iwi Transition Agency headed by Wira Gardiner. The function of Te Tai was to continue running the existing Maori Affairs programmes and manage their progressive transfer to mainstream departments over a five-year period, at which point it would go out of existence. But, before Te Tai had run its five-year course, it was abolished, along with Manatu Maori (Ministry of Maori Policy). They were replaced by the Ministry of Maori Development, otherwise known as Te Puni Kokiri, in January 1992. The heavy cut in Te Puni Kokiri's budget was reflected in over 250 employees of Te Tai and Manatu Maori being made redundant.

The desire expressed by the Hui Taumata in 1984 for a Maori financial institution to fund Maori business enterprise came to fruition in 1987 with the establishment of the Maori Development Corporation (MDC). MDC was launched with a budget of $26 million made up of contributions from government ($13 million), Maori Trustee ($7 million), Fletcher Challenge

($2 million) and Brierley Investments ($2 million). By 1990, MDC had put out 130 loans for Maori businesses totalling $35.2 million (Maori Development Corporation 1990, 11). The chairman of MDC, Robert Mahuta, had a unique combination of mandates as a leader. His primary mandate as a tribal leader stemmed from his whakapapa, his descent line from the ariki of the Tainui confederation of tribes. His hapu constitutes the heart of the King movement to which other hapu of the Tainui waka maintain loyalty through a system of poukai (loyalty feasts). Mahuta was also a graduate, an organic intellectual who had an enormous influence in harnessing other intellectuals to the cause of the people of the Waikato. His mana was both ascribed and achieved.

The chief executive of MDC was Waari Ward-Holmes. He achieved individual success in the commercial world as a corporate manager. Although ethnically Maori, he was not identified with the Maori struggle. But, because of his experience in the business world, he was strategically placed to be appointed the first chairman of MDC. Conflict between Maori needs and Pakeha values within management forced him to decide whether his primary allegiance was to his people or Pakeha associates in the business fraternity. Ward-Holmes had his moment of truth at a meeting with his people hosted by the Tainui Trust Board in Ngaruawahia. He chose to side with his people. When the chief executive who was the cause of the conflict resigned, Ward-Holmes was appointed to the post. He is testimony to Freire's view that professional men are necessary to the reorganisation of the new society and can be reclaimed by the revolution (Freire 1985, 127).

Despite government switches in Maori policy, there was considerable progress in addressing Maori grievances. Fourteen years of radical Maori protest culminated in an amendment to the Treaty of Waitangi Act in 1985 which gave the Waitangi Tribunal retrospective power to 1840. This opened up the way for the negotiation of past grievances concerning land, fisheries and suppression of Maori language. This change, combined with the inclusion of the treaty in 21 statutes, raised the Treaty of Waitangi to the level of a constitutional instrument.

The media

In the early 1970s, Maori groups mounted a strong lobby for a radio station to be established in Auckland. But by the time the move was made to convert one of the existing Radio New Zealand stations for the project, Labour lost the election in 1975. The incoming prime minister, Robert Muldoon, was not in favour. With the rising tide of Maori activism at the time, Muldoon sensed that a radio station in Maori hands would become a powerful political tool against the established order of Pakeha control. He stopped the project on the grounds of financial stringency, an excuse that does not stand up in the light of subsequent expenditure on the government's 'think big' projects.

Despite government denial, Maori persisted with the goal of radio station as vehicle for cultural expression. That persistence eventually paid off. In 1988, Nga Kaiwhakapumau i te Reo initiated the first non-commercial Maori radio station Te Upoko o Te Ika in Wellington. For the first time in the history of broadcasting in New Zealand, the station provided continuous bilingual programmes. The station aimed to promote the Maori language by capturing listeners of all age groups. A year later Radio Aotearoa was established in Auckland. This station has 60 per cent of the Maori population within range of its transmissions. Since the establishment of these two stations 25 iwi stations have been established from Kaitaia in the Far North to Christchurch in the south.

Programmes with Maori content on television were even more meagre than radio offerings. At first there was only the five-minute news programme *Te Karere* pioneered by Derek Fox and Whai Ngata and the fifteen-minute *Koha* programme. But with the Waitangi Tribunal spelling out the responsibility that broadcasting had to promote the Maori language, TVNZ established a Maori Department in 1987. The air time for *Te Karere* was doubled. The hour-long *Marae* and *Waka Huia* programmes fill a two-hour slot on Sunday mornings for 38 weeks a year.

The advances made in radio and television communication by organic leaders such as Selwyn Muru, Derek Fox, Whai Ngata, Merata Mita, Piripi Walker, Hone Kaa and Ernie Leonard in the 1980s did as Robert Muldoon suspected. They achieved status in the communications media as leaders and helped raise the level of political awareness among Maori, as well as adding impetus to the cultural renaissance.

The Maori Renaissance
Although chiefly mana was eroded in the nineteenth century, and the political initiative taken over by prophets, intellectuals and organic lead-

ers into the modern era, it did not die out entirely. The descendants of Te Wherowhero and Te Heuheu, the two paramount chiefs who did not sign the Treaty of Waitangi, kept their mana intact. Sir Hepi Te Heuheu and Dame Te Atairangikaahu are the living repositories of the mana ariki of their illustrious forebears. Encouraged by the modern political and cultural renaissance of their people, they took steps to reassert tribal sovereignty, the principle of tino rangatiratanga guaranteed by the Treaty of Waitangi.

Sir Hepi Te Heuheu initiated the hui at Turangi in June 1989 that culminated in the formation of the National Congress of Tribes at Ngaruwahia the following year. The venues of these hui are politically and historically significant as the power centres of the Tuwharetoa and Tainui confederation of tribes. In the opening address at the Turangi hui, the Maori Catholic Bishop Takuira Mariu was unequivocal in his assertion that the pursuit of justice for Maori was linked to unification of tribes and tino rangitiratanga. Sir Hepi affirmed that position by stating that the hui would not accept government-imposed solutions to Maori problems. The hui would determine its own independent path.[4]

At its inception, the Congress insisted on being based on iwi, ruling out the Maori Council and the League. Iwi who joined the Congress maintained the right to exercise their own tino rangatiratanga. The sole purpose of Congress was to provide a national forum for iwi to address cultural and political issues within tikanga Maori.[5] Given the inherent difficulties of distinguishing between hapu and iwi, Congress refrained from defining iwi for membership purposes. Consequently, Congress, when fully assembled, was a large body of 62 iwi, 14 taura here groups and 25 runanga (Cox 1991, Appendix 22). As the national expression of tino rangatiratanga of the tribes, Congress equated its president with the governor-general, the Congress assembly with parliament, its executive with cabinet, and its officers with ministers (Cox 1991, 189). In this respect, Congress was the analogue to the Maori Parliament of 1892. Nonetheless, despite Congress being a more representative body than the Maori Council, it did not receive recognition from government that it deserved. Congress was formed two years after the Crown entered into negotiations with the Maori negotiators of the Maori fisheries claim. This left Congress on the sideline until 1991, when it was invited to appoint two alternate negotiators to the Maori negotiation team. Both negotiators, Apirana Mahuika

(Ngati Porou) and Professor Whatarangi Winiata (Ngati Raukawa), had tribal mandates. As alternate negotiators, their role was marginal to that of the principal negotiators who had been in place for four years. Winiata attended some, but not all of the meetings of the negotiators. Mahuika attended no meetings but was privy to the papers and proceedings of the negotiators. Because of its marginal role, in the negotiations leading up to the Sealord deal in settlement of the fishing claim, Congress had no option but to line up with the thirteen dissenting tribes against the deal. Thus, Maori were in the classic divide and rule scenario more reminiscent of the nineteenth century than the post-colonial era.

In 1987 the Maori Council, the Tainui Trust Board, Ngai Tahu Trust Board, Te Runanga o Muriwhenua and other tribes lodged the Maori fisheries claim in the High Court against the government's Quota Management System. The court ruled in favour of the claimants. It found that there was no evidence that Maori had sold their fishing right to the Crown and advised the Crown to negotiate with its treaty partners for the use of their resource (Walker 2004, 275–7). The Crown recognised the leading claimants, Tipene O'Regan (Ngai Tahu Trust Board), Robert Mahuta (Tainui Trust Board), Sir Graham Latimer (Maori Council) and the Hon. Matiu Rata (Runanga o Muriwhenua), as principal negotiators for the Maori claim. The negotiators persuaded the government to put up $150 million to assist Maori, in a joint venture with Brierley Investments, to buy Sealord from Carter Holt for $375 million. The Sealord deal, worked out between government and Maori negotiators, exemplifies the politics of expedience and pragmatism. The government wanted to settle all Maori grievances before the end of the decade. Immediately before the deal was signed, and soon after, the Maori negotiators, like a mini-government, went round the tribes belatedly seeking a mandate for what was in effect a *fait accompli*. One of the negotiators rationalised what he had done because it was 'the only deal in town'. In other words the Maori negotiators, for pragmatic reasons, were prepared to surrender the moral high ground of their property rights in the sea, guaranteed by treaty and ratified by a judgment in the High Court, for 150 pieces of silver.

The Maori negotiators, with the exception of Sir Graham Latimer, ostensibly operated from tribal bases. Sir Graham's mandate derived not from his iwi, but from the Maori Council, a statutory body funded by government. His subaltern role in the power structure of the state was also buttressed by his positions of Maori vice-president of the ruling National Party, and chairman of Aotearoa Fisheries Limited. Although Tipene O'Regan had a tribal mandate, he also had a subaltern role in the power structure as chairman of the Maori Fisheries Commission. The third principal Maori negotiator, the Hon. Matiu Rata, was a former cabinet minister. Rata, as a former minister and fisheries negotiator, was the Maori equivalent of a professional lobbyist. He knew what was politically feasible within the parliamentary system.

As the principle Maori negotiators, in a subaltern relationship with the Crown, Latimer and O'Regan, along with Rata, faced a political dilemma. Their function was to negotiate a deal with government that would integrate Maori into the political economy with the least disruption to the fishing industry. That is what they achieved. The inevitable consequence of the dilemma is that they ended up unwittingly maintaining the hegemony of the Crown. They responded to the game-plan devised by the state, which locks Maori into the capitalist extractive mode of a giant company in the exploitation of the sea. The Sealord deal did not provide quota to tribes to create jobs where they were most needed – in places like the Far North or the East Coast. Thirteen tribes, including the Moriori, opposed the Sealord deal on the ground that their treaty rights were not for sale. What they wanted was fishing quota to create jobs for their people.

Conclusion

In the nineteenth century British imperialism destroyed the power of New Zealand chiefs and their tribal structures. Only two ariki lineages survived into the twentieth century, among the Tainui and Tuwharetoa tribes, as figureheads from a bygone age. For most tribes leadership founded on achievement rather than ascription replaced the chiefly class. Consequently Maori leadership became more diverse and dynamic in response to the changed circumstances of Pakeha domination, and saw the rise of the new prophets. The Crown co-opted organic intellectuals to serve as subalterns in Maori councils, trust boards, the Women's Welfare League and as functionaries in general state institutions. In exchange for facilitating governance and social management, the conservative leaders sought concessions for their people from the Crown. Other organic leaders opted for radical protest action against the Crown for infractions against the Treaty of Waitangi. Protest action by radical leaders enabled subalterns to wring concessions from the Crown by way of treaty claims and court action for past and contemporary infractions against the treaty.

---

1   Gramsci (1971, 12) describes the subaltern classes as those subordinated by the ruling elites and excluded from any meaningful role in the power regime.
2   See Hon. Doug Graham (1992) 'Memorandum for Cabinet Strategy Committee, the Crown's Obligations under the Treaty of Waitangi', 1–15.
3   See *Report on the Department of Maori Affairs* (1989), written by Margaret Bazley, Deputy Chairperson, State Services Commision, 8.
4   See the report of the Maori Leadership Hui, Turangi, 24–23 June 1989, 6–8.
5   See the Whakakotahi Task Force Discussion Paper No. 7, 4.

Belich, J. (1989) *I Shall Not Die: Titokowaru's War, New Zealand, 1868–9*, Wellington, Bridget Williams Books.

Benton, R. A. (1979) T*he Legal Status of the Maori Language: Current Reality and Future Prospects*, Wellington, New Zealand Council for Educational Research.

Cox, L. (1991) 'Kotahitanga: The Search for Maori Political Unity', MA thesis, Palmerston North, Massey University.

Department of Justice (1992) *Her Majesty the Queen and Maori: Deed of Settlement*, Wellington, Department of Justice.

Elsmore, B. (2000) *Like Them That Dream: The Maori and the Old Testament*, Auckland, Reed.

Evison, H. C. (1987) *Ngai Tahu Land Rights and the Crown Pastoral Lease Lands in the South Island of New Zealand*, 3rd edn, Christchurch, Ngai Tahu Maori Trust Board.

Firth, R. (1959) *Economics of the New Zealand Maori*, Wellington, Government Printer.

Freire, P. (1985) *Pedagogy of the Oppressed*, trans. M. B. Ramos, Harmondsworth, Penguin.

Gramsci, A. (1971) *Selections from the Prison Notebooks of Antonio Gramsci*, ed. and trans. by Q. Hoare and G. N. Smith, New York, International Publishers.

Greenwood, W. (1980) *The Upraised Hand, or The Spiritual Significance of the Rise of the Ringatu Faith*, Wellington, Polynesian Society.

Henderson, J. M. (1972) *Ratana: The Man, the Church, the Political Movement*, 2nd edn, Wellington, Reed.

Maori Development Corporation (1990) *Annual Report*, Auckland, The Corporation.

McClean, S. F. (1950) 'Maori Representation 1905 to 1948', MA thesis, Auckland, Auckland University College.

Pei T. H. (1960) *King Potatau: An Account of the Life of Potatau Te Wherowhero, the First Maori King*, Wellington, Polynesian Society.

Puketapu, K. (1982) *Reform from Within*, Wellington, Department of Maori Affairs.

Ross, R. M. (1958) *Te Tiriti o Waitangi: Its Origins and Significance*, Wellington, Government Printer.

Sinclair, K. (1969) *A History of New Zealand*, rev. edn, Harmondsworth, Penguin.

Waitangi Tribunal (1989) *Report of the Waitangi Tribunal on the Te Reo Maori Claim*, Wellington, The Tribunal.

Walker, R. (2004) *Ka Whawhai Tonu Matou: Struggle Without End*, rev. edn, Auckland, Penguin.

NINE

Asian New Zealanders: Emergent Political Leadership and Politicised Communities

Manying Ip

When this chapter was being written, New Zealand had three Asian Members of Parliament: two Chinese and one South Asian.[1] Superficially speaking, they should be the most obvious 'political leaders' amongst the Asian New Zealanders. At the 2005 general election one of the Chinese members failed to be returned to parliament.[2] Significantly, this was barely noticed and hardly commented upon by either mainstream or Asian media. The 'Asian MPs' were all list MPs who got into parliament to provide each of their parties with its allotted share of the seats, not on the strength of their campaign or their profile within their constituencies.

In this chapter, I wish to argue that when examining political leadership amongst Asian New Zealanders, one should look beyond the Members of Parliament. While the personalities are interesting in their own individual ways, and their entrance to parliament a noteworthy landmark, to dub them 'political leaders' would be both misleading and extravagant. What is significant is how the Asian communities have, in the recent past, re-forged their political identities and found their political voice. The resulting groundswell has forced the Pakeha power elite to not only take notice, but also to accord them a small share of political power.

This chapter starts with an examination of the shifting balance of Asian New Zealanders *vis-à-vis* mainstream society. The numerical increase of the community is a primary factor to be considered. Equally worthy of examination is the impact of the new arrivals in the period since the new immigration policy of 1987 (Burke 1986). These arrivals tend to be well educated, articulate and highly aware of their rights. They have been at once an injection of energy and a challenge to their own ethnic communities, as well as to the wider New Zealand society (Ip 2003). While the old Chinese and Indian communities have long histories dating back to the mid-1860s and early 1900s respectively, their members have traditionally been very low key and seemingly uninterested in political participation. This chapter will contend that the transformation of the older Asian ethnic communities, in the form of heightened civil awareness among the descendants of the early settlers, combined with the raw energy and fresh aspirations of the new arrivals, has altered the pattern of political participation of the Asian communities in New Zealand. A new political identity has been forged amongst these divergent groups. Given time, true political leaders will emerge among these communities and the pattern of their emergence will take both the conventional path of electoral politics and also the wider spheres of non-electoral politics, when opinion leaders hold mainstream politicians to account, scrutinise public policies and influence the direction of the policy agenda.

What should be of great interest to all political parties is the coming of age of the younger Asian voters whose families arrived in the late 1980s or early 1990s. Because New Zealand's immigration policy favoured skilled middle-class professionals and entrepreneurs, members of the Asian ethnic sector are considerably better educated and younger than their general New Zealand counterparts. The children of these new arrivals, some of them '1.5 generations' and some locally born, have developed considerable cross-cultural awareness and multi-lingual skills (Bartley 2003). In the 2005 election they played a significant role in being prepared to speak out, flex their political muscle and engage with their counterparts in mainstream society. The level of their emergent political acumen is clearly shown by the quality of the debates in the mushrooming Asian blog sites. I will examine the role of the young Asians as a postscript in this chapter.

Current Asian Communities

In a democracy where every citizen has the right to cast a vote for the political candidate to represent him or her, one of the most important variables determining the political influence of any ethnic group is its absolute number. Census 2001 found that Asian New Zealanders consisted of 237,459 persons, or 6.6 per cent of the total population. For the first time in New Zealand history, Pacific peoples, who had long enjoyed the third place – after Pakeha and Maori – in the ethnic number scale, had been overtaken by the Asian population.

Asians also constitute the fastest growing ethnic population of the country in the last decade. The projections further predict that the Asian share of the total population will increase to 13 per cent in 2021.[3]

The term 'Asians' used in the New Zealand context includes a vast range of peoples from over 30 nations. The 2001 New Zealand Census states that 'Asians' include:

- East Asians: i.e. Chinese, Korean, Japanese, Taiwanese;
- Southeast Asians: i.e. Cambodian, Filipino, Thai, Vietnamese, Indonesian, Malay, Laotian; and
- South Asians: i.e. Indian, Sri Lankan, Bangladeshi, Indo-Fijian.

In popular media and public perception, however, 'Asians' are taken to mean mainly Chinese and Koreans, whereas Indians and other South Asians are usually called 'Indians', 'Pakistanis' or 'Sri Lankans'. The term 'Asians' is also often used interchangeably with 'immigrants'. This practice ignores the fact that over 25 per cent of the Chinese and close to 30 per cent of the Indian cohorts are locally born. Among these are many fourth- or fifth-generation New Zealand-born families. The New Zealand identity is not yet inclusive enough to accommodate citizens who are non-white and non-Maori, like the Asians.

However, stereotypes often contain grains of truth. In this case, the popular confusion of 'Asians' and 'immigrants' can be partly explained by the fact that an increasing proportion of the ethnic groups within the Asian community is made up of recent immigrants who arrived within a decade of the 2001 census. This most recent census showed the numerical preponderance of the new immigrant cohort. Within the two oldest Asian ethnic groups, 70 per cent of the Chinese and 59 per cent of the Indian immigrants have arrived after 1991 (i.e., within a decade preceding the most recent census). The percentage of new arrivals with less than ten years' residence among the Korean immigrants is as high as 92 per cent (Ho 2003).

The preponderance of new arrivals within the Asian communities is significant in three ways. Firstly, they gained their residence visas because they belonged to the highly skilled professional and business class which the New Zealand Immigration Service sought. Under the very selective criteria, only highly educated middle-class Asians and their family members can qualify for entry (Ho 1997; Ligard 1998). As a result, new Asians are among the highest qualified cohorts of New Zealanders (Thomson 1999; Henderson 2003). Their new presence has given their community a profile far higher than their absolute numbers would normally command. Secondly, these new arrivals have brought with them the political values and public behaviour that they acquired from their homelands (Friesen 1997; Beal 2001). Since knowledge is power and the bourgeoisie is the pillar of democratic governments, the significant addition of a sizeable number of middle-class, well-educated migrants is bound to have a strong impact on New Zealand. Many of these middle-aged, educated new Asians are well informed and have had a public role to play in their own countries of origin. These two factors have assisted the emergence of the Asian political voice. Given time, this highly educated and ambitious group will undoubtedly develop a capacity for political leadership.

The third factor characterising the new Asian communities, however, may not be a totally favourable one. Within the long-established Chinese and Indian communities, the new arrivals introduced considerable tensions. To the low-key old settlers, the newcomers' culture and public behaviour often appeared too brash and assertive (Ip 1995; Ip 1996). Such tensions between new arrivals and old settlers are not restricted to New Zealand. Scholars of the Chinese diaspora worldwide often analyse the sharp differences that exist between the old settlers and the new transnational Chinese. It is no exaggeration to speak of two different cultural worlds. Chinese political leaders have to carefully negotiate their platform between these two groups with widely divergent interests and agendas.

Qualities of an 'Asian Political Leader'

An ideal 'Asian political leader' of course must be fluent in English in order to debate in parliament and be knowledgeable about New Zealand politics. In addition, as with all 'ethnic minority leaders', they must be supported by their own community network. In New Zealand's established

Asian communities, the challenges to any aspiring leaders are numerous. In the case of a Chinese leader, there is a need to be well versed and fully proficient in the Chinese dialects, at least in major ones like Mandarin and Cantonese, in order to communicate adequately with their constituents. In essence it has to be a person who can move comfortably between the descendants of the early 'sojourning Chinese' and the current transnationals, two cohorts separated by 150 years of different history and divergent value systems.

To be a leader among Indians is probably even more challenging. New Zealand's Indian community is mainly made up of arrivals from the subcontinent and also from Fiji (Leckie 1995). It is a diverse community in terms of culture, language and religion. Take the example of Language Line, a telephone interpreting service recently set up to service new immigrants. There are no fewer than five South Asian languages offered: Hindi, Gujurati, Punjabi, Urdu and Bengali. Besides being aware of the multiplicity of languages, the Indian leader must be very mindful of the tension between the Hindus and the Muslims.

What kind of person can empathise and articulate the aspirations of both the old settlers and the new immigrants within such diverse communities? An interesting point to note is that none of the three Asian Members of Parliament were native born. All three were immigrants, arriving in the 1970s and late 1980s respectively.[4] On the other hand, a sizeable proportion of the Chinese and Indian cohorts are native-born New Zealanders. With their superior knowledge of New Zealand society and politics and with their high educational and professional attainments, one would expect them to play a much more active political role. Why did Asians not play a prominent role in national politics before the late 1990s?

'Apolitical' Old Asian Communities

The established old Asian communities, both Chinese and Indian, were often described as apolitical, unambitious, inward-looking and hardly interested in wider New Zealand affairs. As for the people within these communities, many often prided themselves in being the 'model minority' of their adopted land. They were law-abiding, low key, modest, inoffensive, hardworking and family centred. Outsiders have sometimes criticised them for their apparent lack of ambition. They know that their acceptance by mainstream New Zealand is hard earned. To placate the majority, they have given themselves an extremely low profile to the point of being almost invisible (Yee 2002).

Before the new immigration law change of 1987, which allowed 'quality migrants' to come irrespective of their ethnic origins, New Zealand explicitly favoured the immigrants from Britain and Western Europe. The Asian community was very small. The number of the Chinese was below 20,000, and that of the Indian below 15,000. Even more important was the stable and homogeneous nature of the communities: over 55 per cent of the population was locally born.

Theoretically, the locally born generations should 'know the New Zealand way' and become politically active over time, just like their Pakeha/European counterparts. But that line of thinking fails to take into account the crippling effect of discrimination, both overt and covert, on vulnerable ethnic communities.

The lack of home-grown Asian political leaders is a direct result of the old White New Zealand policy (Price 1974; Brawley 1993). Though unwritten and kept largely secret, it was effective in keeping coloured migration to a minimum. Those allowed in were dubbed 'undesirable aliens' and subjected to various discriminatory policies (Murphy 1997; Ip 2005) During the early part of the last century the Chinese, most of whom arrived as gold miners and market gardeners, were subjected to an exorbitant poll-tax (Murphy 1994; Wong 2003) and had to be thumb-printed on entering and exiting New Zealand. Even locally born Chinese (who held citizenship by right of birth) were specifically barred from pensions and unemployment benefits when these social welfare measures were introduced. But the most serious hurdle for the Chinese was their loss of the right to vote. Between 1907 and 1951 the Chinese were barred from naturalisation. Their disenfranchisement removed any chances to alleviate their plight via electoral and legislative means. In spite of the many inequalities which needed urgent redressing, the Chinese had no constitutional avenue to appeal. As non-citizens they had no right to participate in elections. In spite of their long history as immigrants to the country, the Chinese were mere spectators in the electoral exercise.

Historically, the Chinese were much more interested in political developments in China than in party politics in New Zealand. They obviously felt they could play a part in Chinese politics, since there was no toehold for them in New Zealand. In the 1900s, during the last decade of the imperial Qing Dynasty (1644–1911), the overseas Chinese were courted by both the reformers and the revolutionaries. The Chinese Masonic Society (Chee Kong Tong) was founded in Wellington in 1907. This was a grassroots society with an anti-Qing political agenda (Murphy 1991). Its colourful Triad links and mutual help activities are little known beyond the Chinese community, but the distinctive building of this once powerful tong still stands to this day in Frederick Street in Wellington. The Masonic compass and set square motif and the Chinese characters are still clearly discernible on the building's exterior wall. Dr Sun Yatsen, founder of the Republic of China (1912–), lauded the overseas Chinese actions as the 'Mother of the Revolution'. Branches of his Guomindang (Kuomintang) Nationalist Party were founded in Wellington and Auckland as early as 1913. The party commanded great loyalty among the local Chinese. During World War II, the New Zealand Chinese Association was instrumental in collecting mandatory weekly donations from all Chinese people living in all parts of New Zealand to support the China war effort. The mobilisation of manpower and the organisational efforts were mind-boggling. The New Zealand Chinese ranked a proud second in the list of generous overseas Chinese donors to the motherland (Ip 1990). This was no mean feat when we consider how much more affluent the Southeast Asian Chinese were.

All this shows that the Chinese were far from being apolitical and were fully capable of political organisation but that they had no chance to display it within the New Zealand political framework of the time.

Since the Indians were British citizens, overt legislative discrimination could not be conveniently applied to them. But social discrimination was rampant, and very often such racist reactions metamorphosed into quasi-political organisations and became something much more sinister. Hostility from mainstream society again served to keep the Indians 'in their place'. Gujarati and Punjabi Indians arrived in the early 1900s as drain diggers and farm hands. By the 1920s their presence provoked the Pukekohe locals into forming the White New Zealand League (Leckie 1985). The influential league had allies in the country's leading newspapers, and was supported by the most powerful politicians of the time, both in government and in opposition. The Indians (usually called 'Hindoos' in the newspapers and in the parliamentary debates) were accused of lowering wages and dragging down the standard of living for all honest New Zealand working men. There was widespread public agitation to keep the Indians out.

The Stigma of Being 'Race Alien' and Thwarted Political Development

Decades afterwards, the stigma of being once a 'race alien' continued to bring untold discrimination against the New Zealand-born Asians. Although they know of no other homeland than New Zealand, and although their cultural values are no different from those of their mainstream counterparts, Asian New Zealanders all know that they are not regarded as 'true-blue New Zealanders'. For a start, their yellow or brown skin and dark hair mark them apart as 'foreign'. There is hardly any Asian person who has not been asked the ubiquitous question, 'Where do you come from?'

Neither the British nationality (which the Indians came with, and which the Chinese could acquire through naturalisation after 1951) nor their educational attainment and professional status could protect them from subtle social racism and discrimination (Ip 2005). Right up to the twenty-first century, New Zealand has remained essentially a 'White Nation' (Hage 1998), with a passing nod to the tangata whenua, the Treaty partner.

Asians were taught to 'know their place'. They learnt to bow their heads, not to be tall poppies, and take a low profile in order not to arouse the unease and jealousy of the dominant culture. Keenly aware that their acceptance is 'conditional on good behaviour', many Asians are eager to 'fit in' and to placate (Ip 1996). The power of Pakeha domination is so strong that most ethnic minorities would even measure themselves by Pakeha standards. They have learnt to abide by the 'unspoken contract' by which they would live up to the expectation of the dominant society, trading acceptance by giving up their own standing and identity (Yee 2003). They would try 'to be motivated but not assertive, to excel academically but not be competitive with mainstream New Zealanders, to "know one's place"' (Ip 1996).

For over a century, in trying constantly to step back and bite one's tongue, Asian New Zealanders have made themselves docile and not willing to assert themselves. The words of a Chinese interviewee Kirsten Wong are especially poignant: 'Racism has convinced us that it is a virtue to be passive. We even define ourselves negatively .... We're not criminals, we're not lazy, we're no longer market-gardeners, we don't work in laundries now ...' (Ip 1996).

In the late 1980s, Steven Young, a Wellington community leader, mused about the apparent lack of political ambition among the Chinese in a short community article entitled 'Corridors of Power'. He wondered aloud why there were no political leaders emerging among the Chinese, despite their professional success. His prediction at the time was that the chances of any Chinese people getting into parliament were very remote. In a later article, he pointed out that 'election to Parliament pre-supposed selection to a winnable seat .... A Chinese candidate would probably lose more racist votes than gain ethnic votes' (Young 2003).

While the wider New Zealand political climate was not conducive to the emergence of an Asian leader in national electoral politics, it would be wrong to assume that the Asians were totally docile. The Chinese, in particular, have been reasonably diligent in local politics. Different from politicians at a national level, successful local political leaders need not pay too much attention to party politics. To them, hard work, thorough knowledge and actual 'hands-on' experience of local issues, is more important than populist campaigning. Voter appeal is important, but on a local level that is usually built on an actual track record rather than on electoral promises and rhetoric.

The earliest Chinese leader in local body politics was George Gee, Mayor of Petone (1970–76). Molly Ngan-kee was elected to the Lower Hutt Council in 1977 and became Deputy Mayor in 1980. At the time this chapter was written, Meng Foon was a second-term Mayor of Gisborne and Peter Chin a newly elected Mayor of Dunedin.

An interesting point of contrast with the Asian MPs is that all these local body politicians were/are locally born. Another point of contrast, succinctly and proudly put by one of the mayors, is this, 'We are all actually *elected*. We have real supporters and constituencies'.[5] It is true that all these leaders had long years of council experience and a successful history of involvement in various local community organisations prior to their rise to prominence. Their competence, dedication and demonstrated track record are sufficient to support their ascent to the apex of local government, but probably not enough to propel them into leadership on a national level.

The Anti-Asian Backlash and Changing Political Climate of the 1990s

With the arrival of the new immigrants in the 1990s, the political climate within the Asian communities changed perceptibly. People started to take an interest in both electoral and non-electoral politics. Initially, they were propelled into some quasi-political activities because of the urgent need to bring some cohesion into their own groups. The Asian communities also needed to politicise themselves because of the virulence of the anti-Asian backlash triggered by the influx of new immigrants. Emergent groups and forces capable of leadership were fermenting. Many of these were located beyond parliament, and hence outside of electoral politics.

As explained earlier, the Chinese are a divergent group, with the fault line being drawn most clearly between the old settlers (descendants of the gold miners and market gardeners originating from south China) and the new arrivals since 1987 (the immigrants from the various Chinese home-lands like Hong Kong, Taiwan, the People's Republic of China, Singapore, etc.). The two groups have distinctly different history and cultural tradi-tions. They speak different languages and have different political systems. The People's Republic has a socialist government that is much feared by Taiwan, and it loomed like a large shadow over British Hong Kong. In fact, one major push factor prompting Hong Kong people to emigrate was the fear of 1997, the year that China was to resume sovereignty. The sense of identification with New Zealand (and knowledge of New Zealand politics) also proved very different, with the descendants of the old set-tlers having a strong local identity, and the new arrivals having a more transnational and global identity.

From time to time, especially when the Asians were under attack, the two cohorts tried to understand each other, and to negotiate a 'pan-Chinese voice', in much the same way as the old Gujerati and Punjabi Indian communities and their descendants did when negotiating a 'pan-Indian voice' with the new arrivals, many of whom were from Africa, Fiji and other parts of the Pacific.

A series of events politicised the Chinese community. While the main participants were long-time immigrants, recent immigrants tended to play a strong supporting role, providing the numbers at the public rallies and community meetings. In 1993, the notorious 'Inv-Asian' articles published in the Auckland suburban newspapers (Booth 1993) made Chinese the targets of caricature and racialised criticism. The complaint to the Press

Council by members of the Chinese community was upheld. That incident was quickly followed by another battle with the New Zealand Olympic and Commonwealth Games Association in 1994, which sponsored a series of advertisements 'to encourage New Zealand athletes' by depicting various foreign nationals as detractors from 'true New Zealanders'. A Chinese actor was shown laughing at New Zealand as a small and insignificant country whose athletes would easily be beaten by China, a country both athletically strong and populous. The advertisements were forced off the air within a week of the Chinese complaint to the Race Relations Office. Then, in 1995, when Maori leaders alleged that 'Asians are raping our coasts' because 'their culture is to take everything', the Wellington Chinese led a spirited campaign and met the critics in person, forcing them to withdraw their rash statements (Hunt 1996; Pang 2003).

These incidents all served to politicise the Chinese communities, forcing them to cooperate with each other and giving their leading spokespeople experience in political action. The settler community attained its greatest success in February 2002 by obtaining an official apology for the poll-tax which had been levied on their ancestors by successive governments. When the prime minister, Helen Clark, called community representatives together in the Grand Hall of Parliament on Chinese New Year Day and formally apologised for the poll tax and 'other discriminatory statutes imposed on the Chinese', it marked the culmination of a decade-long process of research and quiet lobbying by the New Zealand Chinese Association (Wong 2003). Never before had the old Chinese community been so politicised as in the several months leading up to the formal apology by the prime minister.

The descendants of those who were forced to pay the poll tax also formed an advisory group to advance the reconciliation process after the apology. Meetings were held around the country, and position papers written to advise government on the best follow-up measures to be adopted. Observers rightly marvelled at 'the sudden political flowering of the old local Chinese community' (Young 2003).

The old settler community attained these successes using all the avenues that they knew as long-time New Zealanders. They actively lobbied parliamentarians and ministers; systematically approached the mainstream media; called high-profile public meetings; and wrote effective press releases. The settler community can get public attention if they wish.

By the 1990s Asian communities also looked to the Human Rights Commission and Race Relations Office to provide redress against opinions or behaviour that was discriminatory. These two offices specified what was, and what was not, acceptable in terms of employment, accommodation, access to services and public places. The social and political rights of the Asian communities, together with those of other minorities, are now clearly spelt out.

MMP and Shifting Power Relationships

The single most significant development that propelled Asians into the realm of politics was the advent of MMP in 1996. With the spectacular influx of Asian migrants, politicians became keenly interested in capturing the Asian vote. At the time, few political leaders and strategists knew much about the Asian communities, and the voting practices of these groups were a great mystery. What better way to entice the Asians to vote for a certain party than to put up an Asian candidate on the party list?

The politicisation of the Asian communities was greatly aided by the country's generous election laws. While many countries restrict the franchise to citizens, in New Zealand qualified permanent residents also enjoy the right to vote. The 1986 Royal Commission on the Electoral System maintained that permanent residents who have the right to live and work in New Zealand are already making a full contribution to the community and its future. For that commitment they have earned full membership of the community.[6] New Asian arrivals are qualified to enrol as electors if they have resided in New Zealand continuously for not less than twelve months. Furthermore, the Electoral Act 1993 allows a person with limited language skills to be accompanied by an interpreter in the polling booth. Returning officers can also have interpreters' help when communicating with voters. The majority of Asian immigrants are therefore able to take part in the elections. The stage is set for some very energetic electioneering and lobbying among the Asian communities.

Under MMP, it is the total number of party votes that determine the number of MPs that each party can send to parliament. An ethnic candidate can attract the party vote of that ethnic group from anywhere in the country. To party strategists, an ethnic candidate became a useful political pawn, a poster boy or poster girl who could attract party votes from everywhere. In 1996, the National Party put Pansy Wong, a Chinese woman prominent in the local Christchurch community, on its party list. Her mentor was Philip Burdon, the then Minister of Trade Negotiations, who has a reputation for being both liberal and pro-Asian. Most probably this astute political move did reap significant dividends for the National Party. Before the 1996 election there was unprecedented fervour among the Chinese, with many stating that they would vote for the party that put up a Chinese candidate (Zhang and Ip 1996).

As the 'New Right' party, ACT also courted the new Asian vote diligently. The party was among the first to establish an Asian branch. Its early Asian members were mostly Taiwanese. The various Asian candidates that the party put up in successive elections were all Chinese, but none got in because the party did not have enough party votes. In the 2002 election, Kenneth Wang, who came from the People's Republic of China in the late 1980s, was given the tenth position on the ACT list. The party had only enough party votes to have nine MPs, so Wang missed out. However, he finally entered parliament in November 2004 following the expulsion of Donna Awatere Huata, becoming the second ethnic Chinese MP in New Zealand history.

Traditionally, the Labour Party has always prided itself in being the champion of the underdog and the natural patron and mentor of ethnic minorities. In the early years of MMP, however, Labour strategists had serious doubts about their chances of courting the Asian vote by placing Asian candidates on the party list. The feeling of the party was that prospective candidates should earn their place by working diligently through the rank and file, thereby proving their commitment and their worth before winning the nomination. Very few new Asian immigrants would fit that bill. Labour leadership also had doubts that a party built on socialist egalitarian ideals could win over the 'new Asians', given the fact that many of them are from the moneyed middle class.

In reality, the class composition (and by inference, the political sympathies) of the 'new Asians' still awaits serious study. Although they are often associated in the public mind with affluence, professional success and entrepreneurship, the Chinese new arrivals (including those who entered through the business investor category) had very low incomes in New Zealand. The 2001 census found that, '[t]he lowest levels of personal median income were reported by those identifying as Taiwanese Chinese

($3,200), Korean ($5,300) and Somali ($7,600)' (Ip 2003).[7] This should be a startling finding. Two Asian groups, the Taiwanese and the Korean, who are routinely cited as middle-class and affluent people, are mentioned in the same breath with the Somalis, who arrived as displaced refugees. Somehow this report did not attract any public attention, probably because very few people could interpret such unexpected statistical findings. Actually, the new Asian groups (including Chinese, Koreans, and Indians) had a lower than average labour-force participation rate in the 1993 and 1999 ethnic profile studies (Thomson 1993; Thomson 1999). For over a decade, unemployment and underemployment have remained chronic problems among the new Asian communities (Ho 2003).

The 'class' affiliation of the new Asians, therefore, might not be uniformly right-wing, as initially expected by the political pundits. Their exposure to economic hardship and an unsatisfactory business environment since their arrival in New Zealand may indeed have given rise to the more egalitarian sympathies espoused by the moderate left and centre-left parties.

In 2002 Ashraf Choudhary, an agricultural and environmental scientist, was placed at a high (winnable) slot on Labour's party list. He had been a long-time party member with an extensive and distinguished working record on race relations. In his own words, he was 'a "grassroots" person who has come from the bottom up through his voluntary work among the ethnic communities of New Zealand'.[8] Choudhary became New Zealand's first MP of South Asian descent.

Asian MPs and Voters on a Learning Curve

These Asian politicians in parliament walked an uneven and narrow path. The three of them belonged to three different parties, and their backgrounds are so vastly divergent that there is very scant chance of them forming an 'Asian caucus' in the manner of the 'Maori caucus'. Besides, three is not an impressive or meaningful number in a parliament of at least 120 members. Furthermore, they are comparative novices in parliamentary politics.

In January 2005, a *North & South* article entitled 'Disappearing Act?' asked whether the ACT Party could survive the election, a question on the mind of many political observers. The writer started the piece with a vivid and somewhat satirical description of Kenneth Wang's first day in parliament. Wang was depicted as naively self-absorbed, and intoxicated by his newfound importance, pumping hands with anyone willing, including the person who brought him a glass of water. Without any experience in public office or government committees, the new Chinese MP seemed oblivious to the reality of politics. That part of the article may be criticised for being a caricature, but the writer's tone was bemused rather than sharply critical. Most probably a more astute person with genuine political ambition would have had more foresight than getting himself into a potentially compromising position by taking up a parliamentary seat in the last few months of a term, with a party on a very slippery downward slope. Genuine political leaders in the true sense of the word have yet to emerge among the Asian communities in New Zealand.

Some brief mention should be made of the abortive attempts of Asian groups to form their own political parties. Since the total population of Asian New Zealanders is 6.6 per cent and increasing, the formation of an independent ethnic political party is a viable option in theory. In 1996, two such parties were formed, the Ethnic Minority Party and the Asia Pacific United Party. Neither gained any significant support,[9] and both folded quickly after the election. Thereafter, the Asians made no further attempts to form parties along ethnic lines.

Meanwhile, the political parties of mainstream New Zealand are quite ready to continue to use some Asian candidates as draw cards for party votes. Mainstream New Zealand political leaders are of course happy to promote suitable 'ethnic' candidates if they are real assets. Asian names certainly arouse community interest and attract donations as well as speaking opportunities for party leaders at Asian banquets and on Asian television. In the 2002 national election, there were no fewer than six Chinese candidates and one each of Korean and South Asian descent on the party lists of various political parties.[10]

In the past, mainstream parties were not above using the Asians to serve as 'electoral cannon fodder'. Probably the most glaring example was Ron Waishing, a leader of the Chinese vegetable growers, who stood for Labour three times between 1963 and 1975. His opponent was no one less than Bill Birch, an experienced and creditable National Party politician. The electorate was affluent Franklin, a true-blue National stronghold. Waishing never had any real chance of winning (Young 2003).

If Waishing's example is to be a useful lesson, then Asians should not enter politics before they are ready for it. The political future of the Asian communities depends largely on the spread of genuine political awareness among the rank and file, and the gradual accumulation of political experience and capital among their key players. Without proper understanding and in-depth knowledge of New Zealand's political culture and environment, the aspiration for political power, not to mention political leadership, remains a distant dream.

Lobbying, Activism and Forging a New Political Identity

Circumstances in 2005 were volatile but full of possibilities for the Asian communities. Many of their resources have not been used or called upon yet. Most of the groups are still new to New Zealand, and individuals tended to be preoccupied with practicalities of settling down rather than charting their political future.

Among the Chinese, the Taiwanese are the most highly politicised, probably because they came from a newly democratised home region.[11] The Taiwanese community embarked on a crash course of New Zealand politics in the 1990s. Emboldened by the unprecedented number of new Chinese arrivals and intrigued by the general debate on the new MMP voting system, they have been the prime driving force behind the major Chinese pre-election rallies, in 1996, 1999 and 2002 respectively. They brought with them the practical skills of organising public rallies, fundraising for political campaigns and lobbying government officials.

By comparison, immigrants from Hong Kong are generally more politically apathetic, probably an attitude left over from their British colonial experience, when all major political decisions were made in London and the Governor appointed by Whitehall ruled with his power unchecked and unshared. Immigrants from the People's Republic of China are numerically the largest group, they are well educated and young, but they are also the most recent and most inexperienced in the workings of a western democracy.

In spite of their varying degrees of acculturation, all these groups are united in their general understanding of the importance of gaining their political voice. Maybe it is still early days to think in terms of political leadership, or playing astute party politics, but Asian communities are certainly matured enough to be ready for lobbying and community-based activism. When the communities felt that they were under attack, for example when New Zealand First rose in popularity on the anti-immigration platform (in 1996 and then 2002), the Asian communities displayed remarkable organisational power. Some wrote articles for newspapers and spoke up on the radio and television, some lobbied their MPs and cabinet ministers, and some organised political rallies to force politicians of major parties to front up to the Asian communities to clarify their stand on immigration and settlement issues. In most of these cases, the sub-ethnic groups (i.e., arrivals from the People's Republic, Taiwan and Hong Kong, and Koreans, too) were able to put their differences aside and cooperate in a united effort of solidarity. Both old settlers and new arrivals worked together to achieve their aims.

Recently, Ashraf Choudhary lamented his acute sense of 'impotence' as a new Member of Parliament. He said he was speaking for all new MPs, '. . . it's a palpable and shocking realisation the moment they hit Wellington and attend their Caucus . . . . They come to change the world but instead discover that they can't even amend the Bellamy's menu. There's years of donkey-dipping and rat-swallowing ahead before real power can even be glimpsed.'[12] It is precisely when one hears such realistic utterances that one feels there is some hope for clear-sighted political leaders to emerge from among the Asian ranks.

By now, the descendants of the old settlers understand that the old self-effacing policy of keeping a low profile and turning the other cheek does not work. In 1993, the pre-election political seminars set up to query senior politicians in both Auckland and Wellington were led by long-standing Chinese settlers' associations (Jones 1993). At that time, only people thoroughly acculturated to New Zealand's socio-political culture would have the skills to run such sessions holding mainstream politicians to account. The Chinese settlers community also led in the 1996 face-off with Maori politicians, when the latter accused 'Asians' of 'raping New Zealand's coast' because 'their [Asian] culture was to take everything'. The community complained to the Race Relations Conciliator and forced a meeting with their Maori critics, successfully asking the latter to withdraw their hasty comments.[13]

Up to now, much has been accomplished through community advocacy rather than formal party politics. Besides the success of the poll tax apology and strong stance shown in the face of racism, most recently younger Asian activists have tried to arrive at some solidarity with Maori leaders. In the anti-racism marches of late 2004 and their confrontation with the National Front, these young Asian leaders sided with Maori and other minority groups (Mok 2004). They advocated abiding by the Treaty of Waitangi as the first immigration document of the country.[14] Time will tell whether this bold and innovative move will establish the legitimacy of the Asian communities as one of the partners in multicultural New Zealand.

Hopefully, in time the Asian communities, especially the new arrivals, will understand that an over-eager plunge into politics does not work – they will just be used as bit players and sideshows. The recent unfortunate experience preceding the 2005 election, when a high-ranking Chinese candidate was removed from the Labour list while undergoing police investigation, was a warning bell to the new Asian community.

The Young Asians and New Zealand Politics

For a real political leader to emerge from the ranks of local-born Asians (the descendants of old settlers), there is now a much greater chance of success because of the numerical strength brought by the arrival of new immigrants. The new arrivals, a group never bowed down by marginalisation and racism, have also given any potential leader much greater confidence, by the example of their assertive behaviour and their strong belief in entitlement.

The emergence of a leader from the new immigrants' group will take time after they have acquired greater English proficiency and political acumen. These can only be gained through immersion and adequate experience in New Zealand society and politics.

As signalled earlier, I will now examine the role of the young Asians as a postscript. These 1.5 generation Asians possess at once the assets and qualities of the two groups discussed above. Educated and brought up in New Zealand, they are proficient in English and well-versed in 'the New Zealand way'. Yet they are very aware of the disadvantages of being a visible minority, and certainly not immune to the various levels of racism directed against Asian immigrants. In the 2005 election, the young Asians played a highly significant role as political commentators and advocates.

From the start, when the election date was announced, the group was very active pushing their peers to get on the electoral roll. But of much greater significance were their political 'blog sites', which discuss and analyse the 'Asian policies' of various parties.[15]

The Labour Party's ill-fated efforts in putting Auckland businessman Steven Ching as number 42 on the Labour list – the third highest non-sitting MP – were widely seen as cynical tokenism. Ching was chosen on his strength as a fundraiser and a generous donor to Labour, although (in the words of a popular Chinese TV anchor) 'many of us [Chinese] found him an obvious embarrassment: he is not very smart, speaks [Chinese] brokenly and hesitantly, and . . . can hardly speak English'.[16] Much more serious and compromising was his failure to disclose a previous guilty plea and an allegation that he asked for a loan of $50,000 from a fellow Chinese whom he offered to help to make a justice of the peace (Ng 2005). Many in the new Chinese community worried about what seemed to be the introduction of undesirable 'black-gold politics' into New Zealand. However, while the new Chinese immigrants mostly grumbled privately, the young Asians fronted up on national television,[17] and wrote angry messages on their blogs which forced the issues into the open. In the end, they probably helped to save the Labour Party from worse embarrassment and further potential scandal.

If the young Asians were disillusioned and angry with Labour attempts to manipulate ethnic votes and for cynically choosing a token candidate, they were equally vigilant and effective towards the scrutiny of the National Party's proposed tax cuts and immigration policy. Nor did they mince words with their very own 'first Asian MP', Pansy Wong. When Brash announced the National Party's plan for a 'four-year provisional residency' period for immigrants, Wong was taken to task by the *Yellow Peril* website and the experienced MP found her party's policy hard to defend. Again, similar to their treatment of Labour's Ching case, the young Asians were much quicker, sharper, punchier and more effective than their elders. For example, when the *Capital Chinese News* queried Brash's policy on its front page on 12 August 2005, it was several days later than the full analysis given in *Yellow Peril.*

Contrary to what some political strategists (of all parties) hoped, the Asians turned out to be much more astute and not readily attracted by yellow or brown faces on the party lists, nor were they easily bribed by promises. There was no evidence of any Asian-bloc voting anywhere. One Chinese newspaper put an analysis of the election results on its front page in a mocking tone. The banner headline said 'Real estate prices the gauge of election winners and losers'.[18] The gist of the long article was that Auckland real estate agents would have been able to give accurate predictions to which party would win or lose in certain electorates: electorates with average house prices lower than $350,000 would vote Labour; otherwise they would vote National. Why waste time checking polls? Its mocking tone notwithstanding, the article pointed to a basic fact which the political parties should know: socio-economic status often dictates the voters' sympathy, regardless of what their ethnicity is. It is self-defeating treating ethnic voters as a separate category. Mainstream political parties should desist in chasing the illusive 'Asian vote'. Ultimately, 'Asian communities' is an artificial construct, and even smaller sub-categories, like 'Chinese voters' and 'Indian voters', are deceptive blanket terms masking distinctive groups for lazy and undiscerning politicians.

In future, political parties have to start treating 'Asian voters' as all other voters who are judicious and capable of independent thinking. The young Asians are scrutinising the parties' every move and intentions, and they are avid participants in the political process even if they are not yet actively campaigning. It is only a matter of time before worthy political leaders emerge from their rank and file.

---

1   Born in British India, Ashraf Choudhary is often referred to as 'Indian' by New Zealand media. His family is actually from northern Punjab, now within the Pakistani territory. Like many Punjabis, he is Muslim.
2   Kenneth Wang of the ACT Party lost his seat because the extreme rightist party polled poorly, as was widely predicted.
3   See www.stats.govt.nz/census.
4   Pansy Wong (National list MP, 1996–) arrived in 1972 from Hong Kong. Ashraf Choudhary (Labour list MP, 2002–) arrived in 1976 from Punjab, Pakistan. Kenneth Wang (ACT list MP, November 2004–September 2005) arrived in the late 1980s from China.
5   Mayor of Dunedin to author, February 2005.
6   See *Towards a Better Democracy*, the 1986 report of the Royal Commission on the Electoral System, Wellington. The liberal and generous recommendations enfranchised the majority of new Asian immigrants. Studies on the voting pattern of Asian Americans found that many were apathetic because sizeable cohorts in their commu-

nities were not enfranchised.
7   Ethnic Groups (2001), 'Highlights', available at: http://www.statis.govt.nz
8   Choudhary (2002), maiden speech, 28 August.
9   According to the *New Zealand Electoral Compendium* (1997, 18–19), the Ethnic Minority
     Party gained 0.12% of the national vote, and the Asia Pacific United Party gained only
     0.002%.
10   Of the six Chinese candidates, National put up two, Labour put up one, ACT put up
     one, and Progressive Coalition Party put up two. The South Asian candidate was nomi-
     nated by Labour and the Korean candidate was nominated by the Christian Heritage
     Party.
11   Taiwan ended the one-party dictatorship in 1988 and started general elections for their
     Legislative Yuan (Parliament) in the same year. Prior to that, authoritarian control was
     justified by the excuse that Taiwan was at war with the People's Republic of China.
12   Ashraf Choudhary (2004) Speech Notes for Awapuni Rotary Club, 20 April,
     Palmerston North.
13   NZPA (1994) 'Asians rape coast, says Henare', *Press*, 20 October, 7.
14   These young Asian leaders' argument is this: Pakeha gained the right to enter New
     Zealand as Treaty partners. By recognising the Treaty, the Asians will also become
     rightful treaty partners in an emergent multicultural New Zealand.
15   See, for example, the *Yellow Peril* blog: http://publicaddress.net/default.yellowperil.sm;
     and the *Poll Dancer* blog: http://publicaddress.net/default.polldancer.sm
16   This is the observation of a WTV (Chinese language Sky TV) anchor on the *Face to
     Face* programme 25 September 2005, commenting on the strategy of various political
     parties in courting the Asian vote. Again, what appears in the Chinese language media
     is considerably later than the reports in the young Asians' blogs and the English media.
17   TV One (2005) *Breakfast*, 24 August.
18   *Asian Voice* (2005) 29 September, 1, 3.

Bartley, A. (2003) '"New" New Zealanders, or Harbingers of a New Transnationalism? 1.5
     Generation Asian Migrant Adolescents in New Zealand', Albany, Auckland, Massey
     University.
Beal, T. (2001) 'Taiwanese Business Migration to Australia and New Zealand', in M. Ip (ed),
     Re-examining Chinese Transnationalism in Australia-New Zealand, Canberra, CSCSD,
     Australian National University, 25–44.
Booth, P. (1993) 'Inv-Asian', Auckland, Suburban Newspapers.
Brawley, S. (1993) 'No "White Policy" in New Zealand: Fact and fiction in New Zealand's
     immigration record, 1946–1978', *New Zealand Journal of History*, 27, 1, 16–36.
Burke, K. (1986) *Review of Immigration Policy August 1986*, Wellington, Government
     Printer.
Friesen, W. & M. Ip (1997) 'New Chinese New Zealanders: Profile of a transnational com-
     munity in Auckland', *Aotearoa/New Zealand Migration Research Network Research
     Papers*, No. 3, 3–19.
Henderson, A. (2003) 'Untapped Talents: The Employment & Settlement Experiences of
     Skilled Chinese in New Zealand', in M. Ip (ed.), *Unfolding History, Evolving Identity*,
     Auckland, Auckland University Press, 141–64.
Ho, E. (2003) *Mental Health Issues for Asians in New Zealand*, Wellington, Mental Health
     Commission.
Ho, E., J. Lidgard, R. Bedford and P. Spoonley (1997) 'East Asian Migrants in New Zealand:
     Adaptation and Employment', A. D. Trlin and P. Spoonley (eds), *New Zealand and
     International Migration: A Digest and Bibliography*, No. 3, Palmerston North, Massey
     University, 42–59.
Hunt, G. (1996) 'Asia takes note of rising NZ xenophobia', *National Business Review*,
     Auckland, 17 May.

Ip, M. (1990) *Home Away From Home: life stories of Chinese women in New Zealand*, Auckland, New Women's Press.

Ip, M. (1995) 'Chinese New Zealanders: old settlers and new immigrants', in S. W. Greif (ed.), *Immigration and National Identity in New Zealand: One People, Two Peoples, Many Peoples?*, Palmerston North, Dunmore, 161–99.

Ip, M. (1996) *Dragons on the Long White Cloud: the Making of Chinese New Zealanders*, Auckland, Tandem Press.

Ip, M. (2003) 'Seeking the Last Utopia: the Taiwanese in New Zealand', in M. Ip (ed.), *Unfolding History, Evolving Identity*, Auckland, Auckland University Press, 185–210.

Ip, M. (2005) *Aliens at My Table: Asians as New Zealanders See Them*, Auckland, Penguin.

Jones, L. (1993) 'Chinese quiz for politicians', *New Zealand Herald*, Auckland.

Leckie, J. (1985) 'In Defence of Race and Empire: The White New Zealand League at Pukekohe', *New Zealand Journal of History*, 19, 2, 103–29.

Leckie, J. (1995) 'South Asians: Old and New Migrations', in S. W. Greif (ed.), *Immigration and National Identity in New Zealand: One People, Two Peoples, Many Peoples?*, Palmerston North, Dunmore, 133–60.

Ligard, J. M., R. D. Bedford and J. E. Goodwin (1998) *International Migration from Northeast Asia and Population Change in New Zealand*, Hamilton, Population Studies Centre, University of Waikato.

Mok, T. M. (2004) 'Race You There', *Landfall*, 208, 18–26.

Murphy, N. (1991) 'Chee Kung Tong: The Hung League in New Zealand', K. Wong, Wellington, Alexander Turnbull Library.

Murphy, N. (1994) *The Poll-Tax in New Zealand: A Research Paper*, New Zealand Chinese Association.

Murphy, N. R. (1997) *A Guide to Laws and Policies Relating to the Chinese in New Zealand, 1871–1996*, Wellington, New Zealand Chinese Association Inc.

Ng, K. (2005) 'Asian Vote', *New Zealand Listener*, Aug. 20–26.

Pang, D. (2003) 'Education, Politics and Chinese New Zealander Identities: The case of the 1995 Epsom Normal Primary School's "Residency Clause and English Test"', in M. Ip (ed.), *Unfolding History, Evolving Identity*, Auckland, Auckland University Press, 236–57.

Park, Shee-Jeong (2004) 'A Study on Political Participation of Asian New Zealanders'. Background paper on a survey as part of a PhD thesis, Department of Political Studies, University of Auckland.

Price, C. (1974) *The Great White Walls are Built: Restrictive Immigration to North America and Australasia*, Canberra, Australian National University Press.

Thomson, B. (1993) *Ethnic Groups in New Zealand: A Statistical Profile*, Wellington, Department of Internal Affairs.

Thomson, B. (1999) *Ethnic Diversity in New Zealand: A Statistical Profile*, Wellington, Department of Internal Affairs.

Wong, G. (2003) 'Is Saying Sorry Enough?', in M. Ip (ed.), *Unfolding History, Evolving Identity*, Auckland, Auckland University Press, 258–79.

Yee, B. (2002) 'Enhancing Security: A Grounded Theory of Chinese Survival in New Zealand', *Education*, Christchurch, 250.

Yee, B. (2003) 'Coping with Insecurity: Everyday Experiences of Chinese New Zealanders', in M. Ip (ed.), *Unfolding History, Evolving Identity*, Auckland, Auckland University Press, 215–35.

Young, S. (2003) 'The background and recent developments in the political culture of Chinese New Zealanders', Stout Research Centre for New Zealand Studies, Victoria University of Wellington, available at: www.stevenyoung.co.nz/chinesevoice/index.htm

Zhang, Y. and M. Ip (1996) *The Chinese Community and New Zealand Politics*, Dept. of Political Studies and Asian Languages & Literatures, University of Auckland.

TEN

The Media
and Leadership

Margie Comrie

Political leaders are created, maintained and brought down by the media. They are as dependent on the 'oxygen of publicity' as media-savvy former British prime minister Margaret Thatcher once claimed terrorists to be. Our politicians not only need the news media to transmit messages, they need media endorsement. Leaders validate their hold on power when the public watchdogs of the media accept their right to lead.

In their turn the media depend on politicians in a symbiotic, but tense, relationship. Political news feeds the daily appetite of the news production machine; and it has automatic primacy as 'important' news. In their role of political messengers, analysts and investigators, the media may claim privileges and respect beyond those commanded by mere entertainers. Journalists take their watchdog role seriously; their news values drive them to be constantly vigilant for political change, conflict and subterfuge. The resulting clash of agendas means both parties constantly test and exploit the other's weaknesses in the name of democracy. In New Zealand, this encounter centres on parliament, with its 120 MPs supported by about 28 parliamentary press secretaries on one side; and around 45 press gallery journalists backed by the power of two dozen media organisations on the other.

McGregor talks of 'news media politics', saying (1996, 8), 'it is impossible to divorce politics from the news media and the news media from politics'. The mixture is volatile and a series of changes in New Zealand has influenced the relationship between political leaders and the media, presenting challenges for both. Transformations in the style and substance of news reporting, the advent of MMP and a growth of professional communication support for politicians have all shaped current news media politics in New Zealand.

This chapter examines this tension between media elites (including managers, editors and high-profile journalists) and political leaders in the light of the political leadership framework discussed in chapter 1. First it tackles the question of context, describing New Zealand's dynamic media environment and the impact it has on political leadership. It looks at how MMP has affected the relationship between political leaders and the media. The chapter then explores the role of political communicators and press secretaries in the processes of political leadership and investigates what leadership involves, identifying the main qualities and strategies exemplified by recent political leaders in dealings with the media. Finally, how significant are followers to a leader's success? This section explores examples of the electorate's response to the interplay between leaders and the media, including some comment on the role of polls.

The Importance of Context – the Media Environment

New Zealand's small population and its competitive, generally centralised media system means that it is comparatively easy to gain near-saturation national coverage. The corresponding downside is that issues can rapidly escalate into media crises. As in most Western countries, our politicians need to perform well on television, with its incomparable reach. New Zealanders are keen watchers of primetime news, with state-owned TVNZ's *One News* pulling in an astounding half to two-thirds of all potential viewers. TVNZ's high-rating nightly current affairs programme has long been influential in making and marring political images. In 2005 two competitors sprang up in the 7 p.m. time slot: TV3 chose John Campbell, a news presenter with a name for putting prime ministers in the hot seat, to front its show; while Australian-owned Prime poached celebrity journalist Paul Holmes from TVNZ. Holmes could not pull in the viewers on Prime and the nightly show was canned in August. Meanwhile *Campbell Live* began eating into TVNZ's audience numbers and, in the scramble for ratings, both channels put the heat on their politician interviewees.

On radio, political performance arguably matters most on publicly owned National Radio's *Morning Report*, with its audience of elites and newsmakers, and on Newstalk ZB's nationwide breakfast show. Political leaders since Mike Moore have also exploited opportunities offered by talkback radio. This populist pulpit is ideal for ACT's Rodney Hide, while politicians John Banks and Michael Laws have found that talkback can keep their profiles high while they are not in office.

Although there is no daily national paper, the four metropolitan dailies have gallery reporters. Provincial papers, served by New Zealand Press Association gallery journalists, also pay attention to national politics and Fairfax in particular encourages sharing of special reports and political commentary among its stable of newspapers.

Many politicians recognise the importance of non-mainstream media. The Maori television service (MTV), TVNZ's long-running *Te Karere*, 21 iwi radio stations and Auckland's ethnic radio stations and newspapers provide a welter of opportunities for leaders to raise their profiles with niche audiences. Helen Clark, for instance, whose weekly schedule includes five calls or appearances on mainstream media before 9.15 each Monday morning, also has a regular date on Radio Tarana. Don Brash is interviewed on Auckland student radio station bfm.

New Zealand's deregulated media market reflects the global picture of growing ownership concentration, competition and drive for profits. Changes in television news have driven changes in other media. Under the stimulus of deregulation and its inherent commercialism TVNZ's network news in the late 1980s became a pacey, visually driven programme where tabloid subjects of crime, accidents, disasters and human interest began to eclipse political and economic coverage. A new style emerged, favouring emotionalism, filmic values, editorialising and sensational headlines (Atkinson 2004; Edwards 1996). The *One Network News* style was mirrored on the new private channel, TV3. In the 1990s, newspapers followed suit with more colour, graphics and white space, and larger pictures and headlines. The televisual approach influenced style and subject matter. Populism sells news and, as former *Dominion* editor Richard Long argues, tabloid-style front-page coverage is important because over half a newspaper's sales can be casual (Luxton 2003, 79).

In this environment politicians receive an increasingly rough ride from the media. Because political issues are rarely visual, emotive, conflictual or intense (Bale 2003, 218–19), political journalists have a problem. According to a former gallery journalist Oliver Riddell (2002, 203), 'News editors want political news that competes with wars, murders, rapes, traffic accidents, corruption, sporting triumphs and disasters, and other news items that are a long way from the traditional reports of what happened and who said what in Parliament.' So, reporters meet demand by accentuating conflict, adding colourful adjectives and becoming more opinionated and aggressive. Personality coverage has increased and political stories emphasise strategy over issues. Political stories are dominated by a 'game frame' of winners, losers and tactics. All this makes it harder for politicians to gain continued positive coverage, increasing the probability that they will come under attack and exaggerating any shift in their fortunes.

Gallery reporters also hunt as a pack. 'If everyone but one reporter has a story, then his or her news editor will want to know why. Reporters therefore have no option but to "beat up" or sensationalise each other's stories' (Riddell 2002, 204). As a result, any minor misdemeanours by the politicians tend to hog the headlines, for instance, Helen Clark's high-speed ride to a rugby test in 2004. Riddell adds that politicians are often in no position to refute sensationalism 'because the real story may also cast them in an unfavourable light'. Even if the story is a fabrication and the politician able to expose it as such, he says, the politician may hesitate because 'reporters and news media do not readily forgive having been shown up' (Riddell 2002, 204).

A further pressure on political leaders is the blurring of the boundaries between the public and private spheres, especially as a result of the enormous growth of celebrity gossip coverage. Media empires, which often own film studios and professional sports teams, stand to gain from any attempt to heighten public interest in their products and players. The result is an interdependent industry of publicity agents, paparazzi and gossip columnists serviced by women's magazines, reality shows and tabloid news. In this environment a politician becomes just another celebrity and has to cope with an often intrusive and judgemental interest in their private life and personal tastes.

The arrival of women as political leaders in New Zealand probably accelerated this attention on the private sphere. When Jenny Shipley and

Helen Clark came to power the media's gaze focused on their partners. Who, for example, was the man behind the woman? TV One's 1999 documentary on the leaders of the two major parties lingered in the kitchen, as well as highlighting the families and investigating the wardrobes of Shipley and Clark. Politicians' partners, past and present, are now being treated as fair game not only by the media but also by their political opponents, as an unedifying spat between Clark and Brash in mid-2004 showed: Brash, in a refusal to speak in Christchurch's Anglican Cathedral, cited Clark's 'indifference to the state of marriage'. In the ensuing publicity, an old affair of Brash's was aired and his former wife sought for comment.

Leaders try to manage this celebrity-style coverage, by agreeing to articles in women's magazines and cooperating in increasingly personalised documentaries, like TVNZ's *Hurricane Brash* documentary on 12 April 2004, which arguably exposed the National leader to derision. Paul Holmes's 2005 pre-election programme *At Home with Clark and Brash* tested the composure of both leaders as he probed beyond the kitchen into the bedroom. In particular, Clark's 'ambiguous marriage' came in for questioning. Among the questions asked of Clark's husband were: 'You found Helen sexy?' and 'Are you very physical with each other?' The media's misuse of the term 'public interest' to justify their actions, by substituting what is 'of interest to the public' for what was originally 'in the public interest', makes it hard for politicians to draw the line about where probing personal questions become an invasion of privacy. This is, after all, an environment in which the Minister of Health came under heavy pressure from reporters to reveal the results of a routine breast scan.

Public broadcasting, with fewer commercial constraints, is one place where political issues could take precedence over political personalities. But the turf of public broadcasting is the site of a different struggle between political leadership and media leadership. State-owned broadcasters are particularly vulnerable to political interference. Charters, like those for Radio New Zealand and TVNZ, are meant to distance broadcasters from direct interference. The situation remains parlous, however, because the government controls the purse strings. Political control tactics include public castigation, board appointments, funding decisions and restructuring.

The Labour Party's market-oriented broadcasting deregulation of 1989 is largely responsible for current tensions between TVNZ and the government. As a result of restructuring, TVNZ became a successful profit-seeking state-owned enterprise competing with private companies for licence fee money. TVNZ's journalists, operating under commercial formats, were notably less respectful to politicians. However, the state-owned broadcaster returned substantial dividends to the government throughout the 1990s and threatened sell-offs did not take place. If National's ultimate weapon was the potential sale of TVNZ, the Labour Party favoured restructuring to restore a public service approach. Ending the 'culture of extravagance' at TVNZ – including such costly blunders as poaching TV3 news reader John Hawkesby, only to fire him weeks later as *One News* ratings plummeted – was one of Helen Clark's opposition pledges. Her concerns about shallow, ratings-grabbing news and current affairs helped drive the restructuring of TVNZ as a Crown-owned company operating under a public service charter (Ralston 2001). Soon after the 1999 election, Clark used further revelations about the Hawkesby payoff to rid TVNZ of its National-Party-appointed board chairperson Roseanne Meo. In December 2004, Clark led the charge against TVNZ's board for allowing news presenter Judy Bailey to negotiate an $800,000 salary. Arguably Bailey's popularity never recovered from the attack and she was dropped from *One News* ten months later. Such clashes underline the contradiction whereby TVNZ is expected to deliver potentially low-rating charter programming while being funded almost entirely by advertising. The structure fuels commercial formats, celebrity salaries and political outrage, with TVNZ's managers regularly on the mat for everything from spending on wine to using public money to pay for top-rating *NZ Idol*.

However, TVNZ is not the only channel to come under pressure from political leaders. In a significant High Court decision in August 2005, Justice Ron Young ordered TV3 to include two political leaders in its election debate line-up. To fit its leaders' debate into the schedule TV3 had announced only six parties would be represented. United Future's Peter Dunne and Progressive's Jim Anderton, who were to be excluded on the basis of a TV3 political poll, then went to court. Justice Young ordered TV3 to include Dunne and Anderton, saying that otherwise they could suffer significant irretrievable electoral damage that could affect the make-up of the next parliament. He added, 'This court is anxious to protect what I see as the fundamental right of citizens in a democracy to be as well-informed as possible before exercising their right to vote and to ensure the electoral outcome is, as far is as possible, not subject to the arbitrary provision of information.' Interestingly for TV3, which has always rejoiced in its separation from constraints of public television, Justice Young said it was a comparatively rare case 'where a private company is performing a public function with such important public consequences that it should be susceptible to judicial review' ('TV3 to fight court debate ruling').

Given the tensions between political leaders and the media, it is perhaps surprising politicians pay so little attention to the internet. ACNeilsen (2002) estimate three quarters of New Zealanders over ten years old have online access. The internet has been hailed as a place where parties with few resources can have an equal presence, and where citizens can form closer links with leaders. Party and individual MPs' websites are becoming increasingly sophisticated and the internet is used to send newsletters and news releases to targeted groups and individuals. However, Barker's survey of 2002 election candidates (2004, 89) found the internet was seen as an additional way to present the party message, but websites were not used as a core campaign tool. Conventional wisdom is that those who access political information on the internet are already interested in politics, whereas the mass media can raise awareness and reach the less committed.

Political leaders, therefore, continue to concentrate on traditional media where they find it harder to keep the focus on issues and policies and are more likely to find themselves under attack. However, paradoxically, mass media's demand for pictures and short 'sound bites' also makes it easier to create and exploit public relations opportunities.

The Media's Changing Role under MMP

The party vote under MMP tends to focus attention on party leaders at the expense of local politicians. This focus means leaders need to pay more attention to building and maintaining a media image. Further, under MMP, more leaders and parties are scrabbling for the media lime-light, intensifying competition for news space. O'Leary (2002, 191) says minor parties hovering around the 5 per cent threshold can be driven 'to what would once be considered desperate lengths to get into the news'. Resulting regular 'mini-scandals' are drummed up by such 'undisputed masters' of the 'time-honoured political art of stirring mud' as ACT's Rodney Hide and New Zealand First's Winston Peters. The pressure on government leaders comes not only from opponents. As elections approach, smaller coalition partners often attack policies in an effort to re-establish their separate identity.

MMP has changed the relationship between the media and politicians. A more complicated political system for the general public to understand, MMP increased the importance of the media in reporting and analysing the political process; this raises the stakes for political leaders to get their media tactics right. Not only are there more parties and viewpoints to cover, constitutional lawyer and former prime minister Sir Geoffrey Palmer argues (2002, 175–7) that complex negotiations between political parties to develop policy and get measures through parliament mean journalists also have 'more to delve into'. His verdict is that reporters now have far more work, which they lack the resources to undertake.

This became very clear when, following the first election under MMP, National's coalition with Winston Peters took the media generally by surprise. Journalists, struggling with the complexities of MMP, were reluctant to grant the National–New Zealand First alliance any legitimacy. Bolger's status as leader grew shaky as strains within the coalition became obvious. Although his deliberate and consultative approach had been rewarded with the National–New Zealand First coalition agreement, this tendency to consult left some journalists with the impression he was not capable of the faster footwork needed under MMP. As Anna Kominik, who joined Bolger's staff from the press gallery in April 1997, observes, 'He would be asking a lot of opinions of a lot of different people. And that was not seen as strong enough.'[1] With MMP, Kominik says, the 'entrails of the political process' are on show and smaller parties use the media to position themselves. Bolger needed to show the media he was acting decisively. Instead, he let conflict simmer on.

MMP also calls for a different kind of leadership. As the media have come to realise, 'strong' leadership of the kind displayed by Sir Robert Muldoon is now less effective. Leaders must be able compromise, to hold disparate coalitions together and to convince media that all is still well if partners fall out. Clark had shown herself able to hold together coalitions and partnerships in her government's first two terms but at the time of writing, the media is alert for signs of stress among the parties she has drawn together to govern for a third term. Media vigilance is more intense because New Zealand First's Winston Peters has taken the role of Minister of Foreign Affairs.

The trick for leaders under MMP is to compromise without seeming like shallow opportunists and to take dissension in your stride without appearing to be lax. All this must be done while convincing the electorate you are still moving towards a clear goal. Mike Munro, Helen Clark's chief press secretary, describes the major challenge of maintaining a balance in the way the prime minister comes across. She has 'to appear the forthright, in-control, in-command leader, at the same time being the compassionate, listening, grassroots democrat'.[2]

Spin and Counter Spin

To help them use the media, political leaders are turning more to professional communicators. News coverage of political leaders reflects their history and their current circumstances as well as their talents and personality. Still, leaders can improve their lot if, aided by an able press secretary, they follow simple rules. There is little mystery and much routine in the work of political press secretaries. Any public relations text outlines the essentials for maintaining good media relations. Those who get good coverage generally fulfil the media's need for clear information and 'quotable quotes'. For example, John Armstrong from the *New Zealand Herald* says (2000, 2) of Helen Clark, '[Her] highly quotable and often acid comments make good copy'. Media trainers emphasise the importance of clients delivering a clear message; of telling the truth and answering media questions while still reiterating the message; and of being themselves (albeit their best selves). Helping media meet deadlines, being available, calling back when requested and not haranguing them about negative stories will pay off. Politicians who treat the media with respect, without becoming doormats, who keep cool under questioning and neither lie nor deliberately mislead, are also likely to get a reasonable run.

With their press secretaries' help, politicians are more systematically exploiting photo opportunities and chances to present positive news stories to build leadership profiles. In a ratchet effect, the sound-bite format and the visual emphasis have increased investment in grooming, media training and organised 'pseudo-events' to present leaders at their best. News media simultaneously lament this tendency and are merciless about personal appearance, clothes sense or verbal slips.

Richard Griffin joined the Prime Minister's Office shortly after Jim Bolger was returned to power in 1993 and said that the 'praetorian guard' of former press secretary Michael Wall and antipathy to the media resulted 'in a sourness and bitterness that reflected on Bolger'.[3] Griffin's openness to the media allowed him to reintroduce the prime minister and 'take him out of the bunker and down to the gallery'. Griffin followed a simple threefold strategy to enhance Bolger's media standing. First he spent a lot of time with gallery journalists. He also worked on Bolger's speeches. Their dry, official tone, Griffin claimed, resulted from the PM's self doubt. Bolger was in fact 'good on his feet' but did not want to be vulnerable. With work, his spontaneity increased, although Griffin believed it was more important to increase the range of issues Bolger spoke on. Thirdly, Griffin concentrated on relationships with editors and radio stations out of the main centres. His communications staff ensured the PM regularly fronted key announcements and events. Referring to the difficult coalition between National and New Zealand First, Anna Kominik described Griffin as the 'glue' between Jim Bolger and Winston Peters. Bolger, she said, relied on his staff to advise him on which interviews to do and when. Griffin says that while Bolger did not want him to be a 'yes man', his relationship with Bolger was stressful. In the lead up to the 1996 campaign, Griffin says, Bolger 'lost faith' in him, bringing back Wall to write his speeches: 'He went back into the "let's snap back and let's portray the media as bastards" mentality, which for eight weeks turned him from a man who could have won the election into a man that just managed to hang in there.'

Poor personal and party ratings pushed Clark into media training in 1996. Press secretary Mike Munro says she recognised the importance of performing well on television and that 'building media relationships was absolutely critical as was playing the media game, getting involved in the issues of the day'. Her media trainer and biographer Brian Edwards (2001, 249) describes her television image as dreadful, 'She allowed herself to be bullied by interviewers, responding to their generally negative questioning with a weak and unnatural smile.' Edwards says his training encouraged her to be 'nothing more than herself'. Clark's improved performance produced positive media comment and paid off during the 1996 campaign's televised leaders' debates.

As well as recognising the importance of media training, political and policy staff have become conscious of issues management: spotting approaching problems and preparing responses or even pre-empting trouble. Mike Munro, who describes himself as the 'bridge' between media and the PM, has a coordinating role 'to watch the PM's back to make sure we are not surprised by announcements and activity in other minister's offices. To make sure that all the government communications activity follows agreed themes and messages.' A weekly plan outlines issues they will respond on and which ministers do what. Coordinated communication helps control the media agenda and conveys an impression of unity and certainty.

Longest-serving gallery member Ian Templeton reports press secretaries using such traditional 'spin' tactics as releasing major stories just in time to meet television deadlines but too late for reporters to seek the opposing view (in Luxton 2003, 81). The *Press*'s Peter Luke (2002) reports, however, that basic tactics like the 'Friday dump', where press secretaries delivered a bundle of papers and reports late on Friday hoping they would be ignored, are declining. Instead, politicians often bypass the press gallery, going straight to journalists in the regional media. Other bypass techniques are regular 'spots' on radio programmes and greater use of the community press and 'new news' providers, like talkback and women's magazines.

Journalists have responded to news manipulation tactics by what Levy (1981) calls 'disdaining the news'. In his previous capacity as a media scholar, politician Steve Maharey once described Bill Ralston, now head of news and current affairs at TVNZ, as the leading exponent of the media's tendency to 'send up or expose what they see as the efforts of politicians to make themselves look good in the eyes of the public' (1992, 96). In the press, the entertaining columns of Jane Clifton are a prime example. This practice brings journalists as commentators to the forefront and on television the resulting 'celebrification' of journalists has become part of marketing the news, where journalist-celebrities are used in network branding (McGregor 2002, 119–21).

What Does Leadership Involve?

The personal attributes of leaders can often be magnified and distorted through the media lens and the resulting leadership image can be hard to shift. The media (not to mention the public) demand a number of, sometimes conflicting, qualities from political leaders. They want vision, honesty, compassion, competence, judgement, decisiveness and experience, all combined with a certain level of attractiveness or people appeal. This is illustrated in the case of Bolger, who was perceived not only as failing to provide certainty, but also as dishonest. Gallery reporter Ian Templeton says: 'He had this tendency to over-egg everything and then it came back to haunt him. He would go beyond what his advisers had suggested often. Over a period the press gallery felt that you had to look deeper than what Bolger had actually said. So the vision of him being in command was eroded almost from the start.'[4]

The media judge whether leaders possess the 'right stuff' and, because few of the complex activities constituting leadership are on show, they, along with the public, often conflate media performance and leadership performance. The media love verbal dexterity, as David Lange proved. They can be merciless over verbal blunders, as Marian Hobbs found in her first stumbling weeks in the broadcasting portfolio when she confused TVNZ's chief executive with the head of the board and became known as 'Booboo, the fifth Teletubby'. But the ability to deliver compelling and inclusive messages is not enough, as the media hunt for cracks in every leader's armour. Any appearance of arrogance – perhaps impatience with media questions – meets with a swift media backlash. Michael Vance, writing in the *Press* (1998, 9), says Bolger retreated from the media because he was not handling exposure well. He described Bolger as 'uninspiring' in news conferences, his good humour and warmth 'transmuted into a shifty tartness'. The resulting coverage ensured the prime minister 'emerged for photo opportunities and for news conferences substantially confined to scripted announcements and with the opportunity for limited questioning only' (Vance 1998, 9).

Bolger was able to attract some positive media coverage later in his tenure, on overseas trips and when delivering a series of social capital speeches from March 1997. This compassionate capitalism – Bolger's attempt to build a visionary leadership position through the 'Millennium Agenda' – was strongly supported by Griffin and had some payoffs. The speeches certainly did not halt speculation about Bolger's pending demise, but were reported and Bolger described as a leader attempting to provide new answers (James 1997, 19). Nonetheless, Kominik described the last months she spent with Bolger as a slippery slope, 'we could only bolster things and try and manage them so it was not quite so quick'.

Through determination, training and experience, current prime minister Helen Clark is now a skilled media performer, although she battled a lacklustre image for years. Press secretary Mike Munro says as a new MP, Clark was serious and aloof from the 'hurly burly of parliament'. Although her style was not 'mediagenic', she came across as a hard-working, competent fourth Labour government minister. It was not until she aspired to leadership that her personality was regarded as an obstacle to success. Clark's gender was a further handicap. McGregor (1996, 181) contends Clark's struggle to gain acceptance as Labour leader was linked to 'media misogyny', noting the 'obsession' with her hairstyle and voice. On 2 December 1993, following the coup in which she toppled Mike Moore, the *Dominion*'s front page featured a photo of Clark and husband Peter Davis captioned 'Leadership Passion'. Clark is leaning back to kiss Davis. The awkward open-mouth kiss, doubtless an inadvertent result of the cameraman begging the couple to 'give us a kiss', was exploited by the paper partly because it reinforced rumours about Clark's marriage. Although the *Dominion* editor described the photo as 'the most suitable shot available', an anonymous *Dominion* staff member had sent Clark another far more flattering picture taken at the same time. Media Women's consequent complaint to the Press Council was upheld. The Press Council said 'the sexual significance identified in the caption introduced elements of ridicule and bad taste that reflected . . . a departure from accepted journalistic standards' (Press Council rules 1994, 10). The photo was a harsh early lesson for Clark that, in a hostile environment, cooperatively 'mugging' for the camera can be a politician's undoing. It is nonetheless a delicate balancing act. Avoiding the camera or attempting overt control of your public image is not only unacceptable in a democratic leader but also encourages a paparazzi-style 'ambush' approach.

Journalists search for any hint of division in party or coalition, partly because divisive scraps make good copy but also because dissent implies uncertainty about policy direction with resulting implications for the country. When conflict erupts, leaders need to act decisively and effectively, but at the same time the media punishes apparent ruthlessness, especially to loyal, long-serving or popular MPs. Clark, so far, appears to have the balance right. While she has been criticised for publicly castigating and discarding a near record number of ministers, John Armstrong of the *New Zealand Herald* (2000, 2) feels her no-nonsense approach works well with the media: 'Unlike Mr Bolger she will not let the media make endless sport of her ministers' embarrassments. She will defend colleagues, but not deny the obvious. The strategy is to own up to failings, deliver one of those milk-curdling glares of disapproval and move on. The story dies.' Clark also managed to ride the storm surrounding Maori MP John Tamihere's diatribe in April 2005, when he insulted his colleagues and made misogynist and homophobic comments. She used a judicious mixture of distancing, scorn and reprimand, followed by a carefully limited reconciliation. In contrast, National's Don Brash, a couple of months earlier, was criticised for dumping loyalist Katherine Rich as welfare spokesperson. Luke (2005, 7), for instance, echoed speculation about Brash being unable to work with women and questioned Brash's 'people-management processes' adapting Oscar Wilde's line: 'losing one spokesperson might be a misfortune, but the loss of a second smacks of carelessness'.

Political leaders are often astute enough to exploit opportunities. Jim Bolger, for example, recognised the rewards to be gained from travelling the country meeting local journalists and editors. On his 'heartland tours', the brainchild of press secretary Michael Wall, Bolger received better provincial press coverage because of direct informal contact with local reporters, who often accompanied him. After failing to form a coalition government, Helen Clark, spent 1996–99 actively campaigning, touring the regions and grabbing media opportunities. Kominik said the Labour communication team's discipline had 'kicked in' by late 1997 and has remained constant since. Munro says: 'We put a lot of work into building media relationships, courting the top political journalists and making sure that Helen was at the forefront of all our major issues, major policy releases. When we had a bit of a scandal, a bit of trouble to cause in Parliament, we made sure that Helen was leading the charge.' To build and keep her positive profile 'meant Helen being quite Stalinist really in the way she ran the caucus and the media strategy'. By the time the 1999 election campaign officially opened Clark's focus on core issues and Labour's 'vision', combined with two years' work building a continued and solid media presence, paid off. After Labour's success in 1999, journalists hailed the return of the Monday post-cabinet press conference. Armstrong says,

'Jenny Shipley preferred "stand-ups", where journalists huddle around the leader. These brief affairs can be wound up quickly before the questioning gets difficult. Allowing sit-down, all-around-the-paddock press conferences is a measure of Helen Clark's self-confidence' (2000, 2). Helen Clark also 'invites Gallery journalists to be only a cellphone away' to the extent that O'Leary talks (2002, 192) of Clark's 'super-accessibility'. She is often home on Sunday afternoons specifically to take journalists calls. Armstrong (2002, 2) comments: 'She has skilfully filled the news vacuum on Sundays, carrying issues through to her regular Monday-morning breakfast slot on Newstalk ZB before raising fresh ones at that afternoon's post-cabinet press conference. It is all consolidated by frequent appearances on National Radio's flagship *Morning Report*.'

The Significance of Followers

Sustained media coverage of leaders is vital in building a following and political polls add complexity to the dynamic interaction between political leaders and their followers. Because news stories of winners, losers and promising outsiders can influence later results, polling experts worry that media coverage is often inaccurate, missing out crucial factors like the response rate or the number of undecided voters. While parties naturally play down the role of their focus groups and polls, they provide valuable guidance, particularly in unknown territory. The Labour Government researched Maori electorates when Turiana Turia left to set up the Maori Party; current National Party's tactics are also clearly poll-driven.

Don Brash's rise in the first half of 2004, following reportage of his Orewa speech, shows polls and media interacting to build a leader. Previous speeches attacking the Treaty by predecessor Bill English had been dismissed by the media as desperate flip-flops. 'Goodbye Mr Blancmange', Audrey Young (2003, 1) wrote. Colin Espiner linked English's tactics to gaining back votes lost to New Zealand First (2003, 3). Brash had already, in the first weeks of his leadership, risen to a respectable 15 per cent leadership rating (Watkins 2003). Ian Templeton cites 15 years as a highly visible Reserve Bank governor as outweighing his lack of charisma and poor performance in parliament. With late January 'slow news' timing and press secretary, former *Dominion* editor Richard Long seeding the idea of a landmark speech, the media gave saturation coverage to the new leader's speech. Within days the polls showed a big gain for National, forcing journalists to reassess Brash. Media consensus was that he had tapped into previously invisible public discontent abut Maori 'privileges'. Clifton concluded: 'We are delighted to see our too-popular-for-its-own-good government given a bit of a rev finally' (2004a, 14). The speech, the polls and the coverage resulted in an upward spiral. But ultimately more substance was demanded. In early July, Brash, still going for the territory claimed by New Zealand First, delivered another highly publicised, tough law-and-order speech to a Sensible Sentencing Trust rally. However, it failed to create a change in the polls and soon faded from the media, a lesson that a winning tactic cannot necessarily be repeated.

Though Helen Clark is widely acknowledged as a skilled 'reader' of poll findings, tactical response to polls is tricky. Following National's rise in the polls, Labour tried to present a response on a number of issues as 'listening to the people'. The media generally decried this as a U-turn; Clifton (2004b, 14) describing it as 'almost obscenely painful to watch'. Even so, later poll results suggest the Labour backdown was effective.

Attention to polls and 'preferred leader' results becomes intense during election campaigns and never more so in the 'too close to call' election of 2005. The narrow see-sawing majority was perhaps the campaign's major media focus. A further difficulty in reading polls correctly is that most are sponsored by media organisations that naturally give their own poll results prominence and downplay results from other polls. Both major parties' policy announcements were almost unashamedly guided by the polls during the campaign. For instance, when it became clear people had expected some form of tax relief in the budget and that National was gaining ground with tax cut promises, Labour revealed a mix of pre-planned and reactive election sweeteners. At such times the media becomes an influential conduit of information between political leaders and their followers.

The televised leaders' debates also generate media commentary that can affect electoral outcomes. Because the debates make news, they influence far more people than actually watch. 'If debates do have an impact on voting,' concludes political scientist Stephen Church (2004, 171), 'then the way the media shape perceptions of who won and who lost must also play a part.' The 'worm', simultaneously graphing response from an audience of undecided voters, has since 1996 further increased the impact of debates. Johnston (1998) called the *Decision '96* debate on TV One the election campaign's defining moment. His research showed viewers clearly judged Bolger the loser and Clark the winner; support for Labour and Clark rose markedly after the debate. From the outset Clark had appeared confident and warm, while Bolger was clearly rattled by the studio audience. A crucial, much-replayed moment was Bolger's response to a question from 'Tony', whose mother had died following the cancellation of her long-awaited heart operation. Bolger began by expressing sympathy, then said, 'I'd have to say that death is always associated with health care and though others . . .' (Laughter and jeers from the audience). 'No! Just let me give you a headline: "52 die on surgery waiting list". That was when Helen was Minister, I'm quoting from that . . .' Clark, however, tackled the waiting-list problem confidently, focusing on Tony. Unfazed by a noisy audience, she attacked the current system: 'We must pay for nurses and surgeons . . . so that no other person's mother, like Tony's mother, dies while she is waiting for that operation.' She concluded with a classic three-part rhetorical flourish – 'I believe we can do that. We can bring the waiting times down. We can save people's lives.'

The 'worm' made its debut in the following analysis programme and dominated media coverage for the rest of the campaign. Particularly potent were repeated images of the worm peaking as Clark told Alliance leader Jim Anderton she would be talking with him after the election and plunging when Bolger said 'death is always associated with health care' (Roper 1999, 8). Two elections later, 'worm effect' recurred when, on 15 July 2002, the worm soared as Peter Dunne of United Future called for 'commonsense' in politics. Vowles (2004a, 37) sees a case to be made that the debate significantly affected election results.

Another single media performance arguably influencing voting patterns was Helen Clark's 'Corngate' interview in 2002. The day before the launch of Nicky Hager's book, *Seeds of Discontent*, TV3 newsreader John Campbell interviewed Clark for a special programme to be played the following evening. The book describes a 'cover-up' of inadvertent importing, planting and harvesting of GM-contaminated maize and the later loosening of strict regulations. Campbell had a pre-launch copy of the book; Clark had no idea about the book or its contents. Clark began confidently but, faced with detailed accusatory questioning about memos and reports, became clearly angry. Next evening, *3 News* featured the furore caused by the book and previewed the Campbell interview, describing Clark's 'controlled fury' about 'attacks on her honesty'. Included were shots of her walking out of a previous ABC *Foreign Correspondent* 'Paintergate' item about her signing a sold-for-charity work actually painted by a professional artist. Before playing the interview excerpts, Campbell stated several times that Clark knew about the release and had covered up and lied about it. In the interview itself, Clark appeared bad tempered and arrogant. The original TV3 audience interview was not large – more people were watching Clark having an easier time on TVNZ's *Holmes*. However, media reports, Clark's 'ambush' claim, a complaint to the Broadcasting Standards Authority and regular replays of its key moments ensured Campbell's interview lived on.

Political scientist Tim Bale (2004, 224–5) dismisses the interview as commercial news-presenter celebrity 'sell' and Campbell as 'a man on a mission' who 'simply didn't know when to stop'. However, the media saw the interview as journalistic toughness in the face of political machination. As Jane Clifton wrote in her 13 July *Dominion Post* review: 'A politician caught without a spin is TV gold – and not half bad for democracy either . . . . Faced with John Campbell in full, righteous gush, her only possible lifeboat was a touch of humility . . . . But no. We got choleric references to "ambush" and "unethical journalism".' While Clark's initial response was unlikely to be a deliberate tactic, the interview and its conduct became the major focus of the Corngate story. The media framing of the interview certainly tarnished Clark's leadership image and Corngate, with its resulting high-profile sniping between the Greens and Labour, damaged both parties. Amid the furore, the original issues of genetic modification and biosecurity were largely forgotten. Media attack and political reaction had become the central news story.

The 2005 campaign may have seen the death of the worm, as both television channels toned down the format of debates. The new tone of civility from Campbell in TV3 debates could possibly be a 'chilling effect' from the High Court decision referred to earlier. The worm did appear in TV3's 11 August debate, along with all eight minor party leaders, but media reports were dominated by the court decision. TVNZ's first debate, between Clark and Brash, made headlines because of the noisy studio audience, particularly hostile to Clark, who had to shout to make herself heard. Clark was also judged to be more 'aggressive' and Brash initiated a national debate, but probably did not affect the electoral outcome, when, in response to questioning about his low-key performance, he replied that it 'was not entirely appropriate for a man to aggressively attack a woman' (Espiner 2005). However, criticism of the strident audience had its effect on TVNZ, and host Mark Sainsbury kept the audience almost too strictly in line in later debates. TV3's eve-of-election *Campbell Live* debate between Clark and Brash made much of the fact there was 'no studio audience . . . no worm'. This new restraint meant television audiences heard more from all the leaders about themselves and their policies, but the lower key debates lacked the feisty appeal that had sparked newspaper headlines in previous elections and the effect on voters remains unclear.

Conclusion

The contemporary environment is a challenging one for political leaders as increasing media competition fuels personalised, sensational, infotainment political news. MMP has forced politicians to become more responsive to the public, other parties and the media. The new political system results in a greater focus on leaders who are fighting with a growing number of political parties for positive media attention. Leaders are more likely to come under fire as their opponents and journalists aim to expose weaknesses and whip up scandals to catch the public interest.

Under this pressure, political parties and their leaders are resorting to increasingly sophisticated and disciplined media planning and strategising in an attempt to ensure regular positive coverage. Parties conduct their own polling to help them interpret the public mood and to guide strategy. In their turn journalists try to wrest back the media agenda by interpreting politicians as overwhelmingly calculating and self-serving. This tendency to media commentary that 'sends up' political motives and parliament has spread to such an extent that journalists are being blamed for undermining trust in democracy and contributing to declining voter turnout.

While a tug of war between media and politicians should be a healthy indication of democracy at work, danger lies in either side gaining the upper hand for too long. The media must guard against dancing to the tune of political leaders armed with populist appeals and clever publicity tactics. The answer, though, does not lie in staged gladiatorial contests, mocking analysis and 'attack journalism'. Atkinson (2004, 146) characterised television's treatment of party leaders in the lead up to the 2002 election as 'recklessly indifferent to public service canons of fairness, impartiality and sobriety'. Such tactics only harden the resolve of political leaders to influence the media through spin or to by-pass traditional news media. Those concerned with the problem in the United States developed 'public journalism', an issues-based, problem-solving approach that some New Zealand papers briefly experimented with in the 1990s. A stronger public service ethos in broadcasting is also suggested as a counterweight to tabloidism. Since the implementation of the charter in March 2003 TVNZ has made some adjustments to news and current affairs programming and the changed tone of the 2005 election debates may reflect this. But it could well prove an anomaly. With TVNZ still dependent on the advertising dollar and locked into a news and current affairs ratings battle with TV3, real public service programming looks unlikely.

However, if media are to maintain credibility and relevance in the political process they need to bring the public as citizens back into the picture and provide them with the quality information needed to choose their leaders and policies.

1 Personal interview with Anna Kominik, press secretary for Jim Bolger and Jenny Shipley, April 1997 to November 1998, 30 June 2004.
2 Personal interview with Mike Munro, chief press secretary for Helen Clark, 31 August 2004.
3 Personal interview with Richard Griffin, former chief press secretary for Jim Bolger, 20 August 2004.
4 Personal interview with Ian Templeton, member of the press gallery since 1957, 16 September 2004.

ACNeilsen (2002) *Internet access over time*, retrieved 30 March 2004 from: http://www.acnielsen.co.nz/MRI_pages.asp? MRIID=11#access%20to%20internet%20-%20any%20location
Armstrong, J. (2000) 'Hundred-day honeymoon still magic', *New Zealand Herald*, 18 March, A2.
Atkinson, J. (2004) 'Television', in J. Hayward and C. Rudd (eds), *Political Communications in New Zealand*, Auckland, Pearson Education, 137–58.
Bale, T. (2003) 'News, Newszak, New Zealand: The Role, Performance and Impact of Television in the General Election of 2002', in J. Boston, S. Church, S. Levine, E. McLeay

and N. S. Roberts (eds), *New Zealand Votes: The General Election of 2002*, Wellington, Victoria University Press, 217–34.

Barker, L. (2004) 'Party Websites', in J. Hayward and C. Rudd (eds), *Political Communications in New Zealand*, Auckland, Pearson Education, 74–91.

Clifton, J. (2002) 'Creep's Ambush', *Dominion Post*, 13 July, B11.

Clifton, J. (2004a) 'A Good Lashing', *New Zealand Listener*, 14 February, 14–15

Clifton, J. (2004b) 'Rebirth', *New Zealand Listener*, 21 February, 14–15.

Church, S. (2004) 'Televised leaders' debates', in J. Hayward and C. Rudd (eds), *Political Communications in New Zealand*, Auckland, Pearson Education, 158–82.

Edwards, B. (2001) *Helen: Portrait of a Prime Minister*, Auckland, Exisle Publishing.

Edwards, B. (1996) 'The "Cootchie Coo" News', in M. Comrie & J. McGregor (eds), *Whose News?*, Palmerston North, Dunmore, 15–25.

Espiner, C. (2003) 'English attacks role of Treaty', *Press*, 23 January, 3.

Espiner, C. (2005) 'Clark scorns Brash's claim to have "gone easy" on her', *Press*, 24 August, 1.

Harris, S. (2000) 'Following the Leaders', in J. Boston, S. Church, S. Levine, E. McLeay and N. S. Roberts (eds), *Left Turn: The New Zealand General Election of 1999*, Wellington, Victoria University Press, 77–88.

James, C. (1997) 'Bolgering with good ideas, the Nats look to 1999', *National Business Review*, 9 May, 19.

Levy, M. R. (1981) 'Disdaining the News', *Journal of Communication* 31/3.

Luke, P. (2002) 'Spin doctors more subtle', *Press*, 28 September, 10.

Luke, P. (2005) 'National disaster?', *Press*, 5 February, 7.

Luxton, J. (2003) *What Makes Political News*, research report, Department of Communication and Journalism, Massey University, Palmerston North.

Maharey, S. (1996) 'Politicians, the News Media and Democracy', in M. Comrie & J. McGregor (eds), *Whose News?*, Palmerston North, Dunmore, 90–100.

McGregor, J. (1996) 'Gender Politics and the News: The Search for a Beehive Bimbo-Boadicea', in J. McGregor (ed.), *Dangerous Democracy?: News Media Politics in New Zealand*, Palmerston North, Dunmore, 181–96.

McGregor, J. (2002) 'Terrorism, War, Lions and Sex Symbols: Restating News Values', in J. McGregor and M. Comrie (eds), *What's News?: Reclaiming Journalism in New Zealand*, Palmerston North, Dunmore, 111–25.

O'Leary, E. (2002) 'Political Spin', in J. McGregor and M. Comrie (eds), *What's News?: Reclaiming Journalism in New Zealand*, Palmerston North, Dunmore, 186–98.

Palmer, G. (2002) 'MMP and Journalism', in J. McGregor and M. Comrie (eds), *What's News?: Reclaiming Journalism in New Zealand*, Palmerston North, Dunmore, 175–85.

'Press Council rules on front-page Clark photo' (1994) *Dominion*, 5 March, 10.

Ralston, B. (2001) 'Prime time', *Metro*, August, 62–8.

Riddell, O. (2002) 'A Gallery of Rogues', in J. McGregor and M. Comrie (eds), *What's News?: Reclaiming Journalism in New Zealand*, Palmerston North, Dunmore, 199–209.

Roper, J. (1999) 'The turn of the worm: The framing of press and television coverage of televised election debates in New Zealand', *Australian Journal of Communication*, 26 (1), 1–20.

'TV3 to fight court ruling' (2005) *New Zealand Herald*, downloaded on 21 October 2005 from: http://io.knowledge-basket.co.nz/iodnews/

Vance, M. (1998) 'Unclogging the capillaries of our democracy', *Press*, 14 March, A9.

Vowles, J. (2004a) 'Estimating change during the campaign', in J. Vowles, P. Aimer, S. Banduccci, J. Karp and R. Miller (eds), *Voters' Veto: The 2002 Election in New Zealand and the Consolidation of Minority Government*, Auckland, Auckland University Press, 33–47.

Vowles, J. (2004b) Jack Vowles on the Polls, an interview with Russell Brown for Mediawatch, accessed on 30 August 2004 from: www.mediawatch.co.nz

Watkins, T. (2003) 'National popularity better with Brash', *Press*, 10 November, A3.

Young, A. (2003) 'Political Review: Ready to tread on some toes', *New Zealand Herald*, 23 January.

Leadership in Legal and Economic Concerns

ELEVEN

Resolving the Foreshore and Seabed Dispute

Matthew Palmer

The question of who has what rights to the foreshore and seabed in New Zealand is a defining issue of national identity at the beginning of the twenty-first century. The way in which we answer it tells us about the maturity of our political system, the identity of our culture(s) and the values of our society. The nature and quality of political leadership is important to this. In this chapter, I apply an approach to leadership developed by Ronald Heifetz, most notably in his acclaimed 1994 book, *Leadership without Easy Answers*. Central to that approach is a four-point diagnostic and normative framework of the principles of leadership that was developed from observations of the practice of leadership. The framework involves identifying adaptive challenges faced by a group or organisation; regulating distress for those involved; directing disciplined attention to the issues; and 'giving the work back to the people'.

There is significant room for disagreement about how Heifetz's framework should be applied to the case of the foreshore and seabed. I should make clear the extent to which its application in this chapter represents an intimately personal view. During the period 1995 to 2000 I was involved in providing advice to ministers on Crown strategy with respect to Treaty of Waitangi and customary rights issues generally, including the foreshore and seabed. My own 'take' on events from 2003 to 2005 is one of sadness and frustration. I understand the incentives operating on all the key actors in the debate and do not believe the party political identity of the government would have changed the dynamics. But I am very disappointed at where they have led, in terms of the health of the relationships between the Crown, Maori and other New Zealanders. We need a system that generates better political leadership.

In what follows, I summarise salient features of Heifetz's prescription for leadership without easy answers and review the events and players associated with the foreshore and seabed from 1997 to 2005. Through this review and analysis, I show how the responses of political leaders to the events of the foreshore and seabed can be seen as rational responses to political incentives. The chapter concludes that that is not good enough. Consequently, I suggest changes to our system of government and politics that might lead to the exercise of constructive leadership, in Heifetz's sense, to the foreshore and seabed issue in the future.

Heifetz's Approach to Leadership

Ronald Heifetz distinguishes leadership and authority as operating in dynamic tension:

> [L]eadership can be usefully viewed as the activity of mobilizing people to do work on their problems, while authority can be viewed as the activity of restoring or maintaining equilibrium in the social system (1989, 541–2).

Heifetz elaborates:

> On one hand authority basically stabilizes, while leadership, in stretching the social system's adaptive capacity, basically disturbs. On the other hand, authority and leadership overlap at those times when authority acts to reduce intolerable levels of urgency into a favorable range for work to proceed. For example, autocratic rule in a chaotic situation may reduce overwhelming disequilibrium and enable the constructive engagement of conflicting factions (1989, 542).

Heifetz's resulting normative conception of leadership emphasises that it is an activity (rather than a status or a set of personal characteristics) and that its purpose is to accomplish adaptive work:

Adaptive work consists of the learning required to address conflicts in the values people hold, or to diminish the gap between the values people stand for and the reality they face. Adaptive work requires a change in values, beliefs, or behavior. The exposure and orchestration of conflict – internal contradictions – within individuals and constituencies provide the leverage for mobilizing people to learn new ways (1994, 22).

Further, Heifetz notes that

The point here is to provide a guide to goal formation and strategy. In selecting adaptive work as a guide, one considers not only the values that the goal represents, but also the goal's ability to mobilize people to face, rather than avoid, tough realities and conflicts. The hardest and most valuable task of leadership may be advancing goals and designing strategy that promote adaptive work (1994, 23).

Heifetz's diagnostic leadership framework can be well applied to the foreshore and seabed controversy in New Zealand.

Events and Players on the Foreshore and Seabed 1997– 2005

Before applying Heifitz's prescription for leadership to our case study, it is necessary to explore the background to the foreshore and seabed dispute.

The issues

Public and political consciousness of the foreshore and seabed issue in New Zealand largely dates from June 2003, when the Court of Appeal's *Ngati Apa* decision came out (see generally Charters and Erueti 2006). The immediate legal origins of the controversy date back to the filing of proceedings in the Maori Land Court in 1997 by eight iwi – Ngati Apa, Ngati Koata, Ngati Kuia, Ngati Rarua, Ngati Tama, Ngati Toa, Rangitane and Te Atiawa – against the Marlborough District Council.

The essence of the underlying legal issue in the litigation was whether the Maori iwi or hapu had common law rights in relation to specific areas of the foreshore and seabed in Marlborough, whether or not those rights had been extinguished by legislation and, if not, what the content of those rights were. However consideration of this underlying issue has not been reached by the courts. At an early stage in the litigation the Crown and other defendants made a preliminary objection that common law and statute had extinguished Maori customary rights in the foreshore and seabed.

Judge Hingston of the Maori Land Court issued a decision in favour of the iwi in 1997. On appeal by way of a case stated to the High Court in 2001, the Crown obtained a determination of answers to eight specified questions regarding the law, the effect of which was that the Maori Land Court does have jurisdiction to examine whether the foreshore has the status of Maori Customary Land; the foreshore cannot have the status of Maori Customary Land unless it is contiguous with dry land that is Maori Customary Land; the seabed could not be Maori Customary Land; and there could be customary rights over the foreshore and seabed short of a right of exclusive possession.

The Maori plaintiffs appealed to the Court of Appeal. In response, in 2003, the Court overruled the 1962 Court of Appeal decision *In Re Ninety-Mile Beach* that the Maori Land Court cannot investigate title to the foreshore. The Court of Appeal found that the Maori Land Court does have such jurisdiction and that Maori customary title to the foreshore has not been extinguished by any general enactment. The Court did not make any finding regarding whether Maori customary title to particular portions of the seabed or foreshore had been extinguished by area-specific legislation or by particular Crown deed purchases.

In paragraph 8 of her judgment issued on Thursday 19 June 2003 the Chief Justice, Dame Sian Elias, cautioned that

> The significance of the determinations this Court is asked to make should not be exaggerated. The outcome of the appeal cannot establish that there is Maori customary land below high water mark. And the assertion that there is some such land faces a number of hurdles in fact and law which it will be for the Maori Land Court in the first instance to consider, if it is able to enter on the inquiry.

On Sunday 22 June 2003, the Prime Minister Rt Hon. Helen Clark and Attorney-General, Hon. Margaret Wilson, issued a press statement playing down the significance of the Court of Appeal's decision, describing it as 'narrow and technical', with 'no immediate practical effect'.[1] However, in the post-cabinet press conference the next day Helen Clark and Margaret Wilson announced that the government considered that the possibility of a court finding that Maori have an exclusive title to the foreshore or seabed 'is not necessarily desirable because it would exclude a traditional interest that all New Zealanders have in access to the sea and the foreshore. Therefore, it is the Government's view that it is important that the legal status of the seabed and foreshore is made clear' and that legislation would be passed to make it clear.[2] In August 2003 the government issued its proposals for protecting public access and customary rights.

The ensuing political storm involved extreme statements, prejudice and racism. As Tahu Potiki, chief executive of Te Runanga o Ngai Tahu, stated in an address to an ACT Party conference: 'Since [the *Ngati Apa*] decision the country has descended into a gutter debate in its most base form slugging each other, caveman like, with clubs of prejudice and racism.'[3]

All political parties had difficulty grappling with the issues. The Labour-led minority coalition government pursued legislation that provided more legal clarity about the public right of access to the foreshore and provided a process for determining the validity of Maori claims to the foreshore and seabed. The resulting Foreshore and Seabed Act 2004 created instruments and processes for the recognition of Maori claims found to be valid but did not extend to requiring compensation for Maori if a common law claim would, but for the legislation, have succeeded. In the course of passage of the legislation, the Labour Party split, with two of its Maori MPs refusing to support the legislation and a minister, Hon. Tariana Turia, leaving the Labour Party and government in April 2004 to form the new Maori Party. There were 11 hui scheduled to discuss the Crown's proposals in September 2003. The National Party and New Zealand First Party made political capital.

The Waitangi Tribunal held an urgent hearing into the Crown's proposals in January 2004 and in March 2004 found (Waitangi Tribunal 2004, xiv–xv):

The policy clearly breaches the principles of the Treaty of Waitangi. But beyond the Treaty, the policy fails in terms of wider norms of domestic and international law that underpin good government in a modern, democratic state. These include the rule of law, and the principles of fairness and non-discrimination.

The serious breaches give rise to serious prejudice:

(a) The rule of law is a fundamental tenet of the citizenship guaranteed by article 3. Removing its protection from Maori only, cutting off their access to the courts and effectively expropriating their property rights, puts them in a class different from and inferior to all other citizens.

(b) Shifting the burden of uncertainty about Maori property rights in the foreshore and seabed from the Crown to Maori, so that Maori are delivered for an unknown period to a position of complete uncertainty about where they stand, undermines their bargaining power and leaves them without recourse.

(c) In cutting off the path for Maori to obtain property rights in the foreshore and seabed, the policy takes away opportunity and mana, and in their place offers fewer and lesser rights. There is no guarantee to pay compensation for the rights lost.

A thousands-strong march on parliament by Maori coincided with the introduction of the Bill. The Foreshore and Seabed Act 2004 was eventually passed. And, as a sort of postscript, in 2005 the United Nations Committee on the Elimination of Racial Discrimination urged the government to resume a dialogue with Maori to lessen the discriminatory effects of the legislation (Charters and Erueti 2005).

Origins and options

The origins of these legal issues are much older than this litigation. They lie in the development of the English common law of aboriginal title and customary rights and in various New Zealand attempts to extinguish or codify these rights in the late nineteenth and early twentieth centuries (McHugh 2004a; McHugh 2004b; McHugh 2005). It has been apparent for over a hundred years that there has been a lack of clarity in the law governing the foreshore (Boast 1993). Attorney-General Sir John Findlay in 1908 observed generally that 'There is no statutory chaos in the world at all equal to the jungle of our Native-land laws today . . .'[4] In 1935 the opinion of the Crown Law Office was that 'The consensus of opinion (in which I fully concur) is that the claim of the Crown [to the foreshore] is weak. The Department would prefer that the matter, if possible, be removed from the jurisdiction of the Native Land Court.'[5]

In academic and legal circles the existence of this uncertainty has been clear. In the 1990s, in relation to this litigation, ministers were advised of that lack of certainty. Yet in 2003 it appears to have come as a surprise to the general public and apparently to politicians. Two sources of surprise can be identified. First, the relevant source of legal authority at issue in this controversy is not the Treaty of Waitangi. The Treaty, through legislation invoking it, was the primary source of legal claims by Maori from the 1980s onwards. The existence of an alternative, potentially more legally binding, source of Maori claims in the common law came as a surprise to the New Zealand public and also, though less excusably, to politicians.[6] The second surprise seems to have been the proposition that there is legal uncertainty as to who 'owns', or has what property rights to, the foreshore and seabed.

At various points since the initiation of the *Ngati Apa* litigation, particularly in reaction to court decisions in 1997, 1998 and 2001, public surprise and political controversy could easily have flared up as it eventually did in 2003. That it did not was probably due to the attitude taken by the then government in dampening rather than exacerbating public concern, and in pursuing further technical legal avenues through the judicial system for legal certainty.

In 2003, the government appeared to be taken by surprise by the Court of Appeal decision and the complexity of the policy and political issues.[7] Alternatives were available. They should have been canvassed calmly, as contingencies, before the Court of Appeal judgment was issued.

The government could have appealed to the Judicial Committee of the Privy Council. But doing so while simultaneously seeking the abolition of the right of appeal to that court may well have lacked political credibility. Or the government could have stuck to its initial line about the lack of immediate effect of the decision, and let the judicial process continue – with consideration by the Maori Land Court of the factual justification for the plaintiffs' case and the ability to appeal and seek judicial review of those decisions. This course was not aided by some inflammatory statements by one or two Maori activists, nor by potential opposition fuelling those flames (potential that was realised dramatically in Don Brash's speech entitled 'Nationhood' to the Orewa Rotary Club on 27

January 2004). Instead, the government clearly reached the view that the continued uncertainty about rights of access to beaches, associated with continuing down the judicial route, would be politically damaging. The Deputy Prime Minister, Hon. Dr Michael Cullen, who eventually acquired carriage of the issue stated in response to the Waitangi Tribunal's report in March 2004:

> The government does not agree that matters can be allowed to drift on, perhaps for many years, to an unknown conclusion. In the meantime great uncertainty will occur. There is a serious risk of injunctions to prevent any foreshore and seabed activity occurring. Already this is beginning to happen.[8]

The government's management of the process of policy-making and legislation-making was, at times, ham-fisted and itself contributed to tension, especially with Maori. In particular, the aggressive tone of the initial government reaction to the Court of Appeal decision was ill-judged and exacerbated the volatility of the situation. Tone continued to be a problem for the government, leading to impressions from all sides of lack of good faith. But those processes were never going to be easy. And opposition politicians, especially Don Brash and Winston Peters, the leaders of the National and New Zealand First parties, were quick to exploit the fear, uncertainty and prejudice that surrounded the issue.

In Search of Leadership

So what can we say about the quality of political leadership in these events? Applying Heifetz's framework, here I discuss the foreshore and seabed dispute in terms of identifying the adaptive challenge, regulating distress, directing disciplined attention to the issues and giving the work back to the people.

Identifying the adaptive challenge

The first step in Heifetz's diagnostic is to identify the underlying gap or conflict at issue. A clue to the nature of the underlying gap or conflict here lies in the two surprises to public and political opinion identified above: that the relevant source of legal authority at issue in this controversy is not the Treaty of Waitangi; and that there is legal uncertainty as to who has what property rights over the foreshore and seabed.

An important source of the distress here lies in the intense cultural values associated with the enjoyment and use of New Zealand beaches (the foreshore) – both for Maori and for other New Zealanders. For Maori, there are often significant, deeply held cultural values associated with specific sites on the foreshore, whether as boundary markers, for fishing, as urupa or other wahi tapu. These values are long-established and cut to the heart of what it is to be Maori. At the same time, access to beaches for boating, fishing, walking, barbeques or Christmas holidays has become one of the few quintessential parts of New Zealand culture more generally. Different regimes, such as private beaches in the United States, evoke powerfully negative gut reactions in New Zealanders. Generations of Pakeha have formed a profound emotional attachment to New Zealand beaches that touches what it is to be a New Zealander.

It is conceivable that Maori and Pakeha cultural values associated with the foreshore could be reconcilable by an innovative co-management regime. However, a more black-and-white perspective could lead easily to the perception that they could conflict. The *Ngati Apa* decision therefore represented a potential threat to be feared by Pakeha: uncertainty as to who has what control over beaches and the corresponding fear that Maori might exclude other New Zealanders from access to beaches. The fear of exclusion from access to beaches came up time and again in the media commentary and in parliamentary debates.

For Maori too there was fear – fear of, and ready anger about, how a potential Pakeha backlash would manifest itself. After 160 years of grievances about Crown breaches of the Treaty of Waitangi Maori were finally making some headway in the resolution of historical claims. Defeated militarily in the 1860s, with accompanying breaches of the Treaty, Maori had peacefully pursued avenues of working within the Pakeha political and legal system to seek redress. The 1980s saw increasing legislative reference to the Treaty of Waitangi and legitimation of the need to resolve historic grievances held by Maori over breaches of the Treaty. The 1990s saw the negotiation and resolution of a number of large historic grievances (e.g., Waikato–Tainui, Ngai Tahu) alongside a number of claims of contemporary breaches that appeared to many New Zealanders as far-fetched – for example, claims to trout, kiwifruit and airwaves. The late 1990s were a time of constant risk of racial backlash over Maori claims.

In addition to revealing uncertainty over the ability to pursue intensely held values, the *Ngati Apa* decision represented a whole new avenue of potential Maori claims, this time legally binding – the other surprise identified above. The Labour-led government was already perceived by some to be too politically correct and over-sympathetic to 'fringe' interests and issues. Opposition parties would be, and were, quick to play on prejudice and fear. Given the state of public opinion the government could not afford to cede political ground by being seen to be 'soft' on Maori. Government rhetoric post-*Ngati Apa* reflected that.

Yet the tone of the knee-jerk reaction that was expressed both by government and opposition politicians in their immediate reaction to the *Ngati Apa* decision symbolised for Maori a hypocritical attitude: pursue your claims through the courts according to law, but if you win we will change that law so you cannot win. Furthermore, political exploitation of prejudice and fear could be seen by Maori to be evidence of racism and cast doubt on the long-term effectiveness of a strategy of peaceful pursuit of claims within the law.

So, the explosive potential of uncertainty about access to the foreshore, generated by the intense values placed on it by Maori and other New Zealanders that could be perceived to conflict, was created by the contemporary context of New Zealand race relations. I have argued elsewhere that the Treaty of Waitangi expresses a desire for healthy ongoing relationships between Maori, the Crown and other New Zealanders (Palmer 1998; Palmer 2001; Palmer 2002; Palmer and Palmer 2004, ch 17; and see Coates and McHugh 1998; McHugh 2004). The challenge is to recognise this, and to create and use mechanisms to achieve it. This is also the underlying adaptive challenge facing New Zealand and its politicians in the foreshore and seabed debate: how to ensure that resolution of this issue enhances rather than degrades the health of the relationships between Maori, the Crown and other New Zealanders.

Regulating distress

Heifetz suggests (1994, 259) that it is necessary to 'identify the tolerable range of distress and discern how to regulate its level within a particular setting' in order that progress is able to be made. He suggests study of the characteristic responses of the community to disequilibrium, when breaking-points are reached, and what actions restore equilibrium.

I believe that these questions are insufficiently studied and understood in New Zealand.[9] They reflect New Zealand culture and one aspect of New Zealand culture is a suspicion that introspection is self-indulgent and yields little of practical benefit. That suspicion is wrong-headed. Greater understanding of the characteristics of our national culture can help us resolve issues such as the foreshore and seabed more effectively and less painfully.

My own instincts are that the key New Zealand values relevant to resolution of disputes at a national level are authority, pragmatism, innovation, flexibility and fair play.

- New Zealand has a tradition of strong, almost authoritarian leadership: 'King Dick' Seddon in the 1890s, the first Labour Government of the Second World War and post-war conscription; the Muldoon administration in the 1970s economic crisis; the fourth Labour Government at the crossroads of 1984. Until MMP arrived in 1996 the 'unbridled power' of New Zealand executive government was the most streamlined form of democratic government in the world (Palmer and Palmer 2004).
- New Zealanders value pragmatism and flexibility but also innovation. The pragmatism usually means we adopt an incrementalist approach to dealing with problems. And we are happy to change things as we need to. But if a problem is big enough New Zealanders are uninhibited about starting from scratch and inventing a completely new way of dealing with it – as long as we can change that too if we want to in future.
- Egalitarian fair play and honesty is also a strong New Zealand value. Everyone should have a 'fair go'. Injustices should be remedied. And those responsible should front up and admit it.

So, New Zealand's characteristic general response to disequilibrium seems to me to lie firstly in an instinctive invocation of authority, a willingness to contemplate change, a distrust of solutions that are 'set in concrete' and a concern for justice.

Historically, disequilibrium in relationships between Maori and Pakeha have been most intense in conflict over land, leading to violence and civil war. Since 1970, the major conflicts between Maori and Pakeha have continued to concern rights to land, particularly Maori grievances over the unjust past loss of land and resolution of those grievances – the 1975 land march or hikoi, the 1986 challenge to the removal of land from the Crown to State-Owned Enterprises (SOEs) and the 1995 reaction by Maori to the 'fiscal envelope' proposals to limit the amount of government funds for resolving Treaty settlements.

Historically, the restoration of equilibrium has come in the form of resort to force and armed conflict – especially in the New Zealand wars of the 1860s. In the 1970s and 1980s, more process-oriented solutions were pursued:

- the Treaty of Waitangi Act 1975 established the Waitangi Tribunal to hear, prospectively, grievances about alleged breaches of the Treaty of Waitangi;
- the Treaty of Waitangi Amendment Act 1985 retrospectively extended Waitangi Tribunal jurisdiction to include historic grievances;
- the State-Owned Enterprises Act 1986 included a general reference to the Treaty of Waitangi, in response to a Tribunal claim; and
- the Treaty of Waitangi (State Enterprises) Act 1988 responded to Maori litigation by enacting a procedure, negotiated with the New Zealand Maori Council, for making land transferred to SOEs available for compulsory resumption by order of the Waitangi Tribunal.

From the 1990s, substantive solutions began to appear:

- a pan-Maori settlement of the fisheries claim was negotiated in 1993 (and has taken more than ten years to implement);
- the terminology of the 1995 'fiscal envelope' proposals were quietly dropped, but their substance continued to be adhered to by governments in case-by-case negotiation of settlements with Maori claimants; and
- settlements of historical grievances have been negotiated on a case-by-case basis since the Waikato–Tainui settlement in 1995.

The characteristics of these substantive solutions to problems reflect the general characteristics of New Zealand culture identified above. In particular, the difficult issues at stake in each set of negotiations engaged leaders on both sides deeply and tended to yield innovative solutions, often involving flexibility and lateral thinking and the setting up of further processes for resolving particular issues.

However, most of the innovation – in devising means of protecting the ability to resolve future Treaty claims in the 1980s and in devising the mechanisms of those resolutions in the 1990s – has tailed off. In the current decade, governments have pursued more formulaic negotiations to resolve historical claims, invoking mechanisms devised previously. Consequently, neither government nor opposition politicians have had to engage in depth with significant challenges to the relationship with Maori. The lack of that thinking and experience showed in the foreshore and seabed debate. This is perhaps the most important lesson for political leadership regarding the relationship between the Crown, Maori and other New Zealanders. If political leadership is to be effective in regulating the distress that issues in these relationships cause, the leaders themselves have to commit themselves to understanding the nature of these relationships. They are much more subtle, complex and multifaceted than other political dynamics in New Zealand – and there is a much higher risk to the nation in approaching them superficially or hastily.

As noted above, consistent with the above focus on process solutions, the initial responses by government in the 1990s to the foreshore and seabed litigation were, also, to seek further process-oriented solutions – within the judicial system. By 2003 the government considered that that option was no longer politically credible. Its instinctive reaction was to resort to the authority of legislation by parliament.

Directing disciplined attention to the issues

Heifetz (1994, 260–2) suggests that if traditionally used mechanisms for restoring equilibrium to social systems do not work, then 'work avoidance' mechanisms will often emerge that divert attention from the real problems. Was this what was going on in the foreshore and seabed debate in 2003?

Before working through the application of Heifetz's framework I would have answered 'no' to this question. Now, having identified the underlying adaptive challenge as the health of relationships between the Crown, Maori and other New Zealanders, and considering the recent pattern of the tailing off of in-depth engagement between the Crown and Maori, I think the answer is a qualified 'yes'.

The current pattern of engagement between the Crown and Maori is stuck. The rocky resurgence of iwi and hapu identity has diminished the legitimacy of the New Zealand Maori Council, with which the Crown negotiated in the 1980s. The major settlements of historical grievances of breaches of the Treaty of Waitangi have been reached. The Clark government took a political hit early in its term, in 2000, of being 'soft on Maori' through its 'closing the gaps' policy to deal with social and economic disadvantage of Maori and reacted by reversing that policy and trying to avoid similar issues. Before the foreshore and seabed issue, it had not had to deal with Maori over a significant generic issue. Opposition leaders in 2003 had either had a pattern of political exploitation of prejudice against Maori or have not seriously engaged with Maori.

Finding a process to resolve the foreshore and seabed issue was undoubtedly difficult. In particular there was no legitimate 'pan-tribal' Maori organisation that government could engage with to negotiate a solution. And the transaction costs of negotiations with every iwi in New Zealand would have been too high for a politically sustainable process. And how would negotiation with Maori over an issue that also mattered to Pakeha sit with Pakeha?

Recourse to the ordinary legislative process, preceded by government consultations over a discussion paper was an understandable option. It resonates with New Zealanders' cultural preference for authority. However, the foreshore and seabed issue is sufficiently important to Maori that the way in which it is resolved directly affects the health of the relationship between the Crown, Maori and other New Zealanders. Adopting an ordinary legislative process ignores that. How to ensure that these relationships are healthy is an underlying challenge with which New Zealand has not yet adequately grappled. In my view the legislative process used by government, and supported by the majority of opposition politicians, and the tone of that process, degraded the health of those relationships. That was foreseeable and should have been foreseen.

Giving the work back to people

Heifetz (1994, 262–3) suggests that 'a community can fail to adapt when its people look too hard to their authorities to meet challenges that require changes in their own ways'. I agree and I think the foreshore and seabed debate exemplifies it. The authoritarian-regarding tendency is well rooted in New Zealand political culture. And politicians respond accordingly. The nature of the political leadership New Zealand achieves is not an accident. If a significant portion of the New Zealand electorate did not respond positively to exploitation of prejudice and fear, politicians would not undertake it.

In Heifetz's framework, leadership involves giving the work 'back to people' to lead them to examine their views and values and the potential gains and losses to be made by keeping them or changing them. Here, I identify the relevant underlying views and values to be those concerning the relationship between the Crown, Maori and other New Zealanders.

The choice is not whether those relationships exist or not. They are inherently present, as long as Maori culture is vibrant. All New Zealanders therefore need to figure out what the qualities of those relationships should be and how they should be managed. Our current political in-centive structures do not easily lend themselves to this.

Neither is the hard work all on the Crown side. The quality of Maori leadership needs attention. In particular, there seems to me to be merit in Maori considering the creation of a democratic, accountable body of Maori leaders with recognised legitimacy in dealing with the Crown over pan-Maori issues. Sir Douglas Graham suggested in 1997:

> What is needed is a redefinition of the relationship between Maori and non-Maori and a recommitment to build a cooperative friendship so that everyone can benefit. It is the future, not the past which beckons us. We must stop talking past each other. The future relationship between Maori and the Crown depends on the trust between the two. If we have learned anything from the past it is that where Maori are likely to be affected by government policy they must be consulted. And to avoid mistakes it may be time to establish a joint council – perhaps up to 10 Maori leaders from Maori organisations, and 10 from government (Ministers or their Chief Executives). It could meet monthly so that each could be made aware of the other's concerns. Meetings could be chaired by a former Governor-General.

In this way potentially difficult issues could be discussed and problems could be avoided before they arise. Such a development would close the gap in communications which still exists despite valiant attempts to close it (Graham 1997, 93).

It may be that the diversity within Maoridom itself is now too widespread to feel effectively represented by such a structure. Certainly it would be criticised by those holding an 'iwi-fundamentalist' perspective. Yet the existence of some authoritative body, developed by Maori, for Maori, might hold out the potential for healthier relationships with other New Zealanders. For example, it might have been possible for such a body to have negotiated a resolution of the foreshore and seabed issues in a way which could have positively enhanced relationships between the Crown, Maori and other New Zealanders. Certainly, it would have been harder for the Crown to ignore.

Conclusion

Questions over the quality of relationships between the Crown, Maori and other New Zealanders can be emotionally fraught. The foreshore and seabed debate demonstrates that – on all sides. Ultimately, the shape of the mechanisms for safeguarding the quality of these relationships is a constitutional issue – in the widest sense of a constitution as the structures, processes, principles, rules, conventions and even culture that *constitute* the ways in which government power is exercised. And New Zealanders shy away from apparently abstract and difficult constitutional issues.

But every time a 'practical' issue arises that puts at stake an issue of importance to the relationships between the Crown, Maori and other New Zealanders, the absence of constitutional mechanisms for dealing with them will encourage the temptation to New Zealanders and their politicians to avoid the real underlying issues. And down that path lies further damage to these relationships and to the fabric of our society. True leadership involves identifying the relationship conflict underlying the superficial issues, and creating a process where all New Zealanders can create mechanisms for managing these relationships. We should demand true leadership.

From 1995 to the end of 2000 I was Deputy Secretary for Justice (Public Law). For part of that period I chaired the Officials Treaty Strategy Committee that advised on strategic issues involving the Treaty of Waitangi and aboriginal title and customary rights. Thanks to Jonathan Boston, Sir Douglas Graham, Gary Hawke, Paul McHugh, Patricia Sarr, Ruth Wilkie and a staff seminar at the Victoria University of Wellington School of Government for comments on a draft of this paper and to Nick Whittington for research assistance. No responsibility for the views expressed here should be attributed to anyone but me.

1   See http://www.beehive.govt.nz/ViewDocument.aspx?DocumentID=17134
2   See http://www.beehive.govt.nz/ViewDocument.aspx?DocumentID=17672
3   See http://www.act.org.nz/item.aspx/24760
4   144 *New Zealand Parliamentary Debates*, 64.
5   Crown Solicitor to Solicitor-General, 30 August 1935 cited in Boast (2004, 1).
6   It is important not to overstate the substantive importance of the distinction between the common law and the Treaty of Waitangi. The same dynamics underlie both (McHugh 2004b).
7   The Ministry of Justice Briefing Papers for the Incoming Government at the 1999 election raised this litigation squarely as a significant set of issues. However, they were not mentioned in the 2002 briefing (see www.justice.govt.nz).
8   Press Statement, 8 March 2004.
9   As an exception, see papers by Bill Manhire, Philip Temple and others presented to the Constitutional Conference in 2000 (James 2000).

Attorney-General v Ngati Apa [2002] 2 New Zealand Law Reports 661 (High Court).
Boast, R. (1993) '*In Re Ninety Mile Beach* Revisited: the Native Land Court and the Foreshore in New Zealand Legal History', *Victoria University of Wellington Law Review*, 23, 145.
Boast, R. (2004) 'Maori Proprietary Claims to the Foreshore and Seabed after *Ngati Apa*', *New Zealand Universities Law Review*, 21, 1.
Charters, C. and A. Erueti (2005) 'Report from the Inside: The CERD Committee's Review of the Foreshore and Seabed Act 2004', *Victoria University of Wellington Law Review*, 36, 257.
Charters, C. and A. Erueti (eds) (2006) *Foreshore and Seabed: The New Frontier*, Wellington, Victoria University Press (forthcoming).
Coates, K. S. and P. G. McHugh (1998) *Living Relationships: Kokiri Ngatahi – the Treaty of Waitangi in the New Millennium*, Wellington, Victoria University Press.
Graham, D. (1997) *Trick or Treaty?* Wellington, Institute of Policy Studies.
Heifetz, R. A. (1994) *Leadership without Easy Answers*, Cambridge, MA, Belknap Press of Harvard University Press.
Heifetz, R. A. and D. L. Laurie (1997) 'The Work of Leadership', *Harvard Business Review*, 124–34.
Heifetz, R. A. and M. Linsky (2002) 'A Survival Guide for Leaders', *Harvard Business Review*, 65–74.
Heifetz, R. A, R. M. Sinder, A. Jones, L. M. Hodge and K. Rowley (1989) 'Teaching and Assessing Leadership Courses at the John F. Kennedy School of Government', *Journal of Policy Analysis and Management*, 8, 536–62.
James, C. (ed.) (2000) *Building the Constitution*, Wellington, Institute of Policy Studies.
McHugh, P. G. (2004a) *Aboriginal Societies and the Common Law: A History of Sovereignty, Status, and Self-Determination*, Oxford, Oxford University Press.
McHugh, P. G. (2004b) 'What a difference a Treaty makes – the pathways of aboriginal rights jurisprudence in New Zealand public law', *Public Law Review*, 87.
McHugh, P. G. (2004c) 'Aboriginal Title in New Zealand: Retrospect and Prospect', *New Zealand Journal of Public and International Law*, 2, 139.

McHugh, P. G. (2005) 'Setting the Statutory Compass: The Foreshore and Seabed Act 2004', *New Zealand Journal of Public and International Law*, 3, 255.

Ngati Apa v Attorney-General [2003] 3 New Zealand Law Reports 643 (Court of Appeal).

Palmer, G. and M. Palmer (2004) *Bridled Power: New Zealand's Constitution and Government*, 4th edn, Melbourne, Oxford University Press.

Palmer, M. (1998) 'The International Practice' in A. Quentin-Baxter (ed.), *Recognising the Rights of Indigenous Peoples*, Wellington, Victoria University Press, 87–103.

Palmer, M. (2001) 'The Treaty of Waitangi in Legislation', *New Zealand Law Journal*, 207–12.

Palmer, M. (2002) 'The Constitution and the Treaty of Waitangi', in C. Wainwright, P. Majurey and M. Palmer, *The Treaty of Waitangi*, Wellington, New Zealand Law Society.

Waitangi Tribunal (2004) *Report on the Crown's Foreshore and Seabed Policy WAI 1071*, Wellington, Legislation Direct.

TWELVE

Promoting Regional Economic Development

**Michael Mintrom
and Luke Williams**

Over recent years, a significant shift has occurred in the ways that local government politicians and officials in New Zealand engage with businesses. There was once a time when business activity within any given jurisdiction was taken for granted by citizens and their councils alike. While it was recognised that the central government in Wellington could affect business conditions through taxes, subsidies, trade policies, and monetary policies, the impacts that local governments could have on business conditions were assumed to be minor. Today, most local government politicians and officials see things differently. A variety of exciting initiatives to promote economic development is now taking place at the local and regional levels in New Zealand. We can gain intriguing insights into political leadership by studying these efforts. Yet to understand the impetus behind changes at the regional and local level, it is essential to recognise the changes that have occurred in the perception of the role of government in the economy since the Labour–Progressive coalition government assumed power in 1999. Jim Anderton, a minor political party leader in coalition government with the Labour Party, has been the driving force behind central government becoming a catalyst for economic development. We examine how political leadership emanating from central, regional, and local government has invigorated regional economic development efforts. The picture that emerges is one of actors at different levels of government undertaking distinctive but mutually reinforcing tasks that, in combination, have resulted in significant changes in policy and practice.

Leadership and Economic Development

Economic development, measured in terms of continually increasing gross domestic product per capita, is a broadly shared goal across communities, regions and states worldwide. With few exceptions, people aspire to being better off than they are, and politicians in democracies are well aware that their electoral fortunes are closely tied to how citizens judge their own financial wellbeing (Anderson 1995; Powell and Whitten 1993). In New Zealand, Prime Minister Helen Clark and other politicians have repeatedly argued that New Zealand needs to get back in the top half of member countries in the Organisation for Economic Cooperation and Development, as ranked by GDP per capita. But what should governments do to promote economic development?

Over the past century, states around the world have experimented with a range of approaches to promoting economic development. In the mid twentieth century, the two most popular approaches taken by national governments were state socialism, where efforts were made to restrict market processes and centralise resource allocation, and Keynesianism, where governments maintained market processes but intervened heavily to achieve desired macroeconomic performance. Industrial policies, designed to promote economic development through the support of large, essential enterprises, were often centrepieces of state socialist and Keynesian policy settings (Frankel 1983; Hall 1989).

Beginning in the 1970s, with the emergence of significant government deficits and high levels of inflation, economists in many advanced economies began questioning the merits of extensive government involvement in the economy and showed renewed respect for market processes. This change of perspective led to policy shifts that tended to remove the visible hand of government and leave more decisions to individuals and firms operating in the marketplace (Yergin and Stanislaw 1998). Under this new policy creed, variously described as monetarism, neoliberalism and the New Public Management, the primary role of government was seen as creating a stable monetary environment, where price signals and exchange rates would reflect the true value of goods and services, and where taxes were as limited and as non-distortionary as possible. Ties between government and business were viewed with suspicion and the separation of political decision-making from commercial decision-making was espoused (Feigenbaum, Henig and Hamnett 1998). But this approach to policy design left little room for national governments to actively promote economic development. The emerging consensus saw government policies towards business as too often descending into efforts to pick winners among existing firms. Worse still, such policies were believed to send perverse signals, encouraging firms to put resources into chasing government support instead of improving their market competitiveness (Buchanan, Tollison and Tullock 1980).

Contemporary prescriptions for government efforts to promote economic development must balance the new economic orthodoxy that rejects industrial policies and picking winners against the will of politicians to appear actively engaged in supporting business growth. In this regard, Michael Porter's *The Competitive Advantage of Nations* (1990) and Robert Reich's *The Work of Nations* (1991) have been highly influential works. Both authors took the intensification of global capitalism as a given. They then explored the kinds of actions that governments in market democracies could take to promote economic development. Since Porter's ideas have long received attention in New Zealand (see Crocombe, Enright and Porter 1991), here we focus on his explanation of the link between political leadership and economic development.

In arguing for active economic development policies, Porter (1990) acknowledged that governments have limited abilities to influence outcomes. 'Because the determinants of national advantage are so deeply rooted in a nation's buyers, its history, and other unique circumstances, it could be argued that government is powerless. Its proper role would then be to sit back and let market forces work' (620). But Porter rejected the powerlessness perspective, and claimed that the nature of government activity is critical. For this reason, Porter urged that '[t]his is a time for political and business leaders, not stewards' (738). Porter contended that the most important contribution a government can make to economic development is as a 'facilitator, signaler, and prodder' (672). Governments should shape the environment surrounding firms, creating the conditions under which competitive industries can thrive. In Porter's view, this can occur when the economic order is based on 'innovation, competition and rewards for effort' (738). Porter stressed the role of leadership, stating that '[l]eaders believe in dynamics and change'. Further, leaders '... do not accept constraints, and know that they can change the nature of outcomes. They are in a position to perceive something about reality that has escaped others, and have the courage to act' (130). While Porter recognises businesses, and business expansion, as the engines of economic development, his perspective requires that government plays a leadership role. That role involves helping existing businesses and would-be entrepreneurs better understand their operating context, perceive opportunities, and position themselves for strong and sustained growth. The emphasis is placed on government as a source of information and advice; more a coach than a source of easy capital or a central planner. The nature of the market game is not questioned. The aim is to help local businesses play that game as effectively as possible.

Often, the argument is made that people in business do not need government officials to help them identify potential business opportunities. That is undoubtedly true for many big businesses that have their own planning and strategy units. But it is not the case for many small to medium-size businesses. Further, many economies, including the New Zealand economy, overwhelmingly comprise small to medium-size businesses. For such businesses, market information may well be a constraint on growth, especially when opportunities for expansion lie primarily in overseas markets. Market failure can then be said to exist, in the sense that businesses that could be expanding are not. In light of this, if government efforts to work with such businesses prompt business expansion, and the overall gains from the policy exceed the costs, then a public good is produced. Of course, the business owners stand to gain from successful expansion, but so do other participants in the economy. The leadership role involves building confidence and helping people to improve the strategic focus they bring to their business efforts.

Michael Porter's notions of how political leaders can facilitate and encourage new business activity fits well with Karl Weick's (1995) comments about the uses that business leaders make of strategic plans. In Weick's view, '[w]hat the leader has to do ... is instill some confidence in people, get them moving in some general direction, and be sure they look closely at cues created by their actions so that they learn where they were and get some better idea of where they are and where they want to be' (55).

Thought of in terms of encouraging economic development, this suggests opportunities for government officials to work with businesses, helping them to build on past successes and explore new opportunities for gain. Porter's perspective on leadership and economic growth is also consistent with Ronald Heifitz's (1994) view that leaders are people who are good at 'getting on the balcony' (252) and who are adept at 'giving the work back to the people' (262). In this case, government officials can play a leadership role in supporting economic development by helping others to achieve a better understanding of their business environment. But, in the end, businesses must take responsibility for their own choices and that is where the leaders – having engaged in their facilitation efforts – step back and leave the decision-making to others. This perspective on government and economic development now informs economic development strategies at the national, regional and local level in many places around the world (Eisinger 1988; Savitch and Kantor 2002; Sweet 1999). As we will show, it is a perspective that is now in ascendance in New Zealand.

A Renewed Interest in New Zealand's Regions

During the years of the fourth Labour Government, the New Zealand economy underwent significant structural adjustments. Some adjustment was inevitable, because under the previous National Government, led by Prime Minister Robert Muldoon, state control of the economy had become excessive, with wage and price freezes and an unsustainable fixed exchange rate regime. Further, government debt had grown to reckless levels as a programme of large-scale infrastructural development projects was pursued. The Think Big projects were designed to reduce New Zealand's vulnerability to world energy price shocks. Inadvertently, spending on them left the country even more vulnerable to global economic conditions. The Labour Government (1984–90) made a series of adjustments intended to free up the marketplace and reduce the role of government in the economy. The exchange rate was floated, many agricultural and industrial subsidies were removed, the tax system was redesigned, government agencies were required to operate as commercial entities and a major programme of privatisation was launched. The fourth National Government (1990–96) continued this reform agenda, seeking to stop the expansion of public spending through retrenchment of the welfare state. The reforms undertaken in this period have been well documented elsewhere (Bollard 1993; Boston, Martin, Pallot and Walsh 1996; Dalziel and Lattimore 2004).

The neo-liberal perspective that underpinned the reforms of the 1980s and 1990s placed faith in markets, and viewed with suspicion any government activity beyond the provision of defence and police forces, basic infrastructure, support of market processes and limited redistribution (Friedman 1962; Kettl 2000; Rhoads 1985). That perspective left little room for government to actively promote economic development. Rather, the prescription was that government should create a stable environment for business where market prices serve as the principal guides to firm-level decisions. This was typically referred to as creation of a level playing field.

Many voices of opposition were heard as the neo-liberal reform agenda was pursued in New Zealand. Among those voices, Jim Anderton was especially vociferous. Anderton had served as president of the New Zealand Labour Party from 1979 until 1984 and entered parliament as a backbencher in 1984. Anderton's opposition to his own party's agenda forced him into the political wilderness. In 1989 he was suspended from the Labour caucus for disobeying party instructions to vote in favour of selling the Bank of New Zealand. In protest at the excesses of the reforms, Anderton created the NewLabour Party, which stood candidates in all electorates in 1990. The party's primary electoral platforms were state intervention in the economy, retention of public assets and full employment. Anderton was the party's only successful candidate in that election. During 1991, Anderton and other left-wing politicians formed the Alliance coalition. The introduction of the Mixed Member Proportional voting system in 1996 laid the ground for a reversal of fortune both for Anderton and his views about the role of government in the economy and society. After the 1999 election, a coalition government of Labour and the Alliance took power, with Helen Clark as prime minister and Anderton as the deputy prime minister. Anderton, the longtime opponent of neoliberalism, now occupied a powerful position at the cabinet table. When the Alliance fragmented in 2002, Anderton created the Progressive Party. He returned to parliament in 2002 as a member of that party, which formed a coalition government with Labour. This time around, Anderton was ranked third in the cabinet after Prime

Minister Clark and Deputy Prime Minister and Minister of Finance Michael Cullen.

Jim Anderton deserves primary credit for the renewal of interest in New Zealand's regions. On entering the cabinet in 1999, along with being given several other responsibilities, he was designated Minister for Economic Development and Minister for Industry and Regional Development. In these newly created ministerial roles, Anderton lost no time championing the cause of economic development and support for the regions. Within six months of being in government, Anderton had guided the establishment of two key budget lines, Vote: Economic Development and Vote: Industry and Regional Development. During 2000, the Ministry of Commerce was transformed into the Ministry of Economic Development. This new ministry was given wide scope to provide perspective both for ministers and other departments on how selected existing or proposed policies could impact on the economic development of New Zealand. These included regional and local economic development issues. Another body, Industry New Zealand, was established as a Crown Entity with a board comprising members drawn mainly from the business community. This body, later renamed New Zealand Trade and Enterprise, was charged with implementing industry assistance programmes. These were specifically intended to contribute to regional development. Although some industry-assistance programmes had been operating under previous governments, they were administered through a raft of different agencies, they tended to be *ad hoc*, and coordination was lacking. The body that came to be known as New Zealand Trade and Enterprise was expected to help achieve greater coordination in programme delivery, both to businesses and to the regions (Anderton 2000).

Three key policies developed under the Labour–Alliance coalition government of 1999–2002 were intended to promote regional economic development. The Regional Partnerships Programme (RPP) was established to improve regional governance focused on sustainable economic development. In practice, the programme has provided matching funds up to $100,000 to councils and other entities to take stock of their regional economic resources and develop strategic plans for the future. The Major Regional Initiatives (MRI) programme has made funding of up to $2 million available for projects that have been planned through inclusive decision-making processes and that are consistent with their region's development strategy. Regions have been able to apply for funding for multiple MRIs. Finally, the Cluster Development Programme has provided region-specific industrial clusters with advice, facilitation and funding with an eye to improving the economic performance of firms within each cluster. Additional programmes, delivered through New Zealand Trade and Enterprise, have been designed to build business skills within the regions.

Along with the initiatives noted above, regional development conferences held biannually since 2001 have done much to highlight regional best practices and create cross-regional networking opportunities for people working on economic development issues. The conferences have been sponsored by the government in association with the Economic Development Association of New Zealand (EDANZ). These conferences have created venues at which Jim Anderton has reflected on recent achievements and showcased his vision for the future. The first of these conferences was held in Rotorua in November 2001 and was attended by over 600 people, representing councils, iwi, economic development agencies, community groups and government agencies. In his opening address there, Jim Anderton observed: 'This conference is significant. It is the first Government sponsored regional development conference since 1969 . . . . [T]here has been a huge cost of doing nothing in regional development over the last 30 years' (Anderton 2001a). Speaking at this same conference, Prime Minister Helen Clark pointed out how the Labour–Alliance coalition government's focus on regional development represented a break from the past.

> I see New Zealand in its modern history as having moved from one strength to another, excepting the carry on that brought our economy to its knees in the early 1980s, but then we went to the extent of hands off and that didn't present sustainable economic growth either. Government opted out, a level playing field was created, but few came to play on it and I think there really was a large gap where leadership from government should have been (Clark 2001).

In this statement, Clark expresses the view that previous economic policy in New Zealand had swung from one extreme to another and that neither extreme had been satisfactory.

Jim Anderton has made a concerted effort to differentiate his preferred style of economic policy from past approaches. In a newspaper opinion piece from 2003, he contended that the Think Big projects of the early 1980s hurt the country economically, socially and intellectually. 'Intellectually, it hurt us in the sense that in the late 1980s and through the 1990s we tried to protect ourselves from the folly of Think Big by going to an opposite ideological extreme, which meant adopting an equally rigid mantra along the lines of: No Government Involvement Is Always The Best Option.' Anderton then suggested that his own strategy has been more moderate. 'To me it makes sense to try to get the most out of our competitive advantages as a society and an economy. Sometimes that will involve a role for the central Government and its agencies.' However, Anderton acknowledged the suspicion that such action evokes. 'I accept that many of our big firms are suspicious of the very idea of an "interventionist" Government. After Think Big, so they should be. And so they should hold the Government and its agencies accountable for every cent of taxpayers' money we spend on mentoring, fostering, and encouraging firms to expand' (Anderton 2003a).

Jim Anderton's vision of regional economic development policy sees a key role for central government, but that role does not involve significant intervention. Speaking at the close of the Regional Economic Development Conference held in Rotorua in 2001, he stated:

> I see Government as the regional development coach. Where we need to help the team get together and when the team is together we can encourage and support it. If the team needs some particular skills we might help provide those. If the team is in dispute we might help mediate. We can find out and share what other teams are doing. If the rules aren't working we might try and change them. If the team is doing brilliantly and is self supporting then we might just step back and watch for a while, our involvement being cheering from the sideline. The key point is that central Government should help you achieve what you want, which is strong, self directed communities and economies (Anderton 2001b).

This understanding of the role of central government is consistent with Michael Porter's prescription for leadership in promoting economic development. It is also consistent with Ronald Heifitz's notion of leadership as an ability to gain perspective, then help others to better understand how they might effectively address the challenges they face.

One of Jim Anderton's clearest expressions of how he sees the relationship between leadership and regional economic development can be found in his closing address to the second Regional Development Conference, held in Timaru in September 2003. There, he stated:

> ... [T]he most important ingredient in reaching our goals is leadership. Leaders make the difference between success and also-ran status. As economic development leaders, we all have a responsibility to make a success of development in our regions. Successful leaders have common characteristics: They are open to ideas – especially audacious new ideas; They aim high – and have high expectations of others; They lead by example and they are consistent. Effective leaders set clear directions; involve all the communities they serve; are action-oriented themselves and unfailingly support the efforts of others. Leadership requires us to engage our heart as well as our head. Leadership in regional development is not something we can leave to politicians, mayors and other civic leaders alone. Every one of us here is a leader of regional development. Each one of us must aspire to achieve more for our regions (Anderton 2003b).

In the remainder of this chapter, we move from this focus on the changes in perspective and policy that have occurred in Wellington since 1999. Next, we discuss the nature of the leadership exhibited by actors at the regional and local levels, who have worked with others around them to promote regional economic development.

Identifying Regional Leaders

There are 26 regions in New Zealand. These do not map neatly onto local or regional government territories. Rather, they represent geographic concentrations of communities with similar economic, social and environmental characteristics. Evidence on the economic performance of New Zealand's regions over the past decade or so reveals that some have been performing much better than others. For this study, we decided to focus on the two largest regions in the country, based on population size, Canterbury and Auckland. Our goal was to compare and contrast the forms of leadership exhibited by those with significant interests in promoting economic development in each region. Canterbury has been deemed a 'star' performer with respect to economic development (NZIER 2004, 33). Auckland, while contributing at a rate of over 30 per cent to the GDP of the country, has been lagging behind the national average with respect to GDP growth and per capita income. For each case, we used public information sources to build profiles of the regional economies. We next identified knowledgeable people in each territorial authority contained within each region. The Canterbury region is divided into eleven territorial authorities. The Auckland region is divided into seven. Through a series of telephone interviews, we identified people in each region consistently mentioned as giving leadership to promoting regional development. We asked about the strategies they used. We also asked about the importance of recent national leadership in promoting regional development, and the extent to which regional and national ties were significant. Interesting differences can be found in the ways that people in the Canterbury and Auckland regions have sought to promote economic development. These differences hold important implications, especially given the differences in the recent economic performance of the two regions.

Initiatives in Canterbury

The Canterbury region is geographically the largest in New Zealand, but second largest after Auckland in population terms, with 520,500 residents. Of those, 66 per cent live in Christchurch. Traditionally, Canterbury has been a strong agricultural region, and that continues. However, there has been growing diversification of the economy over the past few decades. Today, manufacturing, services and tourism all feature strongly in Canterbury's economic profile. Considerable emphasis has also been given to the development of a vibrant information and communications technology cluster around Christchurch. In the year to March 2004, the Canterbury region generated 14.6 per cent of New Zealand's total economic activity. Canterbury's nominal GDP per capita stood at $35,650 in the year to March 2003, making it 11 per cent higher than the national figure of $32,100 for the same period. Between March 2000 and March 2004, the GDP of the Canterbury region grew at an annual average of

4.8 per cent, considerably higher than the average rate of growth for the national economy, which stood at 3.5 per cent (NZIER 2004). The steady diversification and consistently strong performance of the Canterbury regional economy explain why it has recently been described as a regional star performer.

Canterbury has benefited from strong and stable civic leadership in Christchurch during the past two decades. Vicki Buck served as mayor of Christchurch from 1989 to 1998. Buck encouraged job growth in the city and promoted the image of Christchurch as a good place to do business. Through her earlier service as a local government commissioner from 1984 to 1989, Buck gained many insights into the types of administrative changes that local authorities needed to undertake to improve their financial performance. Combining these insights with knowledge gained from being on the Christchurch City Council since the 1970s, as mayor Buck presided over changes that, among other things, saw the city apply the concept of the 'triple bottom line' to its activities. Under this approach, all policies, projects and expenditures in the city have been expected to aim for the three-pronged goal of economic development, social wellbeing and environmental sustainability. During the 1990s, when many local governments were being encouraged to sell off assets, the Christchurch City Council held on to its assets, causing it to be dubbed by a member of the New Zealand Business Roundtable as the PRC, or 'People's Republic of Christchurch' (Meyers 1998). Yet the city's asset base has given it a lot of ability to engage in strategic developments while reforming its financial management and operations. In 2001, *Governing*, a magazine of state and local government published in the United States, devoted a lengthy cover story to Christchurch, declaring it 'the best-run city in the world' (Walters 2001).

Vicki Buck has been acknowledged as a strong supporter of local economic development initiatives. At the Regional Development Conference held in Rotorua in November 2001, she gave a keynote speech on leadership and economic development. She encouraged the audience to take to heart the famous line of anthropologist Margaret Mead: 'Never doubt that a small group of thoughtful, committed citizens can change the world. Indeed, it is the only thing that ever has.' During Buck's term as mayor of Christchurch, the Canterbury Forum was established. This body, consisting of the mayors and chief executives of each of the eleven territorial authorities in the Canterbury region, meets monthly to achieve greater cooperation in the use of resources, to coordinate the representation of the region to central government, and to share perspectives on how best to deliver value to citizens.

Since Vicki Buck stood down as mayor of Christchurch in 1998, the position has been held by Gary Moore. Moore has done much to build upon Buck's legacy. An accountant by training, Moore worked throughout the 1980s in programmes creating employment opportunities for people who had been affected by the reforms of that period. Moore held a range of positions on the Christchurch City Council during the 1990s. While in office, he has worked with his Council to establish an Economic Development Fund of $75 million to support economic and community development. The fund is administered by a joint board of councillors and representatives of the Canterbury Employers, Chamber of Commerce and Canterbury Manufacturers associations. With his passion for employment programmes, Moore established in 1999 the national-level Mayors' Taskforce for Jobs. Now, most mayors in New Zealand are members and all are committed to using the taskforce as a forum for promoting youth employment. Since 2003, Moore has worked with a group of people on the 'Prosperous Christchurch' initiative. Those meeting under the umbrella of Prosperous Christchurch include representatives from educational institutions, manufacturing and the service sector.

The Canterbury Development Corporation (CDC), a charitable trust company wholly owned by the Christchurch City Council and originally established in 1983, offers a significant example of the leadership and foresight on economic development issues characterising Christchurch and its elected officials. The CDC acts as the principal economic and employment development agency for the Christchurch and Canterbury region. It has its own board, comprising a range of key stakeholders, including Council representatives. The organisation's services fall into four main areas: regional economic development, business support, science and technology and employment development. Since 1996, the CDC has been headed by Chris Pickrill, who is widely recognised as a leading light in economic development strategy in New Zealand. Pickrill came to the CDC with many years of business experience in the forestry and apparel industries. Through his past business engagements and his work with CDC, Pickrill has developed an impressive network of corporate and government contacts. He has played a key role in the establishment and development of the Economic Development Association of New Zealand.

Although capacity to promote regional economic development in Canterbury has been strongest in Christchurch, leadership has also come from other localities in the region. The best example is given by Murray Cleverley in Timaru. Cleverley has served since 1999 as the chief executive of the Aoraki Development Trust, which he has built into a strong organisation. In the same way that the CDC serves as the economic development agency for Christchurch City Council, the Aoraki Development Trust serves as the economic development agency for the Timaru District Council. Cleverley describes himself in his role as primarily a relationships manager. As an example of his relationship-building work since entering this role, he has arranged monthly networking lunches, to which he typically invites around fifteen people. These lunches have allowed him to keep up to date on relevant developments in the region and share that information around. They have also allowed him to make introductions and establish relationships among people with common business and economic development interests. Having been a successful businessman, Cleverley also sees himself as a business coach, helping people build strong and growing businesses. He has also led a delegation of local business people to China. In Cleverley's view, leadership is everything in his role. He is supported in his work by a board of successful business people and entrepreneurs. The Timaru District Council has given the trust room to operate independently and in a non-partisan fashion to promote the interests of the region. Aside from his work for the Aoraki Development Trust, Cleverley also serves as the chief executive of the South Canterbury Chamber of Commerce. He has also recently served as the chair of the Economic Development Association of New Zealand

In explaining his efforts to promote economic development in the Timaru area, Cleverley has stressed the importance of having the support of elected politicians. That point is supported by evidence from Christchurch and from several other territorial authorities, such as Ashburton. Further, lack of interest in economic development on the part of mayors and councillors also emerged in interviews as an explanation for why some district councils in Canterbury have extremely limited staffing capacity to promote economic development work.

When the Labour–Alliance coalition government launched its Regional Partnerships Programme in 2000, the Canterbury Forum co-ordinated an effort that saw all the region's eleven territorial authorities resolve to support development of a strategic plan for the region. The Canterbury Development Corporation was commissioned by the Forum to coordinate this work. The result was the Canterbury Regional Economic Development Strategy (CREDS), summarised in a document entitled *Creating Tomorrow's Canterbury* (2000). Five high-level objectives were set out in the document. These involved building an internationally competitive regional economy, bolstering the education and skills of the region's population, social development, environmental sustainability and promoting a positive, collegial attitude among Cantabrians. This document, and activities around it, laid the foundation for a number of regionwide initiatives. In particular, efforts were made to secure funding from the Major Regional Initiatives programme run through New Zealand Trade and Enterprise. Overall, people associated with economic development efforts in Canterbury have expressed positive views towards the central government's recent efforts to promote regional economic development. A range of activities have been initiated in the Canterbury region that would not otherwise have happened. The version of *Creating Tomorrow's Canterbury* produced in 2005 reveals strong strategic focus across the region. It also reveals a high degree of cross-jurisdictional learning since 2000. By comparison, the Canterbury Development Corporation's dominance in setting future directions was more apparent in the strategic plan produced in 2000 (Dalziel, Greer and Saunders 2003).

As noted earlier, the Canterbury region has been performing well economically over recent years. However, there is little complacency about this. People working on economic development issues know that they have to keep things moving forward. The interest in regional economic development on the part of central government has been welcomed across the board in Canterbury, and there is an optimism in the region that was not so apparent in the 1980s and 1990s. The strategic planning efforts coordinated by the Canterbury Development Corporation have led to much more focus on economic development among local territorial authorities. One example is the joint effort on the part of the Waimakariri and Hauranui district councils to establish Enterprise North Canterbury as their economic development agency. Like the Canterbury Development Corporation and the Aoraki Development Trust, Enterprise North Canterbury has an independent board of stakeholders with strong business credentials who share an entrepreneurial vision for their community. One informant observed that, with the creation of Enterprise North Canterbury, information relevant to business growth is now being used much more effectively in the area than at any time in the past.

If there is one concern about recent economic development efforts in Canterbury, it is that the diversity of the region makes it difficult for a sound, region-wide vision to emerge and catalyse regional initiatives. While there is less parochialism in the region than was evident in the past, it still makes sense for a number of sub-regional economic development agencies to exist alongside each other. These agencies enjoy cooperative relations but recognise that they serve communities with different sets of interests and concerns. That said, the diversity of interests in the region has been given as a reason why no Major Regional Initiative funding has been granted to Canterbury since the establishment of that programme. The situation has led some people in Canterbury to wonder if there has been too much rigidity in the way that central government agencies have implemented the regional partnerships programme. It might also be the case that, from the central government's perspective, Canterbury's success as a regional economy, and the strength of its economic development agencies, has made it a lower priority in funding rounds.

Initiatives in Auckland

The Auckland region is the most populous in New Zealand, standing at 1,316,700, or 32 per cent of the population of the country (Statistics New Zealand 2004). The population is more diverse than any other region. In the year to March 2004, the region generated 31 per cent of New Zealand's total economic activity. It is home to two thirds of New Zealand's top 200 companies, and it has the most significant concentration of business services in the country. Auckland's industry profile is complex, with services, manufacturing, trade and tourism all figuring prominently. Yet despite Auckland's comparative economic size and diversity, there are some weaknesses. In the year to March 2003, Auckland's nominal GDP per capita stood at $30,750, lower than the national average of $32,100.

Further, while the national economy grew at an annual average of 3.5 per cent between March 2000 and March 2004, the GDP of the Auckland regional economy grew at the slightly lower rate of 3.1 per cent (NZIER 2004). Compared to other Pacific Rim cities, Auckland has also been performing poorly, particularly when compared to its closest rivals Sydney and Melbourne. Infrastructure constraints, limited domestic markets and distance from global markets have been given as reasons for this disappointing performance (Rowe 2004).

Questions concerning leadership and regional coordination have emerged in the Auckland region because of its comparatively poor economic performance. Traditionally, political support and resources for *regional* economic development in Auckland have been lacking. Until recently the Auckland Regional Council has been constrained legally from taking a leadership role in economic development. However, political collaboration between local actors has also been difficult with strong political personalities and loyalties to local communities getting in the way. These factors, coupled with the diversity of Auckland's cultural make-up and economic complexity, have inhibited the development of strong mechanisms for regional governance. As a result, leadership at the regional level has at best been sporadic and weak.

Recognising that regional leadership and coordination are important for securing Auckland's future economic success, since 2000 an ongoing process of regional economic development institution building has been unfolding. The failure of the Auckland region to secure a bid for the establishment of a Motorola research facility in 2000 delivered a wake-up call to start developing regional coordination mechanisms. Failure to attract Motorola was due in part to competitive bidding among three of Auckland's six local territorial authorities. In the aftermath of Motorola's decision, and prompted by chiding from central government, Auckland's territorial authorities came together in January 2001 to sign a Memorandum of Understanding. The memorandum signalled, at least rhetorically, a change in competition among the region's territorial authorities. The memorandum was intended to '[e]ncourage the local authorities to work cooperatively together and to co-ordinate their endeavours whenever appropriate to achieve beneficial economic development outcomes for the region and for the local authorities in the Auckland region' (quoted in Auckland Regional Council 2002).

Little eventuated from the Memorandum of Understanding. However in March 2001 a private-sector initiative gave further momentum to the development of better regional leadership and coordination. Observing the poor performance of the Auckland region, a small group of Auckland business leaders formed a not-for-profit charitable trust called Competitive Auckland. Richard Dipsbury, the founder of Kiwi Income Property Trust and self-styled 'idea venture capitalist', originated this initiative. Dipsbury built up a small group of like-minded individuals around him. From the beginning, Competitive Auckland was a collaborative project rather than a project pushed forward by one forceful leader. It brought together representatives of local businesses, tertiary institutions and local governments. Bridging the public/private sector divide, Competitive Auckland sought to change the culture of the Auckland region by fostering more regional collaboration. David Irving, the former chair of the organisation, said in July 2001, 'there's a gap . . . for a cohesive economic development plan in the Auckland area. That probably is the most important thing . . . a plan that would bring parties together.' Members of Competitive Auckland undertook one million dollars worth of *pro bono* research work benchmarking the Auckland region against comparable Pacific Rim economies and offering recommendations to promote the competitiveness of the Auckland economy. The organisation was successful in playing a leadership role in the Auckland region by drawing attention to the most pressing economic and social issues and creating an environment in which dialogue could occur.

Renamed the Committee for Auckland, Competitive Auckland continues to have a diverse range of regional actors under its umbrella, including representatives of the private sector, local councils, tertiary institutions and some voluntary sector organisations, like the Auckland City Mission. In recognition of the dearth of cross-sector and regional leadership capacity in Auckland, the Committee for Auckland has established the Future Auckland Leaders' Programme. This programme acts as a 'polishing course' for future Auckland leaders who are already showing promise. Members of the committee select participants from within the organisations they represent. Those selected are typically expected to have already shown leadership skills. The leadership programme is intended to break down the barriers between public and private sectors by building a collaborative culture in Auckland based on high levels of trust, networking and awareness of Auckland issues.

In addition to the role played by the Committee for Auckland, the central government's Regional Partnerships Programme has added impetus to regional institution building. The partnerships programme's funding mechanisms provide incentives for stakeholders to come together to discuss the social and economic issues facing their region and to generate regional development strategies. Building on work undertaken by Competitive Auckland and discussed over four forums held during 2001 and 2002, stakeholders from across the Auckland region entered into a formal partnership to formulate the Auckland Regional Development Strategy – AREDS (see Auckland Regional Council 2002). A Strategy Leaders Group chaired by private sector leader Peter Menzies oversaw the strategy development phase. Tensions between regional stakeholders were evident throughout the AREDS process. However, Menzies was an important figure in bringing partners together. He is credited with working tirelessly to promote and facilitate engagement and commitment across the region's leaders both in government and business. In addition, Manukau City mayor Sir Barry Curtis has been credited with helping to maintain a *regional* focus for the AREDS process in an environment often beset with conflict between 'regionalists' and 'localists'.

Implementation of AREDS began in October 2002. At this point, the strategy process broke down and lost a lot of the community buy-in that had characterised the development phase. Early on, the AREDS leadership arrangements were more akin to private-sector management styles than those found in the public sector. Issues of accountability, ability for the councils to steer the implementation of AREDS and concerns in some quarters that the AREDS process was being subverted by more powerful players undermined the confidence of those funding it – the region's councils. AREDS has since been moved back 'in-house' to the Auckland Regional Council. Now, the Auckland Regional Council is taking on an active economic development leadership role in the Auckland region. It has recently set up a Stand Alone Business Unit intended to provide a regional identity and single facilitation point for the Auckland region. It has also established a Regional Economic Development Forum that brings together twelve regional representatives drawn from the region's stakeholders. The forum is intended to act as a regional coordination and networking arena. These initiatives are widely considered amongst the most important recent developments in Auckland.

Although the Regional Partnerships Programme acted as a catalyst to partnership development in Auckland, the activities surrounding it revealed ongoing friction between central government and regional stakeholders. A widely held view in Auckland is that the programme, while beneficial in bringing diverse partners together, has not been compatible with the needs of a large metropolitan region. Concerns cited involved the cap on funding for major regional initiatives (MRIs), the limited consideration given to local factors and an excessive focus on sector engagement. A significant proportion of the people we spoke with in Auckland suggested that sector engagement at the sub-regional level alongside engagement with regional institutions to address infrastructure constraints would suit Auckland better. Additionally, parochialism on the part of central government policy units and a failure to collaborate with regional and local policy actors were also cited as problems in the partnerships process. However, the recent establishment of a front-line joint central government office for economic and urban development in Auckland suggests there is now a move to more active engagement with regional and local policy actors by central government.

Conclusion

Discussions and debates about economic activity often rarefy the economy to the point where many things about economic relations seem abstract. Since the early 1980s, New Zealand has gone through a major economic transformation. Looking back, it is clear that the reform process sometimes encouraged a greater focus on aggregate statistics and their relationships than on the linkages between local economic activity and broader economic outcomes. Against this backdrop, the move to a greater central government interest and involvement in promoting regional economic development can be viewed as a corrective to that earlier rarefication. At the national level, Jim Anderton made a tireless effort, especially in the period from 2000 to 2002, to see new agencies established that could allow the central government to support economic development in the regions. This effort required both visionary and practical leadership. The vision was to see discussions of economic development routinely informed by greater knowledge of local economic activity. The practical aspect involved Anderton leveraging his role as the leader of a minor political party to secure both policy change and institutional change. Today, regional economic development efforts in New Zealand are supported by well-coordinated central government efforts. Further, the policies that have been put in place are sophisticated in the sense that they are informed by a model of the economy that takes competition as a given, yet sees that low-key government efforts can do quite a lot to promote business growth. Anderton, who has often espoused big government and government ownership of assets, has nonetheless espoused a lighter-handed, coaching role for government in promoting economic development.

Our case studies of leadership and economic development efforts in Canterbury and Auckland further underscore the ways that leadership can make a difference. A number of politicians and appointed officials working on economic development issues in Canterbury were ahead of the government in Wellington in recognising the range of positive ways that government can work with businesses to encourage economic growth. Most often, the leadership role of local politicians and officials has involved helping people in local businesses acquire relevant knowledge, make important contacts with others and seize opportunities. In some instances, people in business can do all these things for themselves. However, there are times when the activities of a local economic development agency can make a significant difference. With time, people in these agencies can build up extensive knowledge about the local economic context and its relationship to the world. In turn, that knowledge can be of real value to new firms or to firms that have been established for a number of years but that are seeking to expand. In theory, the knowledge-broker role could be performed by a private entity. In practice, it is difficult for such work to be undertaken from the outset on a for-profit basis. The model for the economic development agencies in Canterbury noted here has tended to be one where some funding from local governments has been guaranteed, but a degree of revenue-building through consultancy work and other services has been expected. That same model can be found in other regions in New Zealand and in many places around the globe. The model recognises that efforts to promote regional economic development can yield both private and public benefits. In contrast with initiatives in Canterbury, regional economic development initiatives in

Auckland have not been as effectively coordinated. While some of the difference can be put down to the complexity and diversity of the Auckland region, there does appear to have been an absence of the stable leadership and coordination across local governments needed to effectively promote regional economic development.

Overall, we contend that political leadership can make a significant difference when it comes to promoting regional economic development. The leadership is necessary precisely because the operating context for businesses is complex in New Zealand, particularly where businesses are seeking to expand by tapping into export markets. In addition, making and implementing effective regional economic development policy requires that politicians work across a variety of jurisdictional boundaries. With vision and energy, actors at the local government, regional government or national government levels can all make positive contributions to promoting economic development. Things become much more difficult when either the vision or the energy are lacking. Our informants told us that there was now a lot of positive attitude and optimism surrounding regional economic development issues. They contrasted the current situation with the period of the 1980s and 1990s. Invariably, they credited leadership as the central factor having produced that change.

Anderson, C. (1995) *Blaming the Government: Citizens and the Economy in Five European Democracies*, Armonk, NY, Sharpe.
Anderton, J. (2000) 'Implementation of Vote: Economic Development and Voe: Industry and Regional Development', Cabinet Economic Development Committee paper, Wellington.
Anderton, J. (2001a) Opening Address, Regional Development Conference, Rotorua Convention Centre, Rotorua, 28 November.
Anderton, J. (2001b) 'Where to from Here?' Closing Speech, Regional Development Conference, Rotorua Convention Centre, Rotorua, 29 November.
Anderton, J. (2003a) 'Helping Hand Aids Steady Climb', *New Zealand Herald*, 30 September.
Anderton, J. (2003b) Closing Address, 'Where to from Here?', Regional Development Conference, Community Trust Sports Centre, Timaru, 26 September.
Auckland Regional Council (2002) *Auckland Regional Economic Development Strategy 2002–2022*, Auckland, Auckland Regional Council.
Bollard, A. (1993) 'New Zealand', in J. Williamson (ed.), *The Political Economy of Policy Reform*, Washington DC, Institute for International Economics.
Boston, J., J. Martin, J. Pallot and P. Walsh (1996) *Public Management: The New Zealand*

Model, Melbourne, Oxford University Press.

Buchanan, J. M., R. B. Tollison and G. Tullock (eds) (1980) *Toward a Theory of the Rent-Seeking Society*, College Station, Texas A&M University economics series.

Buck, V. (2001) 'Leadership – Its Crucial Role in Regional Development', Regional Development Conference, Rotorua Convention Centre, Rotorua, 28 November.

Clark, H. (2001) Address to the Regional Development Conference, Regional Development Conference, Rotorua Convention Centre, Rotorua, 28 November.

Crocombe, G. T., M. J. Enright and M. E. Porter (1991) *Upgrading New Zealand's Competitive Advantage*, Auckland, Oxford University Press.

Dalziel, P., G. Greer and C. Saunders (2003) 'Regional Economic Development Planning: A Study of its Benefits and Best Practice', Lincoln, Agribusiness and Economics Research Unit, Lincoln University.

Dalziel, P. and R. Lattimore (2004) *The New Zealand Macroeconomy: Striving for Sustainable Growth and Equity*, 5th edn, Melbourne, Oxford University Press.

Eisinger, P. K. (1988) *The Rise of the Entrepreneurial State: States and Local Development Policy in the United States*, Madison, WI, University of Wisconsin Press.

Feigenbaum, H., J. Henig and C. Hamnett (1999) *Shrinking the State: The Political Underpinnings of Privatization*, New York, Cambridge University Press.

Frankel, B. (1983) *Beyond the State?: Dominant Theories and Socialist Strategies*, London, Macmillan.

Friedman, M. (1962) *Capitalism and Freedom*, Chicago, University of Chicago Press.

Hall, P. A. (ed.) (1989) *The Political Power of Economic Ideas: Keynesianism Across Nations*, Princeton, NJ, Princeton University Press.

Heifetz, R. A. (1994) *Leadership Without Easy Answers*, Cambridge, MA, Belknap Press.

Irving, D. (2001) Interview with Kim Hill, *Nine to Noon*, National Radio, 27 July.

Kettl, D. F. (2000) *The Global Public Management Revolution: A Report on the Transformation of Governance*, Washington DC, The Brookings Institution.

Myers, D. (1998) 'Local Government: Time for a New Blueprint', Speech to the ACT New Zealand/Federated Farmers Local Government Reform Summit, Whangarei, 18 April.

NZIER (2004) *New Zealand's Regional Economic Performance*, Report to the Ministry of Economic Development, Wellington, Ministry of Economic Development.

Porter, M. E. (1990) *The Competitive Advantage of Nations*, New York, The Free Press.

Powell, G. B., Jr. and G. D. Whitten (1993) 'A Cross-national Analysis of Economic Voting: Taking Account of the Political Context', *American Journal of Political Science*, 37, 391–414.

Reich, R. B. (1991) *The Work of Nations: Preparing Ourselves for 21st-Century Capitalism*, New York, Knopf.

Rhoads, S. E. (1985) *The Economist's View of the World: Government, Markets, and Public Policy*, New York, Cambridge University Press.

Rowe, J. E. (2004) 'AREDS: A Case Study in Metropolitan Regional Economy Development', *Sustaining Regions*, 4, 30–40.

Savitch, H. V. and P. Kantor (2002) *Cities in the International Marketplace*, Princeton, NJ, Princeton University Press.

Statistics New Zealand (2004) 'Subnational Population Estimates at 30 June 2004', Wellington, Statistics New Zealand.

Sweet, M. L. (1999) *Regional Economic Development in the European Union and North America*, Westport, CN, Praeger.

Walters, J. (2001) 'Urban Role Model', *Governing*, October, 18–23.

Weick, K. E. (1995) *Sensemaking in Organizations*, Thousand Oaks, CA, Sage.

Yergin, D. and J. Stanislaw (1998), *The Commanding Heights: The Battle Between Government and the Marketplace that is Remaking the Modern World*, New York, Touchstone.

Conclusion

THIRTEEN

Political Leadership – Future Challenges

Michael Mintrom, Raymond Miller and Tania Domett

Effective leadership can make a positive difference to the quality of our professional and personal lives. Yet, a precise definition of leadership remains elusive. Leadership can be productively explored from many different perspectives, from general principles about leadership through to the actions of specific leaders. In this volume we have concentrated on leadership in the realm of politics, with particular attention to political leadership in contemporary New Zealand. We take the view that political leadership involves a number of distinctive actions based on a particular set of skills. These actions and skills distinguish the practice of political leadership from leadership in other realms of human effort, such as business, sports, education and science.

What makes political leadership different from other forms of leadership? Clearly institutional settings play an important role in shaping the nature of political leadership. Among the key institutions are political parties, parliament, the public service and cabinet. But political leadership is also heavily influenced by a combination of formal procedural rules and shared norms. Political parties, for instance, are required to follow established rules with respect to spending, advertising and the selection of candidates for office. The actions of party leaders are further constrained by the timing of elections, conventions about how they should be conducted and the legal requirements set down in the Electoral Act (1993). While the attributes expected of a party candidate may appear similar to those of an MP, there are some fundamental differences. For example, whereas a candidate may not be called upon to make public speeches, let alone participate in the cut-and-thrust of extempore debate, these are the tools in trade of an elected member. Indeed, MPs are judged by their ability to make powerful, well-reasoned arguments, combined with the wit to quickly and forcefully expose the weak points in the arguments made by others.

In the past, these adversarial skills were regarded as pre-eminent characteristics of successful leadership. However, with the passing of the two-party system, the advent of MMP and the growing importance of the electronic media, parliamentary leadership in New Zealand increasingly calls for a different kind of rhetorical ability. While debating skills remain important, the ability to conduct studio interviews and the ability to forge agreement across a range of parties have become essential features of effective policy-making and government. Thus, political leadership today is dependent upon the capacity to adapt to the changing technological and institutional context within which politics takes place.

This concluding discussion draws on the insights offered in the preceding chapters. But rather than simply summarising what has already been said, we seek here to identify some implications, especially as they relate to the future of leadership in New Zealand. In particular, we address the question of how people involved in politics may develop their capabilities as leaders. This leads us to consider recent developments in leadership training as well as in the study of political leadership in New Zealand. Even the most cursory review of the leadership literature will reveal the extent to which New Zealand political leadership is both under-studied and under-taught. Taken together, the studies contained in this volume offer a foundation upon which to build political leadership as a strong and vibrant field in New Zealand political scholarship. We hope it will not only provoke discussion around the nature of political leadership, but also encourage new scholarship designed to address the current gaps in our knowledge.

Contemporary Political Leadership in New Zealand

Contextual factors play a key role in determining the kind of issues that political leaders must grapple with. The uniqueness of New Zealand's history, colonisation, engagement with global politics and markets and patterns of immigration has served to define the ways that political leadership is exercised. As a nation with a relatively small population far removed from the global centres of power, politics and commerce, New Zealand has always had a fundamental need to be both outward-looking and willing to assert its relevance to people for whom the question of their own country's relevance has rarely, if ever, arisen. The need to look outward has significant implications for political leadership, especially the leadership shown by prime ministers and others who have been called on to represent the nation in international forums. With the changes in transportation, communications, trade and competition associated with globalisation, New Zealand's engagements with the outside world have accelerated. Globalisation has also led to greater flows of people across national borders everywhere, creating greater diversity in the populations of many countries, including New Zealand.

Several of this book's authors have explored the ways that New Zealand's place in the world, and our perceptions of that place, have created challenges for political leadership. David Capie (chapter 2) considers how the efforts of several prime ministers, beginning with Norman Kirk, have helped to construct both the understanding New Zealanders have of themselves and the perceptions that foreigners have of New Zealand. Clearly, aspects of history, world politics, geography and demographics present challenges for political leaders everywhere as they seek to negotiate the place of their country in the world. But challenges also provide opportunities. Capie explores the degree to which individual political leaders have been able to place their own stylistic imprints on the management of foreign relations and the making of foreign policy.

Since colonisation began in the early 1800s, New Zealand's relative prosperity in the world has been dependent on an ability to produce commodities that attract good prices in international markets. Because of that history, it is tempting to conclude that the challenges associated with globalisation represent nothing new. Jacqui True (chapter 3) dispels that myth. Increasingly, nations that are members of the OECD are recognising knowledge as the new coin of the realm. In the early postwar period, New Zealand enjoyed a very high standard of living built on the strengths of its agricultural and other exports. In more recent times, the challenge has been to consolidate on that past success and find new ways to add value to the commodities and services that the country produces for sale to the rest of the world. Inevitably, that challenge will be met by paying careful regard to the ways that new products can be derived from our agricultural base and how knowledge and creativity can be harnessed in the development of new products and services that sell well in lucrative overseas markets.

Political leaders cannot directly influence people to act in ways that help identify and capitalise on new export opportunities. However, they can help to set the tone of discussions around the drivers of future prosperity. On that score, in recent times, we have seen political leadership coming from a number of quarters outside of government, including business and academe. Michael Mintrom and Luke Williams (chapter 12) identify the linkages between economic policy and political leadership and explore the efforts that have occurred at both the national and local levels to promote regional economic development.

The changing identity of New Zealand as a nation, and how this links with globalisation, is explored through Manying Ip's study of political leadership among Asian New Zealanders (chapter 9). Ip's analysis of the political dynamics within the Asian community in New Zealand highlights two kinds of tension. One is the tension found between immigrants who arrived at different times in the nation's development. Her study shows that while immigrants may have many experiences in common, there are also important differences. Those arriving in New Zealand today encounter a very different country from the New Zealand of the 1950s and 1960s, let alone the 1800s. Once that difference is understood, it becomes clear that the political orientations of recent arrivals may well be quite distinct from those of early immigrants. Moreover, we are reminded that the Asian community is broad-based and consists of immigrants from countries as culturally and politically diverse as China, Hong Kong, Taiwan, Korea, Pakistan and India. With these two kinds of tension in mind, Asian leaders must possess a leadership style that is able to bridge ethnic divides as well as those caused by generational differences.

The presence of a significant indigenous population and the ongoing controversy surrounding the relevance of the Treaty of Waitangi ensure that the issues of race, ethnicity and identity provide a constant challenge for our political leaders. Throughout much of the country's political history, Maori voices have received quite limited attention. Yet, over the centuries, Maori have nurtured and maintained an intricate understanding of leadership and the role that such leadership can and should play in achieving self-determination. The emergence of the Maori Party in 2004 was a direct result of the manner in which discussions over the foreshore and seabed were managed by the government. The subsequent winning of four seats in 2005 has given the Maori Party a significant presence in parliament. It now faces an historic opportunity to develop itself as a strong voice for Maori within New Zealand politics. In light of that, Ranginui Walker's chapter offers a timely review of Maori notions of leadership and opens the way for more discussion that takes into account emerging events and Maori responses to them.

On a similar theme, Matthew Palmer (chapter 9) argues that the foreshore and seabed dispute has yet to be resolved in a way that is both effective and just. At one level, the dispute highlights the political difficulties that inevitably accompany and emerge out of colonisation. While relations between Maori and Pakeha have been remarkably good for much of the history of New Zealand, for the most part those relations have been predicated upon Pakeha domination. As Maori have come to question that domination, so the potential for disagreement and the emergence of political disputes have increased. The foreshore and seabed dispute can be viewed as an indicator of other kinds of disputes that are likely to arise in the future, especially in such areas as self-determination and restorative justice.

Barry Gustafson's review of populism in New Zealand (chapter 4) provides insights into the preoccupations and characteristics of those figures who have loomed large on the New Zealand political landscape. Strong-minded and combative, frequently maverick in their tendencies, these politicians provided colourful models for contemporary politicians to follow. Yet a tension now exists for would-be populists. This tension is explored in Raymond Miller's analysis (chapter 7) of minor party leadership under MMP. Minor parties need strong figures to lead them in order to gain the attention of the media and voters. Yet, in an institutional setting where the ability to compromise and work well with others is essential to achieving power and influence, the very practices that serve populists well with the electorate can hinder them within the corridors of power and prevent them from gaining places at the cabinet table.

An organising assumption in this volume is that political leadership can be exercised in a variety of places well beyond the cabinet or parliament. But the actions of prime ministers, members of cabinet and leaders of opposition parties must receive close attention in any discussion of political leadership. John Henderson and Seishi Gomibuchi's discussion of the leadership styles of Helen Clark and Don Brash (chapter 5) offers a range of fresh insights into the motivations and practices of a prime minister at the height of her powers and a leader of the opposition who has come to the position with an impressive record of accomplishments both in chief executive positions and as a central banker. Like David Capie, Henderson and Gomibuchi effectively demonstrate the ways that political leaders are able to bring their unique stylistic characters to the roles they play, even as the weight of the offices they hold serves to constrain the opportunities and choices they face.

While New Zealand's parliamentarians have been operating within an environment shaped by MMP for a decade now, the election of 2005 gave the strongest indication to date of the considerable negotiating talent that a would-be prime minister must exercise in order to form a stable government that is acceptable to a majority of voters. Elizabeth McLeay's analysis of leadership in cabinet under MMP also provides a fresh exploration of the dynamics of political leadership in New Zealand (chapter 6). McLeay's effort to compare and contrast leadership in cabinet under Keith Holyoake with that of Helen Clark is instructive. As with other chapters in the volume, it indicates the ways that institutional arrangements matter for shaping the opportunities and constraints faced by the prime ministers and other cabinet ministers under MMP. Taken as a group, the chapter on the leadership styles of the leaders of the Labour Party and the National Party, the chapter on the leadership of minor parties and the chapter on leadership in cabinet give a comprehensive coverage of the nature of political leadership in parliament and in government as it is currently practised.

The media represents another key institution that serves to shape and constrain the practice of political leadership in any country. As Margie Comrie points out in her analysis of the role of the media in New Zealand (chapter 10), the electronic and print media can play a powerful role in shaping public perceptions of political leaders, the policies they advocate and the opinions they express. Increasingly, it is only through the media that the vast majority of citizens gain any awareness of politics and the personalities of politicians. Given this, a case can be made for viewing the heads of TV and radio news services, along with newspaper editors, as themselves engaging in forms of political leadership. The choices they make concerning events to cover, and the editorial slants they place on that coverage can strongly influence the ways that citizens make sense of public life and the nature of contemporary politics. Further, budgetary considerations influence the extent to which local media generate their own stories or rely upon reporting from overseas affiliates. That also serves to shape public knowledge of world events and interpretations placed upon them. The decisions news editors make about what material to report themselves and what material to purchase can contribute to how New Zealanders think about their place in the world and the efficacy of their political leaders in shaping global politics.

Future Issues for Political Leaders

The critical task for political leaders, no matter what position they hold, is to make sense of their operating context and to work with followers to coordinate their activities and reflect their goals. The introduction of MMP has had a significant bearing on the composition and influence of parliament. The inevitable emergence of new parties, along with the changing fortunes of both the major parties and the various minor parties, will doubtless ensure that each election produces unique challenges for party leaders, especially those seeking to form a stable and effective coalition government. But electoral change is itself driven by other contextual factors. Looking to patterns and trends on both the domestic and the global fronts, a number of factors are likely to generate challenges for the political leaders over the coming years. Some of these are located beyond central government and include elected and appointed officials in regional and local governments, interest-group leaders, leaders in business and education and leaders of various racial and ethnic groups across the country.

Among the broader economic and social changes is the challenge to transform the New Zealand economy. This is not simply about switching production lines, but rather the ongoing integration of the global economy, the creation of new free trade agreements, and the greater ease with which talented people can relocate from country to country. The future demands of a global economy will require that the workforce be better trained than it is today if it is to remain competitive. Yet, even being well trained is no guarantee of continuous work. As many countries are finding, an array of activities once assumed to require skilled local staff are now routinely being undertaken offshore at much lower cost. These changes are the direct result of improved communication systems and the reduction of barriers to international trade in both goods and services. For New Zealanders to maintain the relatively high living standards to which we have grown accustomed, we must be prepared to produce high-quality goods and services that are valued in other countries. Leadership will be required to get that message across, to identify local role models and to offer helpful advice and training to new and established enterprises alike.

Socially, New Zealand's demographic changes are likely to have profound implications for political leadership. Not only will the elderly require increased care and support, there will also be a relatively smaller proportion of the population generating the income required to pay for it. The ageing dynamics differ across racial and ethnic groups, with the average age of the Pakeha/European population being much higher than the average age of the Maori and Pasifika populations. This means that in the future many jobs and positions of leadership in occupations currently dominated by Pakeha/Europeans will need to be filled by Maori and Pasifika peoples. For that transition to occur smoothly, much more effort will need to be put into ensuring that young people from these groups come to experience more positive outcomes through the New Zealand educational system. Again, the leadership challenges among these ethnic groups are immense.

Multiculturalism brings with it many benefits and New Zealand is fortunate to have an increasingly rich group of cultures finding their identity within the fabric of New Zealand society. But differences within and between cultural groupings need to be taken seriously and efforts must be made to avoid unpleasant tensions. This calls for effective political leadership within those communities, supported by leadership from elected officials at the local, regional and national levels. For example, schools, community groups and local councils can do much to promote understanding and positive interactions between members of different race and ethnic groups. In turn, these actions can promote greater social engagement, the emergence of new understandings of what it means to be a citizen of New Zealand and greater social cohesion. As the foreshore and seabed dispute has shown, good relations among people of different cultures and heritage in New Zealand cannot be taken for granted. The growing desire for self-determination among some Maori, and ongoing calls for the righting of past wrongs due to colonisation, present serious challenges for New Zealand. Good relations between Maori and other New Zealanders are fundamental to the future peace and prosperity of New Zealand society.

Issues of identity will continue to pose major challenges. At the broadest level, there is the issue of New Zealand in the world and the understandings that New Zealanders hold of themselves and their country. Always a task for prime ministers and others who have routinely represented New Zealand internationally, this responsibility is set to become more challenging. Already, we have seen disputes in New Zealand over how involved we should become in international efforts to combat terrorism. These disputes have revealed that for some – especially older – New Zealanders, identity is derived from experiences shared with historical alliance partners, such as the United States and Britain. There have also been disagreements around the degree to which New Zealand should contribute towards efforts to reduce global warming. And discussions concerning the possibility of signing various bilateral free trade agreements have also been particularly heated. Domestically, issues of identity emerge within a range of dimensions. With respect to policy directions, political leaders in the future will need to find ways to balance pressures from those in society who wish to see much more economic development and those who wish to see more environmental preservation. While economic development and environmental preservation need not be in conflict, they often are. For example, in the lucrative tourism industry, two goals must be met. The first involves keeping areas of the country pristine and attractive as tourist destinations. The other involves allowing the number of foreign visitors to grow. Yet the very nature of the experience on offer changes as more and more people crowd in. This presents a significant dilemma, yet it is just one of many that arise when different values come into tension between those who want short-term economic gain in preference to long-term sustainable returns. Other dilemmas of this sort will cut to the heart of what New Zealand stands for and what it means to be a New Zealander, and to have a 'kiwi lifestyle'. One example of such a dilemma is how to balance the work requirements associated with a highly competitive economy against key social goals important to New Zealanders. In the current pursuit of enhanced productivity and economic growth it is essential to ensure that both men and women are able to exercise real choice about how much time they devote to paid work versus work in the home. These choices are negotiated at the family level as well as the organisational level and are mediated by social norms that are bound up in gender, class and culture. Political leaders – in government and business – who want to lay claim to a just society must first address the complexities, and potential sources of inequality, that constitute the work/life dilemma facing many New Zealanders.

The Evolution of Leadership Training

It is often contended that leaders are born rather than made. Because a precise definition of leadership remains elusive, many people believe that leadership requires a mysterious 'something' that some people possess and others do not. Unfortunately, the search for that 'something' often leads to a perpetuation of bias in the selection of people for leadership positions. In developing the organising framework for this book, we came to the view that leadership is best understood as a set of discrete activities. By taking this approach, the study of political leadership is expanded beyond the examination of the actions of people in predefined leadership positions. The *process* of political leadership becomes the central object of study. The contexts in which political leadership occurs remain critical to the analysis, but they are no longer taken as given and it is understood that people can serve as political leaders without holding formal positions of authority. Implicit in this approach is the view that many people in many locations can engage in and contribute to political leadership. *What people do* becomes more important than *who they are*.

When the ability to be a leader is understood as something that people either do or do not possess, then the notion of leadership training is treated sceptically. In New Zealand, as elsewhere, until recently very few opportunities have existed for people to receive systematic training for future leadership roles. Where training has occurred, it has tended to be on the job and *ad hoc*. Mostly, the expectation has been that people can learn by doing, augmented with a few pointers from seasoned leaders prepared to share their insights with the chosen few.

As we have noted above, many important issues call for political leadership. Consequently, we think there is a need for training programmes that impart political leadership skills to people aspiring to be involved in politics. Among other things, the exercise of political leadership requires that people have the ability to build and maintain relationships within and across particular political contexts. Good interpersonal skills, good negotiating skills and entrepreneurial savvy are crucial for helping people to work with others and achieve collective goals. The ability to work closely with the media and to effectively convey key ideas is also critical. Importantly, these are skills that can be learned. While the exercise of such skills cannot guarantee success – there are no guarantees in most areas of politics – we believe people who have acquired such skills will be more likely to demonstrate effective political leadership than people who have not.

In 2004, two significant programmes were launched in the Auckland area designed to impart leadership training to people coming from a range of fields of human endeavour. The New Zealand Leadership Institute based at the University of Auckland, and also known as Excelerator, offers several leadership programmes. The Future Leaders Programme is a leadership development programme for 17–25 year olds from all corners of New Zealand. It is designed to develop their leadership capacity so that they can make a difference. Participants are challenged to think about themselves, about how they relate to and work with others and about the context or environment in which they live, work and play. So that participants can grow and develop from the experience, the course runs over an 18-month period, allowing time for networks to be established and for real and sustained development to occur. Meanwhile, the Hillary Leadership Programme brings together senior leaders from business, government and community organisations. Offering a range of training experiences, this programme allows participants to work with other like-minded people from a variety of backgrounds, industries and communities to challenge and stimulate their leadership abilities.

In a separate initiative, the Future of Auckland Committee has established the Future Auckland Leadership Programme. This programme runs for two years, and includes bi-monthly workshops offered by a number of tertiary institutions in the Auckland region. It is intended to build leadership skills and a knowledge of the Auckland region within a select group of young people, in line with the Committee's concern that Auckland be led with vision and imagination in the years to come. The participants in the programme are selected for their potential to become future civic, corporate or community leaders. In the early cohorts, they have come from a range of backgrounds including commerce, education and local government.

In the future, we would like to see more effort made to offer political leadership training in New Zealand. Building on some of the initiatives now under way, and joining these with new initiatives inspired by overseas examples, we envisage a programme that brings together the best of practice and scholarship. For example, it could involve workshops where seasoned political leaders share their insights with aspiring political leaders. These could be augmented with opportunities for participants to learn from relevant scholarship. The programme itself could begin in quite a modest way, with perhaps two or three weekend workshops being offered each year. But once the programme developed, networks became established, and the reputation of the programme grew, we believe that it could be developed in a variety of fruitful directions.

The Study of Political Leadership

Political leadership in New Zealand remains under-studied. The chapters in this book help to fill some significant gaps, and suggest some future lines of inquiry. Here we wish to make some brief observations about potentially fruitful topics for future study and useful analytical strategies. Substantively, there are many areas that deserve close scrutiny. Most of the topics covered in this volume could benefit from ever more detailed study, building on the work of the chapter authors. In addition, we think there is a pressing need for more work on political leadership among New Zealand's minority ethnic communities, focusing in particular upon the ways that these groups seek to engage with the formal systems of politics found at the local, regional, and national levels. Further, we would like to encourage new efforts to explore aspects of political leadership in areas that have received limited attention from political scientists. Examples could include the study of political leadership as it is exercised by business groups, environmentalists and entities such as the Human Rights Commission and Equal Employment Opportunities Trust.

In terms of useful analytical strategies, we think that more case study work of the kind included in this volume could do much to add to our knowledge of political leadership in New Zealand. Leadership is difficult to study in more quantitative ways, and often such studies do not produce significant insights. Yet the comparative method has its merits. For this reason, we suggest that more studies that compare political leadership in New Zealand with political leadership as it is exercised in other countries could generate new and important insights of interest both in New Zealand and elsewhere. Political leadership can be successfully studied both through a focus upon discrete leadership contexts (such as within political parties, or within cabinet) and through a focus on substantive issues (such as the construction of a nation's identity in the world, or the promotion of regional economic development). Most of the contributors to this volume, if we had requested it, could have treated the subject of their chapters in a comparative way, drawing out points of similarity and difference between the exercise of political leadership in these substantive fields in New Zealand and elsewhere. That would have resulted in a very different set of chapters, but we think that work of that kind would have a lot of merit. In particular, through the accumulation of evidence, such comparative work would allow us to better understand the instances in which political leadership as practised in New Zealand is distinctive from political leadership elsewhere and where it is the same, and the reasons why similarities and differences exist. With globalisation, political leaders in all countries are increasingly being required to wrestle with a set of common issues, like multiculturalism, the transformation of their economies, integration into regional political and economic blocs, and so on. The scope for comparative studies of political leadership is broad. But such work should be treated as an accompaniment to studies focused squarely upon political leadership in New Zealand. We have to have a sound understanding of the local scene before we can really engage in powerful comparative work.

Conclusion

In every country, political leaders do vitally important work on behalf of their fellow citizens, and their actions frequently draw intense media attention. At a personal level, we look upon these leaders with awe and wonder at how they can possibly manage the complex task of balancing their public commitments and their private worlds. Often, the crises over which political leaders preside offer a kind of entertainment to the masses. We look on and imagine how difficult and messy it must be to survive in the world of politics. At other times, we imagine what it must be like to have power and to be so apparently efficacious in the world. In this volume, we have shown how careful political analysis can help us to better appreciate the range of contexts in which political leadership occurs and the ways that political leadership can be exercised. For a variety of reasons, now is a fantastic time to be analysing political leadership in New Zealand. Up until this point, the study of political leadership in New Zealand has been dominated by biographical works that have tended to combine narratives concerning the private lives of leaders with analysis of their public actions. Such works make very important contributions to our understanding of political history and, to an extent, political leadership. But we believe that other research strategies that pay more attention to political context and the interactions between leaders and followers can shed important new light on the exercise of political leadership. Taken together, the contributions gathered here offer a variety of insights into contemporary political leadership in New Zealand. We hope that this volume will inspire a new generation of thinking about the nature of political leadership and its practice in New Zealand. That is indeed an exciting prospect.

Contributors

Margie Comrie teaches public relations in the Department of Communication and Journalism at Massey University. Before joining the Massey staff in 1990, she worked in the media for 18 years. She has co-edited two books on the New Zealand news media, most recently *What's News?: Reclaiming Journalism in New Zealand* (2002). She has also written on public participation in government decision-making, communication with Maori and various public relations issues. She holds a Diploma in Journalism from the University of Canterbury, wrote her PhD thesis on the restructuring of TVNZ and contributes regularly to National Radio's *Sunday Supplement*.

David Capie is a lecturer in international relations at Victoria University of Wellington. His research interests focus on international relations theory and conflict and security issues, particularly in the Asia-Pacific region. His books include *The Asia-Pacific Security Lexicon* (with Paul M. Evans) and *Under the Gun: The Small Arms Challenge in the Pacific* (2003).

Tania Domett has recently completed her MA in Political Studies at the University of Auckland; her thesis explored the politics of work/life balance policies in New Zealand organisations. In 2004, she won the Australasian Political Studies Association's award for the best student paper on women and politics. Her work has been published in the *Australian Journal of Political Science*.

Seishi Gomibuchi holds a PhD from the University of Canterbury. His thesis examined the leadership crises in the New Zealand Labour Party between 1990 and 1996 with specific focus on Helen Clark and Mike Moore. His research interests lie in New Zealand and Japanese politics including political leadership.

Barry Gustafson is former professor of politics at the University of Auckland. He is a leading political historian and biographer whose books include biographies of Michael Joseph Savage and Robert Muldoon. He is currently completing a biography of New Zealand's longest-serving postwar prime minister, Keith Holyoake.

John Henderson is an associate professor in the Department of Political Science at the University of Canterbury. His doctoral studies at Duke University were supervised by James David Barber, a pioneering researcher in the field of presidential leadership and character. John Henderson has produced a large number of studies on political leadership in New Zealand. He is a former director of the Prime Minister's Office.

Manying Ip is an associate professor in the Department of Asian Studies at the University of Auckland, as well as being an associate dean of the Faculty of Arts. Her most recent work is an edited book, *Unfolding History, Evolving Identity* (2003), which provides a comprehensive overview of the history and experience of the Chinese in New Zealand up to the present day.

Elizabeth McLeay is an associate professor of political science at Victoria University of Wellington and is a member of the New Zealand Political Change Project. Her book *The Cabinet and Political Power in New Zealand* (1995) remains the most authoritative work on the subject. She has also written on political representation, and her most recent work is a co-edited book on the 2002 election (2003).

Raymond Miller is an associate professor and head of the Department of Political Studies at the University of Auckland, where he specialises in New Zealand politics, comparative parties, coalition government and political representation. His most recent books are *Proportional Representation on Trial* (co-author, 2002), *New Zealand Government and Politics* (editor, 2003), *Voters' Veto* (co-editor, 2004), and *Party Politics in New Zealand* (2005).

Michael Mintrom is an associate professor in the Department of Political Studies at the University of Auckland. He has written extensively on political leadership, policy design and efforts to prompt local innovation. His most recent books are *Policy Entrepreneurs and School Choice* (2000) and *People Skills for Policy Analysts* (2003).

Matthew Palmer is Pro Vice Chancellor, Dean of the Law School at Victoria University of Wellington. Among his numerous publications on the constitution, the political system and the leading political actors is *Bridled Power: New Zealand's Constitution and Government* (co-authored with Geoffrey Palmer, revised edition, 2004).

Jacqui True is a senior lecturer in the Department of Political Studies at the University of Auckland. She has published widely on cross-national institutional efforts to promote gender equity and the differential social impact of global economic restructuring. She has also written on national identity formation in a globalising context. She is the author of *Gender, Globalization, and Postsocialism* (2003) and a co-author of *Theories of International Relations* (1996, 2nd edition, 2001).

Ranginui Walker is a professor emeritus and former head of Maori Studies at the University of Auckland. Among his many publications on Maori politics are *Tradition and Change in Maori Leadership* (1993) and *Hi Tipua: The Life and Times of Sir Apirana Ngata* (2001).

Luke Williams has recently completed his MA in Political Studies at the University of Auckland; in his thesis he explored the politics associated with the development of knowledge-based partnerships in the Auckland region.

Index